FRESHWATER ENVIRONMENT

Encyclopaedia of Geographical Science and Environment Series

FRESHWATER ENVIRONMENT

Edited by

Ravi Mishra

ANMOL PUBLICATIONS PVT. LTD.

NEW DELHI - 110 002 (INDIA)

ANMOL PUBLICATIONS PVT. LTD.
4374/4B, Ansari Road, Daryaganj
New Delhi - 110 002
www.anmolbooks.com

Freshwater Environment

First Edition, 2002

ISBN 81-261-1102-X

PRINTED IN INDIA

Published by J.L. Kumar for Anmol Publications Pvt. Ltd., New Delhi - 110 002 and Printed at Tarun Offset Press, Delhi.

Contents

Preface

Language forces us to express ourselves in a one dimensional stream of words. But nature is seldom so simple and tractable; instead, it has many different dimensions. This is particularly true of geographical environment because its subject matter includes many complexities, inter-related concepts and phenomenon involving several heads of organization. Thus, there is no such thing as an "ideal" outline or a perfect sequential order for presecutation of the subject treated here. To obtain an overview of modern geographical environment, a student needs to assimilate a great many ideas. Ideally, a reader would knew everything in this present title before beginning to read it. Perhaps the only solution is to read it twice. To help a reader follow a train of thoughts different from the authors have chosen to use here, various chapters and sections are cross-referenced.

Our approach throughout is critical and evaluative; neither old nor new theories are taken to trust but are examined rigorously and often critical; the student should be aware of what material is sound and what untested or controversial. Those principles which survive such analysis we have put together in a new and current synthesis of the 'state of the art.' We have deliberately avoided a descriptive habitat a taxonomic approach to the material, feeling that geographical environment must be shown to be quantitative exact science, with certain underlying principles and laws as fundamental as the laws of pure physics.

The present title is aimed to bring together in one place and in a simple way the fundamentals of geographical environment with special emphasis on the modern viewpoint of the science. The potential scope of this branch is very great and no attempt of any exhaustive treatment of the subject is made here.

In the preparation of such a title we have obviously had a great deal of help from a great many people. We would like to take this opportunity to thank many friends and colleagues with whom we have thrashed out the ideas. All of them are most warmly acknowledged.

We have freely consulted a large number of foreign books and journals in the preparation of the present title and also to make it comprehensive and uptodate and to that extent it is not claimed to be our original work.

Any worthwhile criticism and suggestions for improvement would be thankfully acknowledged.

Editor

Chapter 1

FRESHWATER ENVIRONMENTS

The aquatic systems of the terrestrial environment are, per area, among the most productive systems of the Earth. The purpose of this chapter is to examine the features and processes that contribute to their high productivity.

The freshwater environments include streams and lakes, as well as wetlands such as peatlands or bogs, marshes, and swamps. Aquatic features such as lakes and wetlands depend upon climatic conditions, geologi.al events, or biological actions to develop and maintain bodies of water. These sites are thus geographically restricted. Estuaries develop where fresh and sea water meet and are also highly localized: their location is limited mainly to the mouths of rivers. Streams are far more common, and because they are the most ubiquitous terrestrial aquatic feature on the Earth, they will be the main focus of the chapter.

THE WATER CYCLE

The water cycle, or hydrologic cycle, refers to the exchange of water between the ocean and atmosphere. On the Earth, the oceans, which cover 71 per cent of the surface, are the major reservoir of the water. The oceans lose water by evaporation and gain water by precipitation. This is where the process becomes intriguing. The oceans only gain about 90 per cent of the water that the evaporated. The remainder is transferred to the land and returns to the oceans as runoff. The total amount of water involved in the cycle, about 0.04 per cent of the Earth water, represents all of the water that appears in the atmosphere (some of which appears as rain), the rivers, lakes, wetlands, soil moisture, and ground water. At any one time, under present climatic conditions, 97.5 per cent of the water on the planet occurs in the oceans. The remaining 2.5 per cent is divided among the following categories. About 8,0 per cent is in the ice caps and glaciers and about 20 per cent is ground- water. Lakes contain about 0.7 per cent of the water soil moisture holds about 0.44 per cent of the water, and the atmosphere and streams contain about 0.05 and 0.005 per cent respectively of the non-ocean water. Table lists the approxiit illustrates the time, percentage, and amount of each reservoir; mate residence relatively small portion of total water involved in the land part of the cycle. The land area occupied by open water also provides perspective of the water cycle. Lakes occupy about 2.5 million km^2 1.7 per cent of the surface area of the continents of the Earth (*Czaya* 1981). They contain about 241,000 km^3 of water. The major lakes of the Earth, *i.e.,* Lake Baikal of Asia the Great Lakes of North America, and the Rift Valley lakes of Africa contain almost three- quarters of the freshwater. All of the remaining lakes, ponds, and wetlands share the remaining portion. Streams on the other hand occupy less than 0.1 per cent of the area of the land (*Hynes* 1970). Annually, rivers, which occupy about one- seventeenth of the land area of lakes, discharge about 1,000 km^3 of water back to the ocean, or nearly one-tenth as much water as stored in lakes. Annually, streams, with only a fraction of the depth of lakes, handle about 2.6 times more volume of water per occupied area in lakes. That in essence describes the stream-a large volume of water flowing among a narrow ribbon of land.

Table 1.1. The Major Water Reservoirs of the Earth

Reservoir	*Per cent*	*Residence time*	*Amount (1,000's km^3)*
Total water	100.0		1,382,000
Oceans	97.5	1,000's years	1,347,000
Ice	2.0	1,000's—1,000,000's years	276,000
Groundwater	0.5	10—100's years	6,908
Lakes	0.0175	variable	241
Soil moisture	0.011	months	152
Rivers	0.0001	days	1.2
Atmosphere	0.001	10's days	12.3

STREAMS

At any one time, streams and rivers contain about 1,230 km^3, or about 3.3 per cent of the annual volume of water which returns to the seas. Stated differently, during the course of a year, the Earth's streams transport to the sea about 30 times more water than they contain at any one time. There are many possible transfers of water from streams. Some water undergoes evaporation and some steeps as ground water into the spaces between particles of sediment. Some of the groundwater enters the root some to become available to plants and thence undergoes evapotran spiration. The relationships between soils, plants, and the hydrologic cycle are described in greater detail in the next section. However, before these relationships are examined, the characteristics of streams will be considered.

Streams are located at virtually all latitudes and in all climates. Climate delivers the crucial ingredients which determine the regional characteristics of streams. Streams form under conditions where precipitation exceeds evaporation and infiltration. There are several types of streams. Perennial or effluent streams occur in humid climates where the supply of water is sufficient to flow in every season. The smallest drainage basins of the upper reaches of a large effluent river system often have intermittent streams. These small drainage basins characteristically have large variations in stream flow because they have too little storage of water to continuously supply the stream with water. They may flow, for example, for only a few days after each input of precipitation. Ephemeral streams occur in arid climates where infrequent precipitation and high evaporation leads to inadequate water for sustaining stream flow over long periods of time or along extended channel courses. The water in these streams tends to soak into the channel bed and such streams are called influent streams. In reality, these categories are complicated by the fact that the Earth's largest drainage basins extend across several major climatic zones.

The Drainage Basin

Stream channels occur in a seasonably well ordered pattern. Most streams are part of a drainage network that, connected, remove water from a drainage basin. Generally, geological conditions determine the geometry of the drainage network. Thus, the drainage network provides important clues to the geologic nature of the terrain.

For biogeographical purposes, the most important pattern of the drainage basin shows up in the longitudinal profile of a stream. Most of the major streams and rivers of the Earth have a slope profile that is steepest at its headwaters, and has an exponential decrease in slope toward the mouth.

The drainage basin of a large river consists of many smaller drainage basins containing smaller streams. A scheme has been devised to classify drainage basins according to their position within the hierarchy of the drainage network. The classes of streams are called orders. A first-order stream basin has no tributaries. It is the top of the stream profile. Its slopes tend to be the steepest and with small tributary area, it tends to have low flows. A second-order stream basin is formed when two first-order stream basins join; a third-order stream basin occurs where two second-order basins join, and so on. Higher order streams are associated with low slopes. Because of the number of streams that have joined to create high order streams, these streams usually have large volumes of water.

The relationship between slope and stream flow rate provides an interesting insight into biologically significant properties of streams. Intuitively, the relationship may seem straight- forward. That is, one might expect that on steep slopes, streams flow rapidly and on low slopes they flow slowly, and that the different sized streambed sediment at both segments matches expectations (i.e., larger sized materials in steeper segments and finer materials in flat segments). Streams, however, behave very differently than intuition suggests and there are many physical processes which need to be taken into account to describe the difference between upper and lower reaches of a stream. Upper reaches of a stream are found in highlands. The water source of streams is directly related to climate. Certainly, orographic precipitation in upland areas is important in contributing water to streams, and depending on elevation or latitude, may be stored in the form of ice and snow and appear in the stream as melt water. The bed material of the stream generally includes an assortment of boulders and other coarse materials. The valley which the stream traverses is generally a narrow, steep-sided, V-shaped valley. Under these conditions, a stream encounters much resistance as it flows over the streambled. Much turbulence is apparent in the formation of various eddies and standing waves. While the water may appear to be moving swiftly, in reality, streamflow is restricted by channel resistance in its downstream progress. In the upper reaches, boulders and pebbles undergo grinding and wear as they are moved down stream (*Adams* 1979).

The lower reaches of a stream. *i.e.,* high-order stream, occur near base level, either at a lake or at sea level. Here, there may be expanses of flat land on either side of the stream which periodically become flooded, hence the name floodplain. The stream in these places is both wide and deep and the streambed particles consist of silts and clays. The streambed surface is thus relatively smooth, providing little resistance to streamflow which is less turbulent in appearance. In addition, the volume of the stream water in the lower reaches creates the condition whereby most of the mass of water comes into contact with only water. Only a small fraction of the volume comes into contact with the stream bottom and sides. Under these conditions, the stream velocity on low slopes is higher than it is on steep slopes in the upper reaches (*Leopold et al.* 1964). Based on a continuum of bedload characteristics, slope, amount of turbulence, and flow, the stream is naturally divided into upper and lower segments. These physical divisions have distinctive properties that are important to organisms.

Regional variation of Drainage Basins

The previous section dealt with stream characteristics that generally apply to all drainage basins. There are some characteristics that distinguish drainage basins from each other. In general, most of the major distinctions occur as a result of variations in climate and geology.

Climate clearly influences the characteristics of a given drainage basin. In both the Blue and White Nile headwaters, there is ample precipitation. In the headwaters, the Nile is a normal effluent stream which receives a portion of its flow from soil and groundwater. However, as the Nile flows across the wet-dry Tropics and into the desert the situation changes. The last major tributary entering the Nile is the Atbara, over 2000 km from the mouth of the Nile. From thereon, the Nile becomes an influent stream, whereby it feeds groundwater reservoirs and undergoes evaporation during its entire journey across the Sahara Desert. In this manner, runoff is continuously diminished from the flow that originates in the upper reaches of the stream. A stream which passes through a desert for a major portion of its length is called an exotic stream. Historically, much confusion arose about the nature of streams because of the fact that the Nile appeared to come from a desert, and even more amazingly, annually flooded the land even though it came from the desert.

The major streams of the Earth listed in Table are not exotic. They receive ample rainfall at their source and throughout most of their course, thereby gaining volume on their route to the sea. Most of the great rivers exist in humid environments. Some of the most voluminous rivers such as the Yenisei and Lena are not located in particularly humid environments. They drain an exceptionally large region, however, and they exist in a cool climate with a relatively low rate of evapotranspiration.

These drain into interior basins such as the Dead Sea, Death Valley, Caspian Sea, and Lake Eyre. With the exception of Australia's Lake Eyre, these lakes are located below sea level. They all exist in climates where, overall, evaporation exceeds precipitation. These inland basin lakes of the Earth are the recipients of stream water from surrounding drainage basins. They illustrate the point that if a stream does not receive enough precipitation, it cannot carve a path to the ocean. Many interior basins of the Earth are intriguing because they contain a biota that is relict from a time when the drainage basin was connected to a larger network of streams during more humid times. These basins provide an opportunity to study evolutionary trends that occur in isolation, in addition to those presented by oceanic islands (*Naiman & Soltz* 1980).

In addition to influencing the flow volume of a stream, climate plays a related role in establishing the physical conditions that cause weathering and consequently the accumulation of various minerals in soils. Tropical soils tend to be rich in aluminium and iron oxides and poor in cations such as calcium, magnesium, sodium, and potassium. Tropical streams tend to be devoid of base minerals and are thus very soft water. During flooding the sediments carry the aluminium and iron oxides into tropical rivers. Likewise, middle latitude dry soils are enriched in a variety of base elements. The streams of these regions tend to be rich in base elements and thus are hard water. During flooding, the stream sediments are enriched in base-rich elements. In humid middle latitude climates, the soils may be heavily leached and the waters arising from them poor in base elements and therefore soft. High-latitude soils are rich in silica and the streams reflect this fact.

Streams may tend to mirror soil-forming processes but generalizations do not reflect the complexity of the actual chemical characteristics of streams. Streams are strongly influenced by regional or local geologic conditions. The water quality of the stream is determined by minerals with which it comes into contact. For example, the Colorado River passes through a salt dome in its course to the Gulf of California. In doing so, the river picks up sodium chloride. In an arid climate, the sodium chloride becomes concentrated during evaporation, and this influences water quality and the type of organisms that can exist in the river, especially during droughty years. Some rivers flow through limestone formations and pick up calcium carbonate. The dissolved carbon dioxide (CO_2) in water readily reacts with calcium carbonate to form soluble calcium bicarbonate. Calcium bicarbonate, however, stays in solution only as long as there is a certain level of free CO_2. Any condition, such as photosynthesis, which removes carbon dioxide from water also causes the precipitation of calcium carbonate. The calcium carbonate precipitate builds up a crystalline deposit around cells of algae. These deposits of calcium carbonate are called travertine (Hynes 1970). Such rivers have an unusual flora and fauna. Apart from physical conditions that arise from various regional and geological influences, drainage basins also have characteristics that result from organic activity within the basins. The next sections will further develop the connections between organisms and drainage basins.

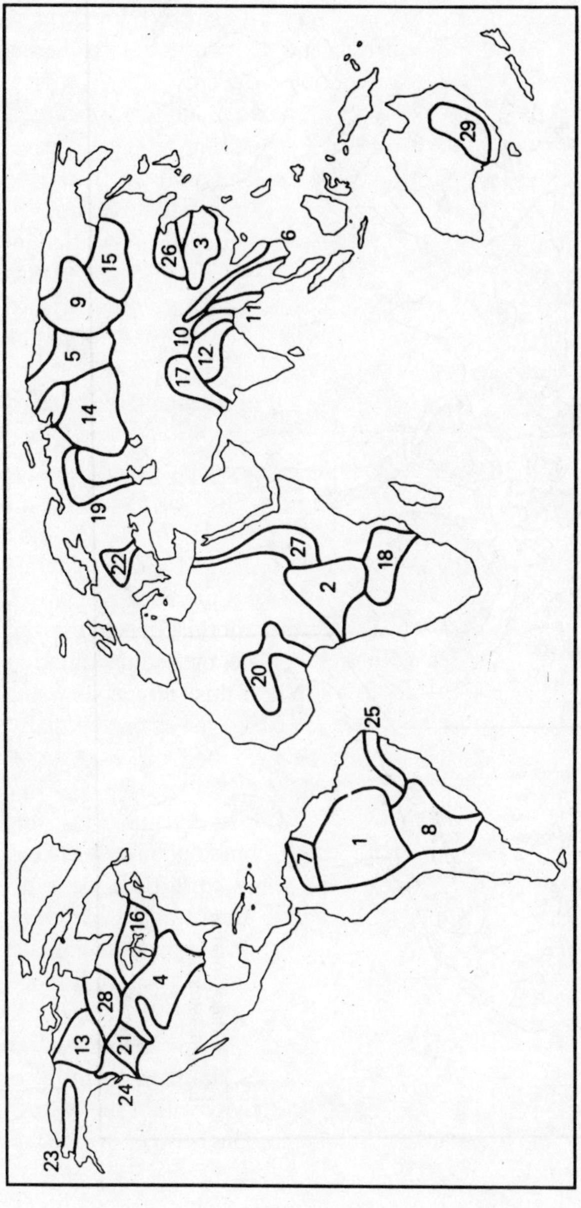

Fig. 1.1. A map of the earth's major river basins as listed in Table 1.2.

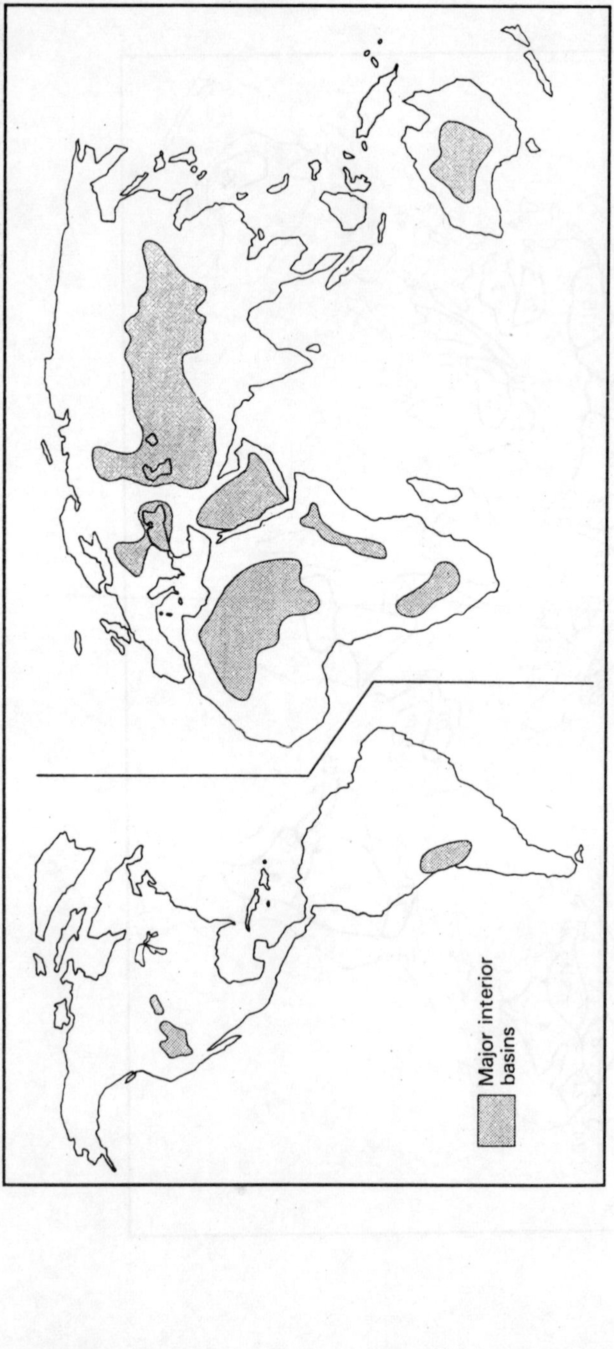

Fig. 1.2. The major interior basins of earth.

SOIL-PLANT-ATMOSPHERE CONTINUUM

The soil-plant-atmosphere continuum refers to the many interconnections between the physical and organic components of the landscape. The atmosphere provides the major energy and hydrologic inputs and also creates the conditions (wind, water vapour, and heat) for a large percentage of the output (evaporation) from a location. Plants respond to the conditions provided by the atmosphere, although the atmosphere too is influenced by albedo (the reflection of light energy from the Earth's surface) and water vapour handling properties of plants. Soils play a significant role in the hydrological cycle because of their water-holding capacities. Due to their requirement for water, various plants are both influenced by water availability and influence the amount of water in soils. Plants also play a role in soil formation. The drainage basin has been the key unit of the landscape that has provided opportunities for experimental observations of the relationships between soils, plants, and the atmosphere, and their influence on the movement of water (*G. S. Brush* 1982). The next two sections examine these relationships.

The Soil Factor

The basic point of reference to begin a discussion of the movement of water in the landscape is soil. Soil has varying capacity to absorb water. Infiltration of water depends upon several physical properties of soil, particle size is the most important. If the particles are sand sized, water generally infiltrates rapidly. Smaller particles such as silt and clay tend to pack together and have much reduced infiltration rates. The existence of roots, soil fauna, and organic matter can moderate the infiltration rate considerably. Because of the relationship between volume and surface area, particle size strongly influences water-holding capacity. Larger particles such as sand adsorb water freely and then, because of a lack of surface area, be unable to retain soil moisture. Clays generally have a higher water-holding capacity because of the large surface area of the clay particles. But, if infiltration is poor, and spaces between clay particles too confined, then water-holding capacity is also reduced. Silts and loams (that is, mixtures of clay and sand-sized particles) have the largest amount of available waterholding capacity reserve for plant growth (*Brady* 1974).

Three different types of bonding between water and soil particles are important to plants. Gravity water is that which occurs in liquid state and fills the spaces as it permeates the soil. This water is freely available to plants and moves through the soil under the influence of gravity. Capillary

Table 1.2. The Major River Basins of the Earth (Ranked by Discharge)

River	*Length (km)*	*Basin area (km^2)*	*Discharge (km^3/y)*	*Rainfall intensity (mm/y)*	*Dissolved transport (t/km^2/y)*	*Solid transport (t/km^2/y)*	*Amount transported (t× 10^6/y)*
1. Amazon	6,303	7,049,980	3,767.8	534	46.4	79.0	290.0
2. Congo	4,373	3,690,750	1,255.9	340	11.7	13.2	47.0
3. Yangtze	5,529	1,959,375	690.8	353	NA	490.0	NA
4. Mississippi-Missouri	6,215	3,221,183	556.2	173	40.0	94.0	131.0
5. Yenisei	4,991	2,597,700	550.8	212	28.0	51	73.0
6. Mekong	4,186	810,670	538.3	664	75.0	435.0	59.0
7. Orinoco	2,066	906,500	538.2	594	52.0	91.0	50.0
8. Parana	3,874	3,102,820	493.3	159	20.0	40.0	56.0
9. Lena	5,853	2,424,017	475.5	196	36.0	6.3	85.0
10. Brahmaputra	1,610	934,990	475.5	509	130.0	1,370.0	75.0
11. Irrawaddy	2,152	431,000	443.3	1,029	NA	700.0	NA
12. Ganges	1,610	488,992	439.6	899	78.0	537.0	76.0
13. McKenzie	3,276	1,766,380	403.7	299	39.0	65.0	NA
14. Ob	5,508	3,706,290	395.5	107	20.0	6.3	50.0
15. Amur	4,347	1,843,044	349.9	190	10.9	13.6	20.0
16. St. Lawrence	2,512	1,010,190	322.9	320	51.0	5.0	54.0

17.	Indus	2,898	963,480	269.1	279	65.0	500.0	68.0
18.	Zambezi	2,737	1,329,965	269.1	202	11.5	75.0	15.4
19.	Volga	3,689	1,379,952	256.6	186	57.0	19.0	77.0
20.	Niger	4,186	1,502,200	244.3	149	9.0	60.0	10.0
21.	Columbia	1,955	688,220	210.8	316	52.0	43.0	34.0
22.	Danube	2,861	816,990	197.4	242	75.0	84.0	60.0
23.	Yukon	3,186	865,060	193.8	224	44.0	103.0	34.8
24.	Fraser	1,368	219,632	112.4	512	NA	NA	NA
25.	San Francisco	3,199	625,680	107.7	165	NA	NA	NA
26.	Hwang-Ho (Yellow)	4,671	1,258,740	104.1	83	NA	2,150.0	NA
27.	Nile	6,693	2,849,000	80.7	28	5.8	37.0	10.0
28.	Nelson	2,576	1,072,260	76.2	71	27.0	NA	31.0
29.	Murray-Darling	5,427	1,072,908	12.6	12	8.2	30.0	2.3

Note : NA—not available

water clings to small particles and fills small spaces of the soil. It is also available to plants as it slowly moves into the water table. The third type of water is called hygroscopic water. It is so tightly bound to soil particles by molecular forces that it is unavailable to plants which wilt without other water. This water does not move through the soil (*Brady* 1974).

Soil releases water to streams and groundwater when two conditions are met. The soil must have sufficient water, and the water must be under the influence of gravity. When precipitation occurs at a rate that is equal to or greater than the rate of soil infiltration, the excess water flows under the influence of gravity as runoff toward the stream. If more water infiltrates the soils than can be held by it, the surplus flows as groundwater and reappears in springs and streams, or enters an underground aquifer.

The Vegetation Factor

No discussion of the water cycle or the properties of a drainage basin is complete without inclusion of the organic processes and, in particular, plant modification of the movement of water. Plants influence the operation of the drainage basin to such a large extent as to be inseparable from it. The effect of vegetation on the quality and yield of water from a drainage basin is a topic that has received considerable attention (Colman 1953).

One recent study is the Hubbard Brook Experimental Forest Study (*Bormann & Likens* 1979). The experimental design of the research made it possible to determine the degree of management of drainage basin commodities by the biotic community. The commodities in this case include water and the major plant nutrients both in the soils and the atmosphere. A major purpose of the research was to measure the exchanges between bedrock, soil, plants, the atmosphere, and rivers. The research was conducted on six drainage basins in the White Mountain National Forest in New Hampshire. The drainage basins rest on impervious gneiss bedrock.

The studies began with the measurement of the water budget of the six undisturbed drainage basins, from 1955 through 1968. Through the use of specialized dams designed for measuring the flow rare of streams, runoff was measured. Also, the settling ponds behind the dams were used to measure sediment movement. Provisions were made to measure precipitation, as well as dissolved mineral load of both incoming precipitation and outgoing runoff waters. The major water budget results of Hubbard Brook Forest are as follows.

Measured inputs and outputs
Average annual precipitation = 123 cm
Average annual runoff = 72 cm
Difference
Average annual evapotranspiration = 51

From these results it can be concluded that the combination of evaporation (i.e., water loss from all wetted surfaces) and transpiration (water movement from soil and groundwater to the atmosphere via plants) accounts for 41 per cent of the total annual amount of water entering the water basin (*Bormann & Likens* 1970). The removal of water from the soil by plants is relatively straightforward. The amount of energy required to extract soil water is small compared to the amount of energy needed to evaporate water from the leaf. Thus, up to the wilting stage, all soil water can be assumed to be equally available.

Provided there is soil moisture available to a plant, hydrostatic pressure within plant conducting tissues reaches maximum values. Stomata are openings in the leaf that control leaf ventilation. When light is not limiting the stomatal apertures of the leaf open to the maximum. In this way the leaf obtains the greatest possible flow of carbon dioxide. However, this condition also allows the rapid outflow of water vapour. Because of the limitations in the amount of carbon dioxide which a plant can obtain from the atmosphere, plants use much more water during ventilation than they actually require for physiological purposes (*Penman* 1970).

In the humid mid-latitude climate of New Hampshire precipitation is relatively evenly distributed throughout the year; runoff, on the other hand, is unevenly distributed. Most of the runoff occurs during March through May. Peak runoff is attributed to the spring melt of accumulated winter snow. Thus, 57 per cent of the total runoff occurs during one quarter of the year. April alone accounts for 35 per cent of the total when rain often falls on top of the snow. At the other extreme, during August, only 0.7 per cent of the annual average runoff takes place. The extremely low runoff during the mid to late summer can be explained by the effect of plant growth and transpiration on soil and groundwater (*Bormann & Likens* 1970). In spring, as the air and soil temperatures warm up, the vegetation begins to leaf out, ending the period of winter dormancy. Evaporative losses of water increase with rising temperatures, and plants begin to draw soil and groundwater at rates which exceed replenishment by precipitation.

During the peak temperatures of summer, soil and groundwater are being withdrawn by plants to the extent that almost no water is available for runoff. During low flow, small streams undergo a diurnal oscillation. During daylight, streamflow drops as evapotranspiration increases and during darkness streamflow increases. In autumn, as temperature decreases, large reductions occur in plant transpiration as plants shed their leaves and become dormant again. At this time of the year, rainfall replenishes the soil and groundwater reserves and runoff from the water increases. The ground freezes and snowfall accumulates during the winter leading to a repeat of the sequence of the annual runoff cycle.

In the Hubbard Brook study, the role of plants in modifying the movement of water was further demonstrated by deforestation of one of the six drainage basins. Following deforestation, the annual runoff of the drainage basin increased by about 30-40 per cent over the amount of runoff of the previously forested drainage basin. The greatest difference occurred during the spring and summer months when runoff values were about 400 per cent higher than expected from the basin in its vegetated state. The difference represents the amount of water which was normally transpired by vegetation in an undisturbed drainage basin. Unvegetated, drainage-basin runoff becomes more evenly distributed during the year because it closely reflects precipitation and becomes disconnected from the influence of plant processes (*Likens et al.* 1970).

Another major thrust of the Hubbard Brook study was on the biogeochemical cycle of a forested drainage basin. Comparison of disturbed and undisturbed basins demonstrates the degree of control that organisms exert on the landscape. The chemical quality of both precipitation (input) and runoff (output) were studied on the forested and disturbed drainage basins. Table lists the precipitation inputs and runoff elements in outputs of elements in undisturbed and disturbed basins.

Table 1.3. Comparison of the Chemical inputs and output (kg/ha) of Undisturbed and Disturbed Drainage Basins.

	Forested		*Disturbed*	
Element	*Precipitation*	*runoff*	*Precipitation*	*Runoff*
Calcium	2.6	11.8	2.3	77.3
Sodium	1.5	6.9	1.3	18.1
Magnesium	0.7	2.9	0.6	16.2
Potassium	1.1	1.7	0.5	23.0
Nitrates	4.6	1.3	5.8	104.0

In the forested drainage basin, the ratios between the input and output of the elements calcium, sodium, magnesium and potassium range from

0.2 to 0.6. In the case of nitrates, the atmospheric contribution is about 3.5 times larger than the amount appearing as runoff. An important discovery of the research was that the loss of cations, i. e., the nutrient ions of Table is balanced by the input of positively charged hydrogen ions delivered by precipitation. A large proportion of the hydrogen ions are associated with sulphates and nitrates that apparently originate with industrial activities. When the water containing hydrogen ions enters the soil, the hydrogen ions replace the nutrient cations attached to the exchange sites of the soil, and the nutrients are flushed out of the soil with runoff.

Water quantity and quality variation due to disturbance can be more fully appreciated by comparing drainage-basin outputs before and after deforestation as shown in Table. Several key points can be made. Most striking is the fact that the disturbed drainage basin biota loses control over the movement of elements in a local region. All of the nutrient elements were being released at a rate which was between 14 and 46 times greater than gained via precipitation. Many other changes were also observed in the stream system.

Physical qualities of the water undergo fundamental changes. In the forested basin, the streams are in deep shade during summer. As a result, there is a very small daily fluctuation of temperature of the stream water. Within a disturbed drainage basin, direct sunlight warms the soil during daytime and radiation losses during night cool the runoff. The overall change in warmer runoff which undergoes relatively large diurnal temperature fluctuation. It was also observed that the release of nutrients into the stream in large quantities (or eutrophication) caused severe deterioration of stream water quality. The combination of large quantities of nutrients and warm water triggered the rapid growth of algae in the stream. The algae in turn died and sank to the bottom and the bacterial decay processes consumed large quantities of oxygen. The stream became anoxic and unable to support higher forms of aquatic life. In conjuction with eutrophication there was increased erosion. In the deforested drainage basin, without a source of leaves, the layer of litter was lost from the land surface and stream bottom. These leaf-litter substances are extremely important to the stream because they form a biological barrier to erosion. Leaf-litter loss, coupled with increased runoff, caused a significant increase in stream channel erosion. In sum, the drainage basin functions as a whole system in which plants and their litter play a critical role in tying the parts of the system together (*Likens et al.* 1970).

Experimental work in several locations has revealed that not only is the drainage basin influenced by plants but that the amount of streamflow

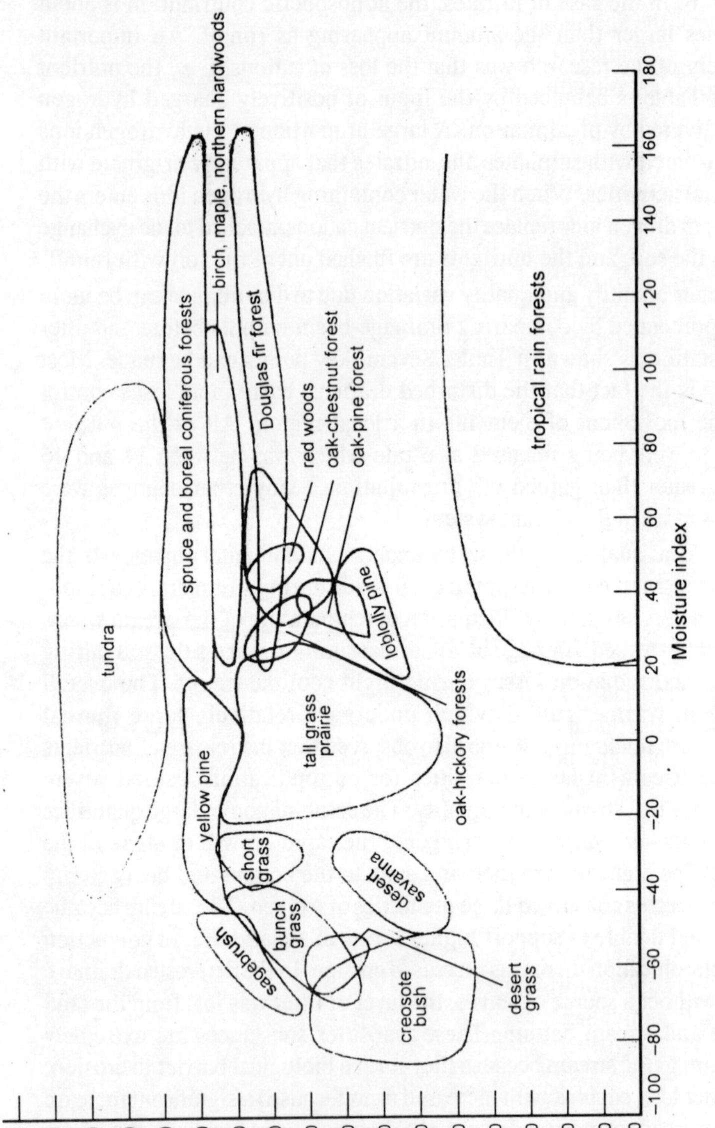

Fig. 1.3. Natural communities a function of potential evapotranspiration and moisture index.

is a function of the species of plant present in the basin. One long-term, study, has been conducted in the southern Appalachian Mountains of southwestern West Virginia (*Swank & Douglass* 1974). The naturally occurring deciduous oak-hickory forest was cut and replaced with a stand of white pine (Pinus strobus). The study demonstrated the physical differences between basins vegetated with different species of plants. The soils within a basin vegetated with conifers tended to be much drier than those vegetated with hardwoods. Conifers photosynthesize and evaportanspire much earlier in the spring than do broadleaf deciduous trees. One measure of leaf surface is the leaf area index, which is a measure of the area of leaf surface compared with the area of ground the plant is occupying. During the dormant season, conifers have a much larger leaf area index than broadleaf deciduous trees (9.9 compared to less than 1) and thus intercept and subsequently evaporate much more rainfall. Overall, the evaporation and transpiration by conifers results in a stream- flow reduction of 20 per cent compared to drainage basins composed of the broadleaf deciduous forest (*Swank & Douglass* 1974). The reduced soil moisture resulting from higher transpiration rates among conifers also limits the growth of ground cover. The reduction in ground cover resulted in changes which influenced flooding cycles and water quality. During heavy precipitation, runoff of the sparsely vegetated surfaces caused an increase in soil erosion. Stream channels were deepened and slopes became steeper as an adjustment to the influence of a conifer forest. Also, the natural acidity of pine needles resulted in the leaching of cations and hence, water contained greater quantities of various elements. Type of vegetation controls basic characteristics of soil moisture, ground cover, and chemical regime, which in turn influence drainage basin characteristics such as water quality, sedimentation transport, channel depth, and angle of slope.

Vegetation cover can influence local water availability by acting as a cloud droplet inpaction network which deposits water and aerosols. Examples of this phenomenon are reported from several elevations of the northern Appalachians (*Lovertt et al.* 1982) and Lomas de Lachay in coastal Peru (*Holdridge* 1967). In the subalpine forests of the northern Appalachans, inputs from cloud droplets account for about 46 per cent of the water, and from 150-430 per cent more chemical inputs than bulk precipitation. In the Peruvian forest, precipitation recorded under the tree-crown yielded 17 per cent more water than was recorded in the open. The mechanism that causes this increase in precipitation is the condensation of moisture or deposition of cloud droplets on the aerial portion of the tree. The leaves act as large nets that capture droplets of moisture which do not otherwise have a possibility of coalescence to form precipitation. Thus process attests to the capacity of the tree canopy to influence and enhance its own microclimate. When all aspects of the relationship between plants, albedo, precipitation, and soil water are taken into consideration it becomes apparent that vegetation plays a major role in modifying the Earth's climate (*Shukla & Mintz* 1982, *Lockword* 1983).

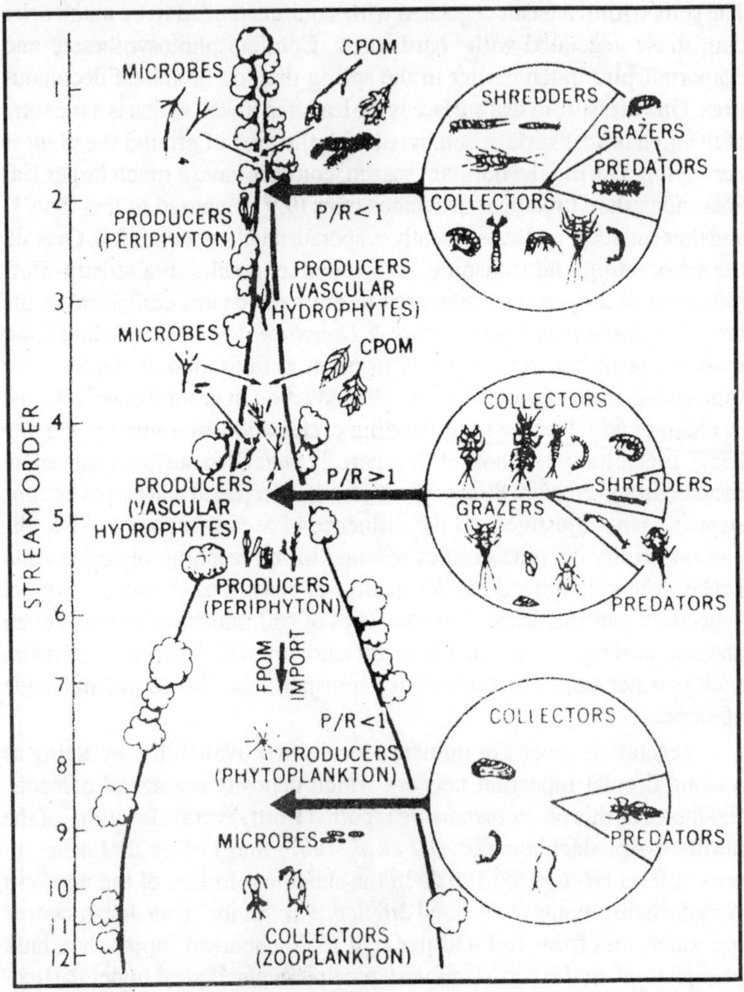

Fig. 1.4. The stream organism as a function of the stream order and position in the vertical stream profile.

Soil Moisture Balance

The above discussion of the relationships between precipitation, vegetative cover, soil moisture, evaporation, transpiration, and runoff provides reason to consider alternative methods of classifying climate beyond the simple use of temperature and precipitation. *C.W. Thornthwaite* (1948) developed a method for classifying climates on the basis of energy and moisture criteria. Thornthwaite's soil water balance analysis uses month- by-month values of precipitation, potential evaporation, actual evaporation, and soil moisture surpluses or deficiencies to determine the water available for plant transpiration and growth at a given locality.

Potential evaporation (PE) is the amount of soil moisture which could be used by the vegetation if there was no limit to the supply of water. The principal determinant of PE is solar radiation. PE is usually expressed as the depth of liquid water that could be transpired per month. The value changes with seasons. When soil moisture is depleted and only hygroscopic water remains, the estimated actual rate of evaporation (AE), will fall below the potential rate of evaporation. By using these two estimated moisture parameters, *Thornthwaite* was able to chart the local deficit or surplus of soil moisture. Several problems have been observed in the calculation of water balances in various places (*Major* 1977, *Schulze & McGee* 1978). Calibrations have been developed to enhance the reliability of the *Thornthwaite* method in localities where they need adjustment (*Schelton* 1978).

One particularly useful measure for evaluating the long- term availability of water resources is the moisture index (*Thornthwaite & Mather* 1955). The moisture index is calculated in two ways. It is the ratio of the difference between water surplus and deficit and the potential evaporation 100[(S-D)/PE]; and it is the ratio of the difference between precipitation and potential evaporation and the potential evapotranspiration 100[(P/PE) – 1]. In general, when the potential evaporation of stations bearing particular natural vegetation-types is plotted against the moisture index of the same stations, as shown in different vegetation associations become distinguishable from one another (*Mather & Yoshioka* 1968). A forest requires an index of about 20, while grasslands and deserts exist where the moisture index is negative. Likewise, the great rivers of the Earth arise from regions with positive moisture indices, while inland basins are associated with negative moisture indices.

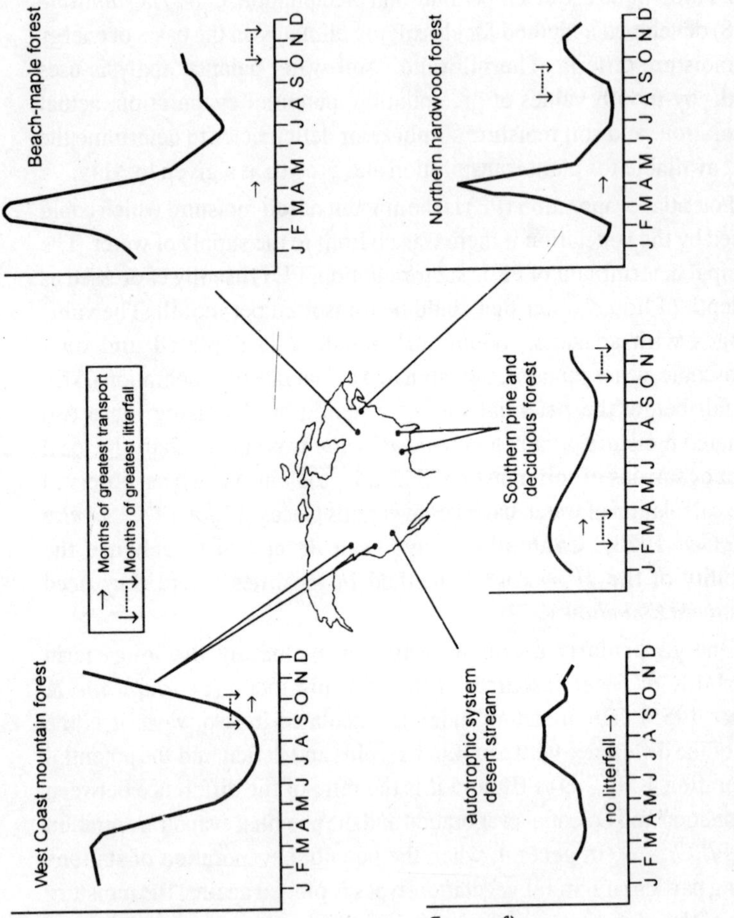

Fig. 1.5. Streamflow, litterfall, and peak particulate organic matter as a function of geographic location.

General Characteristics of Stream Organisms

Comparisons have been made between stream organisms and their marine counterparts (*Patrick* 1975). In general, stream organisms as a group are smaller than their marine relatives. For example, porpoises of the Amazon, though fairly large for stream organisms, are smaller than marine porpoises. Also, it has been observed that fish living in large rivers are usually larger than fish inhabiting small streams. The small size of stream organisms is probably related to the conditions found in the small streams. Narrow channels and seasonal fluctuations promote the survival of small as opposed to large animals.. Small streams undergo greater fluctuations in water due to small catchment area and lack of storage capacity. Large numbers of small animals have a greater likelihood of surviving the inevitable fluctuation of small streams. Under these unstable conditions small numbers of large freshwater animals would be comparatively prone to extinction.

In one way, freshwater environments of the Earth are remarkably similar. They support the same four types of insects: water striders, whirligig beetles, backswimmers, and springtails (*Milne* & *Milne* 1978). Water striders glide or dart across the water surface by rowing with their middle pair of legs. Gerris is a genus found on freshwater surfaces in all parts, of the Earth. Whirligig beetles (Gyrinues and Dineules) live half in the water and half out, set up ripples as they move, and can dive or fly, and crawl on solid surfaces. Backswimmers (Nolonecta) live in ponds and the relatively quiet pools of streams. They swim belly-up and live on the underside of the: surface film of the water. Their major food is the midge or mosquito. The fourth cosmopolitan surface-film aquatic insect is the springtail (Podura and Sminthurus). These latter are the most ancient surface-water insects and first appeared about 375 Ma ago. They alone inhabited the surface film until 250 Ma ago. Springtails feed on plant spores that settle onto the water surface.

Stream organisms generally have short life cycles compared with deep-lake or marine organisms. Many species have life cycles that last only one day. Since life cycles are short, the reproductive rate tends to be very high.

Stream communities tend to have long food chains that include four or five transfers of energy. Algae are important both as a food source and as a substrate for the growth of other epiphytic food sources. Rooted plants are not as important as a food source as they are as a substrate or shelter for other organisms. They thus serve to increase habitat diversity (*Patrick* 1975).

Table 1.4. Comparison of Physical and Chemical characteristics of Peat and Mineral Soil (Values in Per cent Based on Dry Matter, modified from Brady 1974)

Source	Nature	Organic matter	N	P_2O_5	K_2O	CaO
Michigan	Low lime	77.5	2.10	0.26	—	0.16
Michigan	High lime	85.1	2.08	0.25	—	6.80
Germany	Low lime	97.0	1.20	0.10	0.05	0.35
Germany	High lime	90.0	2.50	0.25	0.10	4.00
Austria	Low lime	93.3	1.40	0.10	0.06	0.45
Austria	High lime	83.8	2.10	0.18	0.13	2.13
New York	Low lime	94.2	1.26	0.15	0.10	0.60
New York	High lime	81.5	2.56	0.19	0.28	6.51
Minnesota	Low organic	59.7	2.35	0.36	0.17	2.52
Minnesota	High organic	94.0	1.70	0.16	0.04	0.31
Florida	Sawgrass peat	87.1	2.79	0.41	0.04	5.20
Canada	Pest soil	74.3	2.19	0.20	0.16	—
Washington	Woody sedge peat	89.2	3.52	0.43	0.90	1.29
Mineral soil (typical)		4.0	0.15	0.04	1.70	0.40

Streams commonly contain very large numbers of species. Many species have developed specialized organs or appendages for surviving in currents (*Vogel* 1981). Hard-water streams tend to support fewer species of algae, larger number of protozoa and insects, and slightly fewer species of fish than soft-water streams (*Patrick* 1975). Along a single river, the number of species in common during a single collection time between different collection sites tends to be higher than the number of species in common found at a single site during different collection times (*Patrick* 1975). Overall, there is a high species turnover in time and space. Examination of the physical characteristics that influence biotic qualities of streams provides insight into the biogeographic patterns of the stream habitat.

Photosynthesis and Respiration Rotio of Streams

The traditional way of considering a community of organisms is to regard them as a locally self-sustaining entity to which radiant energy is supplied. The energy passes through the various trophic levels, that is, the primary producer, primary consumer, secondary consumer levels, and so on, and the decay chain breaks down the organic materials so that the constituent elements can be subsequently returned to the organisms to be recycled. This biogeochemical model may be a reasonable conceptual framework for many terrestrial and even lake communities, but it is inappropriate for the stream system. In the stream, everything released into solution moves down stream and cannot be locally recycled (*Hynes* 1970). A generalized approach that succeeds in conveying the dynamic features of the stream is based on the longitudinal profile of the stream. There are physical features of the stream which change from the headwaters to the mouth that influence the ratio of photosynthesis and respiration. Some stream segments have almost no photosynthesis and thus a ratio of photosynthesis and respiration (P/R ratio) less than 1. The organic matter, usually leaves or needles, which supports the growth of organisms here must be imported into the stream segment. These segments are principally the domain of heterotrophic organisms. Other segments of the stream may have more photosynthesis than respiration and thus a P/R ratio greater than 1, and large numbers of autotrophs (*Cummins* 1975). The physical and biological properties of the upper and lower segments of a large stream are sufficiently different that the two parts of the stream have been subdivided into to rhythron and potamon.

RHYTHRON

The turbulent flowing stream in the elevated area, *ie*., head- waters and mountain streams, of the drainage basin is known as the rhythron (also called rhithron), literally flow plus elevation. The general changes occurring in the longitudinal profile of a stream and their influence on stream organisms. The rhythron is the coldest part of the stream from the source to the point where the monthly mean temperature rises to about 68-75°F (20-24°C), where water flow is turbulent, oxygen concentration is always high, and the streambed is composed of rocks, stones, or gravel. The head- water region of a stream is typically densely vegetated and, because of the narrowness of the stream, dimly lit. The food chain of the headwater consists of inputs of organic matter from the vegetation via leaf fall. Because the stream valley is typically steep sided in the headwaters, the quantity of leaves per cubic meter of stream per year far exceeds the quantities in lower reaches of the stream. The nutrient values vary with the type of vegetation. Species of Alnus (alder) have root nodules and a symbiotic relationship with bacteria similar to legumes. Thus Alnus leaves contain about four times more nitrogen than other deciduous species. Conifers are relatively poor nutrient suppliers to streams (*Hynes* 1970). The rhythron supports large numbers of benthic (bottom-dwelling) organisms specialized in shredding organic matter and another group specialized in capturing coarse particulate organic matter (CPOM). The CPOM in turn is further digested by these organisms and becomes line particulate organic matter (FPOM) of the water and sediments. The shredders obtain their food source from microorganisms and hyphomycete fungi growing on leaf tissue (*Williams* 1981). One group of shredders that are important are aquatic hyphomycete fungi of the genus Ingoldia (=Gyoerffyella) which colonize leaves that fall into streams during the autumn (*Barlocher* 1982). Along with shredders are collectors which either trap the FPOM as it passes in the water or collect it from sediments. Caddisflies spin nets which capture suspended organic matter. The most ancient caddisfly taxa live in turbulent currents (*Alstead* 1982). Other organisms feed on the microorganisms that colonize the surfaces of organic particles and thus return the particles, minus microorganisms back to the FPOM pool to be utilized repeatedly by other benthic organisms down stream. Because of the fact that primary productivity is low, grazers are poorly represented. Predators such as stoneflies and fish species such as salmonids and sculpins are also present in these well-aerated, organically rich, high-protein rhythron waters.

Potamon

As one descends along the longitudinal profile of the stream, several physical and biological changes occur. The potamon (means river) is the lower stream segment where the monthly mean temperature rises to over

68-75°F (20-24°C), where oxygen deficits occur at times, where flow quickens and the channel deepens, and where the bed consists mainly of sand, silt, or clay. There is a gathering of water resulting from the confluence of additional streams, and the stream broadens to the extent that the middle becomes exposed to sunlight. In humid climates this happens when streams become-third-or fourth-order. The character of the stream shifts from a predominantly heterotrophic to an autotrophic condition. Planktonic forms are common in the surface waters, and in the benthic community, grazers and collectors predominate. Shredders become less common. The caddisflies of more modern taxa have evolved to live in the laminar currents which have greater concentrations of particulate food (*Alstead* 1982). Predators include both invertebrates and vertebrates. Collector species dominate the river benthos as a result of the inflow of large amounts of FPOM produced up stream, and locally produced FPOM from planktonic forms. Overall, the P/R ratio becomes less than 1 because high turbidity blocks sunlight. However, high turbidity may be a modern problem because many early accounts of streams along the east coast of North America indicated clarity where now there is turbidity (*Trimble* 1974).

The transition zone between the cooler, turbulent, shallow, and aerated rhythron and the warmer, deeper, smooth-flowing potamon generally has the largest number of species because of overlap in the ranges from both segments of the stream. The total number of fish tends to decrease while the weight per unit fish tends to increase in the downstream reaches of the stream. The weight per unit area remains more or less constant in the stream (*Hynes* 1970). North American rivers have many more species of fish than do northwest European rivers, though there are many similarities between the two funas. Glaciation had an unequal influence on the faunas of the two areas. In North America, as the climate changed, the river fauna was able to retreat to warmer climates in the south. In north- western Europe, species were caught between the ice sheet building in the north and the glaciers forming in the Alps, resulting in the extermination of many species (*Hynes* 1970).

The above discussion is based on research conducted primarily in humid mid-latitude climates. There are many factors which influence the productivity of a stream. For example, the seasonality of precipitation and streamflow changes with such factors as altitude, latitude, continental position, that is, all of the variables that influence climate. These same factors, because of their role in productivity, also influence the amount of organic matter available in a stream. In addition, the composition of vegetation, whether coniferous or broadleaf deciduous forests (and even the species such as alder or oak), also affects the amount of organic matter in a stream. This brings the discussion back to the water balance idea discussed earlier in the chapter. A comprehensive view of the complexity of the stream biosystem requires combining the principal factors which govern the operation of the regional water balance with factors that influence litter production and organic matter availability in the stream. The average timing of streamflow, litterfall, and peak particulate organic matter transport into streams is shown for several North American regions.

The influence of latitude is equally profound. Middle- latitude streams include rhythronic and potamonic zones and support both cold and warm water adapted species. Potamonic species are capable of surviving-but not thriving-in rhythronic waters. Rhythronic animals cannot survive in the warm, oxygen-depleted waters of the potamon (*Williams* 1981). In high-latitude environments, the streams are typically rhythronic, supporting species adapted to cold, well-aerated water through- out the entire length. In tundra freshwater systems, organic matter has accumulated in the form of terrestrial peat, and is transferred to higher organisms via aquatic insect larvae (*Schell* 1983).

In lower latitude streams, the rhythron may be very short or absent, with the potamon dominating the river. Large tropical lowland rivars have distinctly high fish species diversity, and the fish are characterized by having many adaptations to low oxygen supply (*Welcomme* 1979). The Amazon undergoes seasonal fluctuations of as much as 20 m (*Gentry* and *Lopez-Parodi* 1980) and floods large areas during high water stages. The total efflux of organic carbon for the Amazon has provided a basis for estimating the total organic carbon input to the oceans from the Earth's rivers. The Amazon contributes about 10^{14} g of carbon and the total for the Earth's rivers must exceed 10^{15} g (*Richey et al.* 1980). One source of organic carbon is from swamp hardwood forests and floodplains. This organic carbon enters the river during flooding. The influx of organic carbon tends to be moderated by biological processes because the carbon promotes increased organic activity which in turn removes organic carbon from the river at a faster rate. The overall result is a relatively constant transport of organic carbon (*Richey et al.* 1980).

The floodwaters of the Amazon open up extensive habitats to aquatic organisms. During high water periods, the forested lowland floodplains are inundated, forming extensive varzea forests. These forests are the base for the aquatic food chain. Many common fishes move into the inundated forests and voraciously consume fruits and seeds. During low water periods, the same fish move back into the main river channel or floodplain lakes and consume little food (*Goulding* 1981). There are many fascinating examples that provide insight into the biogeographic patterns of streams and organisms.

Natural Impoundments

Several physical processes form water-holding depressions in the landscape. These include glacial action, stream meandering, tectonic forces, and structural weaknesses. During Pleistocene times, continental glaciers formed lake-pitted kame and kettle landscapes in many areas of the Northern Hemisphere, such as the lake areas surrounding the Great Lakes of North America or dotting the landscape in European countries around the Baltic Sea. Enormous blocks of ice were buried in glacial till and when they melted left depressions or kettles which filled with water, as well as ridges which are known as kames. Rivers play a role by creating oxbow lakes as they cut and fill their sedimentary banks and undergo course changes in their flood- plains. Tectonic processes have formed the intermountain basins in western North America as well as coastal subsidence in the Atlantic and Gulf coasts of the continent. Structural weaknesses that have resulted from the weathering and dissolution of the underlying limestone formations have created sinkhole depressions in several regions, such as south Florida.

Rift Lakes

The rift valley lakes of East Africa are spectacular for their size and for the diversity of their fish fauna (*Fryer & Iles* 1972, *Beadle* 1981). Lake Malawi is the southern-most rift valley lake; it is 620 km long, 80 km wide and has a single large basin which is 750 m deep. Lake Tanganyika is even larger and deeper and has three basins, but has a smaller diversity of fish.

Lake Malawi has more, species of fish than any other lake in the world. About 300 species of fish are currently known but many new species are being described, and it is estimated that at least 1,000 species probably exist in the lake (*Ribbink et al.* 1983). The most fascinating biological feature about Lake Malawi is that nearly 95 per cent of the fish are members of a single family, Cichlidae.

Cichlids are a large family of freshwater fish and are found in Southern Africa, Sri Lanka, India, South America, and one species is found in Texas. Their distribution (with the exception of the member found in Texas) suggests a long history which extends back to a time when the continents of Gondwana were connected. All but four of the cichlids found in Lake Malawi are endemic to the lake. All species except one are mouth brooders. The exception is the red-bellied bream, Tilapia rendalli, which digs and broods in tunnels.

The density of cichlid species is truly amazing. On Domwe and Thumba Islands near Cape Maclear, in Lake Malawi National Park, there are rocky areas where densities of 15 to 20 different species of cichlids exist per 10 square metres (*Reinthall & Lewis* 1986). The fish have adopted a large number of specialized feeding behaviours. For example, algae and diatoms grow in the water column, on rocks and sand; different species have specialized their feeding behaviour to live in each of these conditions. In addition, some cichlids feed on the scales and fins of other fish. Lake Malawi is anoxic at about 230 m, and bacteria are the dominant organism in anoxic waters. In addition to nutrients sinking to depth and being lost, another way in which there is a loss of nutrients from the lake is through the hatching of midges (Chaoborus and Chironomus). So many midges hover in the air at one time that they form dark clouds above the surface of the lake. When the midges hatch and blow onto the land they carry valuable nutrients from the lake.

As in the case of the finches and turtles which *Darwin* found in the Galapagos Islands, the many related fish species existing within Lake Malawi raises questions regarding the development of new species.

Wetland Communities

One common successional hypothesis treats open bodies of water as ephemeral features of the landscape which over time fill in and disappear. Starting with an open body of water, there is a submergent stage (submergent water plants become dominant), an emergent stage (shallow water herbaceous plants dominate), and then "climaxes" with a closed stage of either a wet prairie or a wet forest. There are situations, such as within the floodplain, where this sequence may be appropriate. However, because of the qualities of the organic materials that have filled the depression, organisms may continue to play a role in maintenance of the body of water. There are a number of wetland communities of plants and animals which thrive within and are an inextricable component of the drainage system. A few of these communities, the bog, marsh, and swamp, are briefly described below.

Bogs

Two broad groups of soils are commonly recognized: mineral and

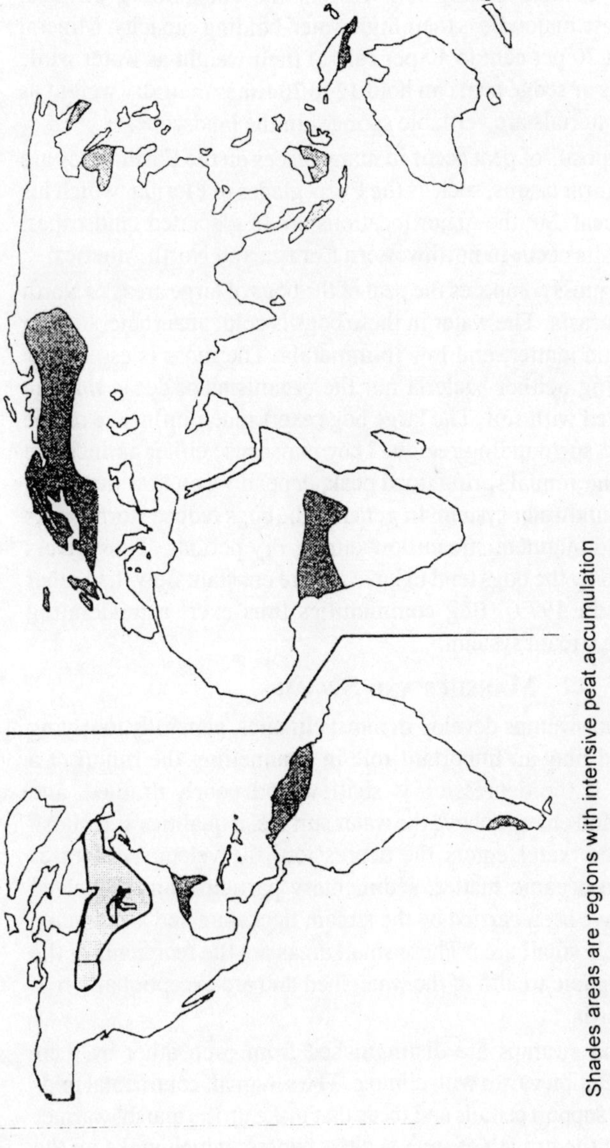

Fig. 1.6. Location of the major peat soils of the earth.

organic soils. Organic soils are composed of large accumulations of mosses or sedges, and are commonly referred to as peat. They have the highest organic matter content of any soil. One of the outstanding physical properties of these materials is their high water-holding capacity. Mineral soils hold about 20 per cent to 40 per cent of their weight as water while undecayed moss or sedge peat can hold 12 to 20 times their dry weight as water. These materials are veritable sponges in the landscape.

Organic deposits of peat occur in many places on the Earth. They are located in structural basins, such as the Ever- glades of Florida, which his sedge-derived peat, but the major locations are in glaciated landscapes. Extensive deposits occur in northwestern Eurasia and North America.

Sphagnum moss composes the peat of the bogs of large areas of North America and Eurasia. The water in these bogs is cold, anaerobic, high in dissolved organic matter, and low in minerals. The moss is essentially sterile, containing neither bacteria nor the organisms of decay that are usually associated with soil. The large bogs exert much influence on the hydrology of the surrounding region. They may cause either an increase or decrease on the annual spring flood peak, depending on how the bog is tied into the groundwater system. In general, the bogs reduce storm peaks significantly and augment streamflow during dry periods. Thus, rivers that are supplied by the bogs tend to have a more constant flow than other streams (Novitzki 1979). Bog communities thus exert a moderating influence on the stream system.

Marshes and Swamps

Marshes and swamps develop in moist climates, generally low lying depressions, and play an important role in channelling the runoff of a stream system. If the depression is shallow and poorly drained, and supports plants and emerge above the water surface, it qualities as a marsh or swamp. When water enters the depression, the velocity decreases rapidly, and the organic matter, sedimentary particles, and dissolved minerals that have been carried by the stream flocculate and accumulate within a relatively small area. These small areas are the recipients of the nutrients and organic wealth of the watershed and are exceptionally rich places on the Earth.

Marshes and swamps are distinguished from each other by their vegetation. Vegetation varies with climate. The seasonal, continental mid-latitude climates support cattails and reeds that make up the marsh; warmer climates support the growth of trees such as cypress which make up the swamp vegetation.

Emergent marshes are extremely productive environments. They annually produce between 450 and 2,320 g/m^2 (dry weight) of above-ground material and compare favourably with saltwater marshes in their productivity (*Good et al.*, 1981). In order of their productivity are cattails (Typha), reed canarygrass (Phalaris arundinacea), reeds (Phargmites communis), sedges (Carex), and bulrush (Scirpus) (Pratt & Andrews 1981). Marshes can undergo enormous fluctuation of productivity from year to year. Prairie marshes have been described which vary by as much as 18-fold over a period of 5-20 years (*Good et a.,* 1978). Marsh variability is related to two major factors. First, weather fluctuation leads to changes in water depth that strongly influence the plants which can be supported within a body of water. During wet years, high water may flood out emergent plants, while dry years may result in the filling in of a marsh with emergent plants. Severe drought may even lead to the drying up of a prairie pothole, whence the unprotected bottom may become deepened by wind erosion. In North America an animal plays a major role in marsh vegetation, the muskrat (Ondatra zibethica). Muskrats are rodents that have an impressive capacity to reproduce. They have six or more young per litter and under optimal conditions, can have four litters per year. Muskrat populations have been reported to grow so rapidly that they literally "eat out" the plants from the marsh (*Weller* 1981).

The muskrats use the plants for food and construction. The rootstocks, rhizomes, and tips of the plants are eaten and the stems are used to construct a platform and left to rot. In the early stages of reestablishment in a marsh, muskrats tend to construct lodges nearly 2 m high and 4.5 m in diameter. However, the lodges are half that size when the muskrat population has removed a large proportion of the plant material. Reproduction rates have also been reported to undergo changes that reflect the conditions of the marsh. Thus, as the marsh becomes crowded, lodges decrease in size, and the number of surviving young decreases. These dynamic activities affect the numbers and species of birds which inhabit a marsh. The greatest number of individual birds are supported when the whole marsh is dominated by a thick growth of emergent plants. However, when there is a roughly equal balance between open water and emergent vegetation, then the maximum number of species can be supported by the marsh.

When muskrats open up the vegetation around their lodges, they create habitat diversity that attracts an increased diversity of bird species (*Weller* 1981).

The most extensive swamps in North America occur along the Atlantic and Gulf coastal plains. The most notable examples include the

Great Dismal Swamp, Okefenokee Swamp, and Everglades. The Great Dismal Swamp consists of nearly 200 km^2 within the Atlantic coastal plain. The swamp, is believed to be at least 80,000 years old (*Kirk* 1979). The oldest pollen is from pines and spruce. The modern vegetation consists of a variety of tree species including cypress, white cedar, and tupelo gum (Nyssa aquatica). The swamp acts to stabilize the groundwater table in the region. During periods of very heavy rains, the swamp controls floodwaters by temporarily storing excess runoff and releasing it slowly as runoff or into the groundwater system. The area abounds with an amazing variety of plants and animals, some of which are poorly known (*Kirk* 1979).

Within the Everglades of South Florida and the Gulf Coast swamps, one organism has had an especially important role within the environmental system, the American alligator (Alligator mississippiensis). Alligators are active diggers. They dig out channels and build large mounds for nest sites. They also dig deep pools or "gator holes" in the swamp. During periods of extreme drought these pools provide the last remaining inhabitable sites in the swamp for birds and other animals to survive. When the drought breaks repopulation of the swamp takes place from the animals which have survived alligator holes. The nesting mounds of alligators contribute to the variety of the swamp environment by providing nest sites for several bird species, such as herons and egrets. Thus, marshes and swamps are complicated habitats that depend on energy expenditure and behavioural adjustment of specialized water-dwelling animal inhabitants. The activities of these animals create conditions that provide opportunities for-existence of the larger plant and animal community.

Beaver Impoundments

Beavers are a sine qua non of the influence of animals on streams. They have an unusually large impact on stream systems and the development of valley soils and vegetation of the Northern Hemisphere. Two species are recognized, the Eurasian beaver, Castor fibre, and the North American beaver, C. canadensis. The beaver is a large rodent, second in size to the capybara (Hydrochoerus hydrochaeris), a relative of the guinea-pig and inhabitant of tropical America. The beaver attains a length of between 90 and 120 cm and a weight of up to 30 kg. The present range of the beaver is only a fraction of its former range. In the Old World the range of C. fibre once extended from Scandinavia to Spain and from Britain to Siberia. Now there are only limited populations in the lower Rhone, the middle Elbe, and the southern part of Norway. The former range of C. canadensis included the northern half of North America with extensions into the southern Appalachians and the southern Rocky Mountains. They numbered in the thousands of millions and were an attraction to early traders who sought their pelts. In general, beavers were hunted for food (because of the scales on their tails they were defined as fish and could be consumed by Catholics on Friday and during Lent), for fur (they have magnificent coats which are durable and easily tailored), and for castoreum, a scent gland substance which was highly valued for its medicinal properties during medieval times. For these reasons and because they occupied flood plain soils that humans valued for agriculture, the populations of beavers were cut to a fraction of their former numbers by hunters and trappers. But, many soil and vegetation features can be understood only by considering the influence that beavers have on river valleys.

The activities of the beaver are entirely bound up with trees, flowing water, and the construction of dams. Beavers create deep ponds or maintain water levels in preexisting depressions by building dams across streams. These are usually made of logs and sticks, although dams made of boulders have also been described (*Chapman* and *Chapman* 1937). The impoundment stores water and serves the beaver by providing a site for a lodge which is safe from predators. The food of the beaver consists of the bark and shoots of poplar, willow, alder, elm, or oak, plus vegetation which is favoured by the expanded riparian environment that the beaver pond creates. The beaver obtains food by chopping down trees. The bark is stripped and the inedible portions of the trees are moved to the river for the construction of the beaver dam or the lodge which is built in the impounded waters behind the dam. In order to move large logs, beavers construct canals.

Castor canadensis is acknowledged as the superior dam builder . The largest recorded dam built by C. fiber was found in the Voronezh region of Russia. It was 120 m long, 1 m high, and 60-100 cm wide (*Frisch* 1974). One of the largest structures constructed by C. canadensis was on the Jefferson River in Montana; it was 700 m long and could bear the weight of horses and then riders (*French* 1974). The largest dams were probably maintained by generations of beavers for centuries. Beavers regulate the water level of the beaver pond by constantly adjusting the dam. During high water, the dam can be adjusted by lowering the crown. During low water the beavers tighten up the dam to reduce seepage. The splendid teamwork of beavers building and maintaining a single dam is, itself magnificent. A series of dams within a number of tributaries of a drainage basin operate together to create an impact on the landscape.

The concerted efforts of many beavers must have changed many valleys of the Northern Hemisphere during the Holocene from relatively physically and biologically homogeneous habitats into heterogeneous environments supporting diverse groups of organisms. The process can be imagined within the high valleys of the Rocky Mountains. Prior to the movement of beavers into high valleys, conifers probably dominated the landscape. As beavers move in and construct dams, the impounded waters flood out the conifers. Each pond creates a site which is attractive to migrating waterfowl and other birds. The riparian environment of the shores of the pond supports new types of plants (poplar, willow, alder), that supply the food for the beaver population. The pond checks the movement of sediments down stream and these particles and to the richness for the aquatic organisms of the pond. The enlarged surface area of the enriched pool of water supports high levels of photosynthesis and releases increased amounts of organic carbon that in turn enhances the food supply for aquatic organisms down stream. Eventually, the impoundment becomes filled with sediments, and beavers abandon the site. As the beaver pond drains it becomes a thick lens of rich humus that supports the rapid growth or grasses and forbs (non-grass species) and establishes the beaver meadow. These soils have high water-holding capacity and slowly release water to the water table and the stream. The activity of the beaver becomes the primary force in the evolution of the soils in the riparian zone. They influence the diversity of habitats and establish structures which argument the slow but steady movement of water through the drainage basin. These feats, give the beaver its reputation as the unparalleled engineer and builder of the animal kingdom (*Hodgdon & Larson* 1980).

The Estuary

Eventually, most freshwater streams flow to ocean level and meet the sea. Under special conditions, the flow of fresh water to the ocean is partially enclosed and the outlet to the sea restricted to a relatively narrow opening. These places are referred to as estuaries. The most important estuaries include drowned river valleys, such as Chesapeake Bay; down-faulted sections of the Earth's crust, such as San Francisco Bay; drowned glacial troughs, or fjords, found in Norway, Alaska, New Zealand, and other glaciated mountainous coastal regions: and saltmarshes and lagoons that are formed behind barrier beaches.

Within the estuary, fresh water from the land flows upon and meets the denser salt water of the ocean. The interface between the two different types of water is a nutrient-rich and highly productive site for organisms.

But these sites are also physically demanding and only a few species can tolerate the rigors of successive exposure to fresh and sea water, and the wide fluctuation in temperature associated with these environments.

One component of the estuary is shallow saltmarshes that play an important role for organisms. Saltmarshes are regularly rinsed by the ebb and flow of the tides. Waste products are diluted and removed and nutrients are brought in from the land and the sea. The materials of streams flocculate as the mixture of clay-size particles and algae meets the sea waters. They settle out, leaving the water clear (*Avnimelech et a.,* 1982). In the saltmarsh, plants need not expend energy in collecting minerals. They are assisted in obtaining minerals from many organisms. Clams, oysters, and mussels trap nutrients as they feed, and deposit the wastes as pseudo-feces. In these nutrient-rich waters, plants grow, die, and cycle rapidly as they are consumed by the inhabitants of the estuary. The base of the food chain of the estuary is marsh grass or Spartina. The major energy flow is by way of the detritus food chain rather than the grazing food chain. In estuaries along the coast of Georgia, U.S.A., for example, Spartina alterniflora dominates, and organic detritus (over 90% of which originates with the growth of Spartina) is the link between primary production and consumption. Only a small portion of the grass is consumed as a part of the grazing chain (*Ranwell* 1972).

Estuaries are one of the most productive habitats on Earth. They provide huge food supplies as well as sanctuary for many species of waterfowl. They serve as a breeding ground and nursery for many marine fish species. They store nutrients for larval and juvenile marine life. As various species mature, they leave the estuary and head out to sea. Thus, there is a constant movement of the rich organic and nutrient materials to the sea (*Honjo* 1982). As tides move in and out there is also a movement of the sea and enriches the shallow coastal waters of the marine environment.

CONCLUSIONS

In this chapter, the hydrologic cycle, and especially the terrestrial remifications of the cycle as seen in the organization of the drainage basins and the mayriad of organisms that exist along the path of the stream were examined. The path of water from the atmosphere to the land, and across or through the soils to the stream and then through a number of specialized stream, marsh and pond communities within the flow of water were described. At all points, the climate and geologic setting provide primary conditions, but organisms moderate and alter the flow of water, minerals, and organic carbon of the stream. Thus, we have followed the flow of water from the atmosphere to the soils, from the soils to the stream, and along the streams to lakes and wetland communities and finally to the estuary. At every juncture of the path from the land to the sea the stream supports thriving group of organisms.

Chapter 2

Freshwater Environments in Polar Regions

The chronic aridity of both polar heartlands has already been noted. Though the antarctic ice-cap is estimated to contain 90 per cent of the world's water, only a tiny fraction of it becomes available each year for living material. Similarly the arctic desert, with or without ice sheets, has very little water available during the short summers, and none in waters. On the polar fringes warmer air brings in moisture and deposits it as hoar-frost, snow or rain. Though water is solid for much of the year, the annual thaw in spring and summer provides a wide range of aquatic habitats that support biological activity, and may even allow high productivity for a few weeks each year.

Wet soil is essentially a freshwater habitat, above. Melting snow and ice surfaces provide transient substrates which bacteria and algae colonize, forming patches of pale green, red or yellow several hectares in extent. Snow-melt and rain gather in runnels, streams and even small rivers, that flow for a few hours, days or weeks in summer but are stilled by freezing for the rest of the year. Ponds and lakes form in poorly-drained rolling country, accumulating debris and nutrients, freezing partially or completely in winter but providing a limited habitat for plants and animals in summer.

Polar Freshwater Habitats

Snow and Ice Habitats

Freshly-fallen snow surfaces are virtually sterile, though bacteria are present in detectable quantities even on the southern polar ice-cap (*Meyer-Rochow*, 1979). Older snow surfaces become adulterated; damp snow attracts wind-blown particles electrostatically (*Benninghoff and Benninghoff*, 1985), acquiring films of rock dust, bacteria, spores and plant propagules. These accumulate as the snow melts under spring sunshine, and the resulting discoloration hastens the melting. Fragments of moss and algae that land on snow surfaces survive well in the moist environment, and may settle through the remaining snow to colonize the ground beneath.

Ionization and other atmospheric processes add nitrates and ammonium compounds to the snow in nutritionally significant quantities (*Parker et al.*, 1978). Snow close to the coast is often additionally contaminated by mineral salts and organic material from the sea. In summer these are carried inland in sea spray; in winter impregnated snow from the sea ice deposits them on coastal rocks and snowdrifts. In late spring, snow surfaces within a few hundreds metre of the coast often show a flush of colour, usually pink, green or brownish-yellow, caused by patches of unicellular or colonial algae. On the South Orkney Islands Chlamydomonas, Raphidonema and possibly Ochromonas are implicated (*Fogg*. 1967), similar accumulations of algae in a wider range of species have been seen at many other points around the coast (*Akiyama*, 1979; *Kol* and *Flint*, 1968; for a recent review see *Vincent*, 1988). Their productivity is low, fixed carbon being of the order of 10 mg m^2 of snow per day; colour differences are due to different stages in development of the cells, and their sudden, often dramatic appearance during warm spells is more probably due to progressive loss of covering snow than to rapid proliferation (*Fogg*. 1967). Snow algae are widespread in alpine and polar regions, but require persistent banks of melting snow to form spectacular coloured patches; they are rarely seen, for example, on the colder coasts or interior ice-cap of Antarctica. Their ecology has been reviewed by *Hoham* (1975, 1980).

On the lower reaches of glaciers and on ice shelves close to the sea, where ablation exceeds snowfall in summer, wind- blown dust and rock fragments encourage local melting. The resulting shallow pits and pools, often extending over many hectares, accumulate salts and nutrients from year to year. Many are rich enough to support a distinctive cryoconite flora of algae and cynanobacteria, which survive winters encapsulated in the ice (Wharton et *al*, 1981; Vincent, 1988) and flourish briefly the during the summer thaw.

Still-Water Habitats

Over much of the Arctic, surface drainage is poor; permafrost seals the subsoil, and snow-melt provides a flush of water in late spring. In the northern desert there is rarely enough snow for melt-water to accumulate, and ponds are rare. Where winter snow is plentiful, ponds and shallow lakes occupy large areas; over much of the tundra they form networks of static waterways that make walking difficult after the thaw. On ice- scoured uplands and coastal flats there may be more ponds and lakes than dry land. Coastal plains often feature long, shallow lakes, separated and aligned by raised beaches and occupying up to 90 per cent of the terrain. Antarctica has relatively little standing water. Large lakes, many of them strongly saline, are reported from several of the oasis areas; freshwater lakes are also present even in high latitudes, and temporary lakes form in summer alongside many glaciers. Small coastal summer ponds are rare on the mainland but plentiful in the maritime and peripheral Antarctic regions.

Lakes form also on poorly-drained ice, alongside glaciers and ice-caps, on snow-covered ice-sheets, and between ice-sheets and ice-filled moraines. Some are long-lived, fed by annual influxes of melt-water. Others are temporary, flooding during the summer melt and liable to sudden drainage through rifts in the ice and other causes (*Hambrey*, 1984).

Polar lakes and ponds are partly or completely frozen and snow-covered for much of the year. Large ponds and lakes, especially those in high latitudes, stay frozen all the year round, accumulating snow-melt water from rocks nearby and part-thawing only in exceptional seasons. Large lakes thaw round the edges but tend to retain a core of ice in summer; in consequence their waters never warm far above freezing point. Small lakes and ponds thaw completely. Lakes that owe their volume to a balance between inflowing and outflowing water may change radically between seasons, almost draining in winter when the inflow slows down, and overflowing when summer melt brings in water than cannot escape through still-frozen outlets.

Lakes that are ice-free in summer begin cooling at their surface late in the season. The cooled waters sink and circulate until the water mass reaches the critical temperature of 3.98° C, at which fresh water is densest. Thereafter cooler waters overlie warmer, and the surface freezes while bottom waters are still relatively warm. Shallow ponds freeze to the bottom in winter; deeper ones may remain unfrozen at depth, providing a still, protected habitat for overwintering fish, larvae, eggs and spores.

Conversely, spring warming begins immediately under the ice as soon as sunlight penetrates usually, in early summer after the surface snow (which is relatively opaque to solar radiation) has ablated or melted. Water that is warmed a degree or two above freezing point sinks into the colder water below, and is replaced; the resulting density currents stir the lake into turbulence and spread warmth, a process that is enhanced by wind-stirring as the ice disperses. Thus the water quickly becomes isothermal, at temperatures close to those of the air or ground surface nearby. Some stratified hypersaline lakes are permanently warmer in their lower layers than at their surface, sometimes because of volcanic heating, more often due to solar warming through the ice and upper layers of water.

Most polar lakes are highly oligotrophic, with clear waters and a very limited range of species inhabiting them. Notable exceptions are arctic oxbow and other remnant lakes formed on river plains, which may be muddy and well endowed with minerals. Ponds range from oligotrophic to highly eutrophic, according to their situation and history. The poorest are the clear waters of ice-scoured uplands, where there is little soil or vegetation. Those on low-lying land invested by tundra vegetation are usually richer, with a seasonal turnover of minerals and slightly higher productivity. However, such important nutrients as nitrates and phosphates are generally scarce, because rates of bacterial decomposition in the soils of the catchment areas are low, and very little leaches out into the water.

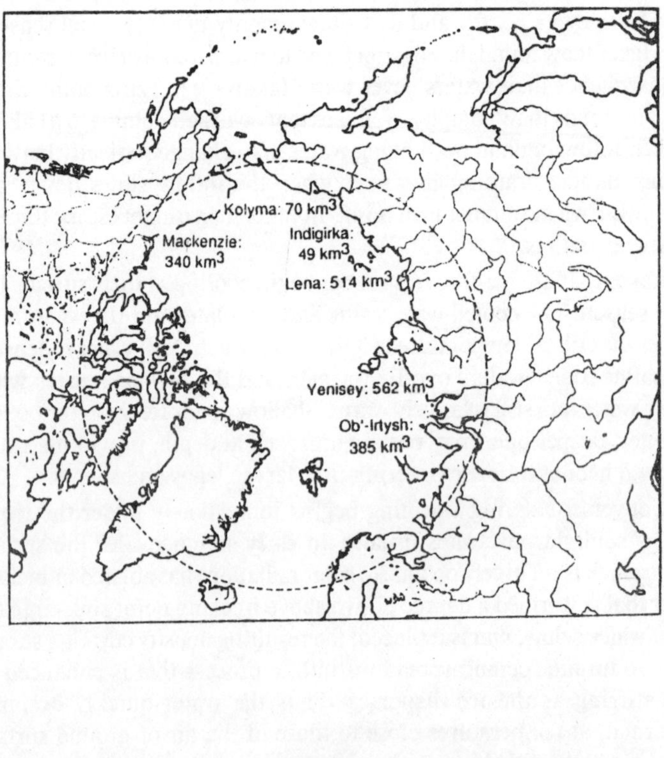

Fig. 2.1. Major inputs of fresh water into the Arctic Ocean.

Ponds and lakes that are frequented by birds often have an enhanced productivity, based on nutrients from the birds droppings and decaying feathers. Even the richest polar ponds and lakes have fewer species and lower productivity than most ponds of similar size and shape in temperate latitudes.

A few polar lakes are saline, their salts originating either from sea water and spray or from rock weathering in their own catchment areas. Sea water on chilling precipitates salts sequentially, first calcium carbonate, then sodium sulphate at —8.2°C, sodium chloride at —22.9°C, and magnesium and potassium chlorides at —36°C. leaving a residual solution rich in calcium chloride (*Nelson* and *Thompson*, 1954; *Thompson* and *Nelson*, 1956). Deposits of many of these minerals, notably halites (hydrated sodium chloride) and mirabilite (hydrated sodium sulphate) occur in the sediments and surrounds of many existing lakes, and in dried-out lake deposits. Saline water reaches its maximum density at temperatures below 3.98°C: at 27 ppt and above the maximum is reached at freezing point, which is also determined by salinity.

Running-water Habitats

Few rivers start in polar regions, though some very large ones flow across arctic and subarctic lands to discharge into the Arctic Ocean. The great northwards-flowing rivers of Siberia and the lesser ones of North America bring year-round flows of water and warmth from the south. They bear thick ice in winter and their flow is strongly seasonal, especially so in those that rise or have much of their catchment area in tundra or boreal forest. Over 35 per cent of the annual flow of the Lena, in Siberia, is delivered during the peak month of June, less than 1 per cent in each of the three months of February, March and April.

More characteristic of the regions are small graded rivers and streams fed by springs and surface runoff, and seasonal, short-lived torrents that flow from glaciers. In these up to half the annual output may occur in the three or four weeks of springtime thaw. Like the larger rivers they are erosive, undercutting and destroying their banks to form wide, braided channels. They carry heavy loads of sediment, abandoning it along their course and inextensive deltas; the finer deposits are often colonized by vegetation, providing some of the richest and most productive communities in the tundra mosaics. More characteristic still are the thousands of tiny meltwater streams that trickle from ice-sheets and snow-banks for a few days or weeks each summer, often following the same channels year after year, and sometimes building up mats of vegetation along their course.

The Arctic is well endowed with running-water habitats. Continental and maritime Antarctica have no large year-round rivers, and only a very few smaller ones, mostly glacier-fed torrents, to match the smaller tundra rivers of the north. The periantarctic islands have many permanent or seasonal streams, spring-fed and carrying run-off from the peaty vegetation throughout the year.

Aquatic Ecology: Food Webs and Productivity

Arctic Aquatic Communities

Still-Water Communities. Arctic ponds and lakes freeze to depths of 1—2.5 from September onward, and accumulate a layer of compacted snow on top of the ice during winter. Thawing occurs slowly in May and June; generally the larger the water body, the longer it takes to thaw out in spring, and the cooler it remains through summer. In a study of lakes and ponds on Truelove Lowland, Devon Island (75°30N), *Minns* (1977) found the smallest lake (16 ha) free of ice by 17 July, while a larger one of 95 ha retained ice until early August. Temperatures at the lake-beds in about 6 m depths were higher than at the surface when ice was present, rising from 1°C in mid-May to about 3°C in late July. When most of the ice had gone, wind stirred the waters; by later summer temperatures became a uniform 4–5°C at all depths. Temperatures of nearby ponds rose higher, to 8°C.

Char Lake (72°42'N), the subject of long-term studies on Cornwallis Island, with an area of 52.6 ha, was typically ice-free from early August to mid-September. The waters were layered from October to May while ice was present, with temperatures close to freezing point near the surface but at 1—1.25°C near the bottom in 26 m. From June onward warming through the ice set up circulation currents which gradually raised temperatures to a uniform 4°C throughout the water column (*Rigler*, 1974).

Biological activity starts long before the ice has melted. In Truelove Lowland lakes aquatic algae and bacteria begin photosynthesis as early as February, when snow still mentles the ice and less than 1 per cent of available light penetrates (*Hobbie*, 1962, 1964; *Holmgren*, 1968). Often the algae accumulate in a thin layer on the underside of the ice sheet, dispersing when the ice melts. Measuring chlorophyll a in water samples as an index of phytoplankton abundance, Minns (1977) found it already plentiful under the ice by mid-May and reaching peak values in late May and June; *Kalff et al.* (1972), working on Char Lake and a neighbouring lake in the Canadian Arctic, recorded active production from February onward.

Algae that are capable of photosynthesis at very low levels of light intensity proliferate early in the season, to be replaced by a succession of other species as light intensity increases (*Kalff*, 1970). Primary productivity is generally low, averaging 10–50 mg Cm^{-2} daily in May and June and rising to 70–30 mg Cm^2 daily during the summer peak of production; on average only 6–12 g Cm^{-2} fixed throughout the year (*Kalff*, 1970; *Minns*, 1977).

Table 2.1. Annual and Quartely Flows of Six Majo River Systems into the Arctic Ocean. After Mackay and Loken (1974)

	June—Aug.	*Sep.—Nov.*	*Dec.—Feb*	*Mar.—May*	*Annual flow (km^3)*
Ob'-Irtysh	57	20	9	14	385
Yenisey	57	18	7	18	562
Lena	71	22	4	3	514
Indigirka	85	14	<1	1	49
Kolyma	73	17	2	8	70
Mackenzie	38	27	19	16	340

Lack of nutrients, rather than low temperature or incident radiation, is the single most important factor restricting primary production. Production is often highest in early summer when nutrient levels are maximal, though the water is still close to freezing point. By the time the water warms, all available nutrients have been absorbed and productivity falls. Only a few lakes show a second, late-season peak of production. Shallow lakes sometimes have a bottom layer of aquatic mosses, which by photosynthesis add oxygen to the water close by. Deeper lakes are likely to have the bottom sediment-covered, and the lower water layers may remain unstirred and stagnant.

The fauna of these lakes is usually restricted to rotifers, tardigrades and other small detritus-feeding invertebrates, a few species of copepods and other crustaceans, enchytraeid worms and the larvae of chironomid flies. The planktonic copepods Limnocalanus macrurus produce eggs from September to November; the nauplii which hatch after about one month mature in the following June (*Roff*, 1972, 1973; *Roff* and *Carter*, 1972). Mysids Mysis relicta by contrast have a two-yearly cycle; females require the same species in warmer climates, but take a year longer to acumulate it (*Lasenby* and *Langford*, 1972, 1973). Chironomids; including several species which bite man and other warm-blooded animals, are plentiful in the lake, forming the main food of arctic char, the single species of fish.

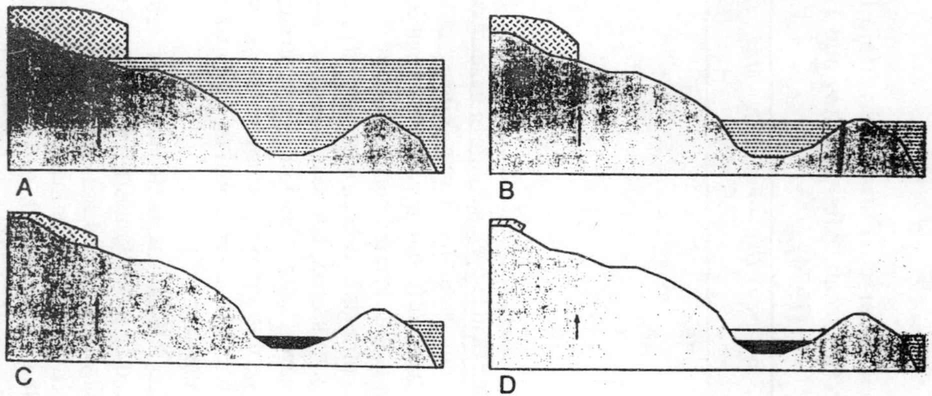

Fig. 2.2. Development of saline lakes on polar coasts. After depression by late Quarternary ice caps. (A) the land rises, isolating hollows and arms of the sea (B) . In dry areas, salinity of the isolated water rises through evaporation and other causes (C), producing (D) a dense bottom layer that subsequent inflows of fresh water fail to disturb.

Faunal relationships in Char Lake are reviewed by *Rigler* (1974): studies of individual species or groups include those of *Morgan* and *Kalff* (1972) on bacteria. *Nurminen* (1973) on oligochaetes, *Welch* (1973) on chironomid larvae and *Holeton* (1973) on arctic char.

Hypersaline lakes are fairly common in coastal areas of the Arctic which have until recently been ice covered, and since liberation have risen isostatically from below sea level; see *Hattersley-Smith* and others (1970). One Garrow Lake, a hypersaline lake of 418 ha on Little Cornwallis Island, northern Canada (75°N) *Dickman* and *Ouelett* (1987) found an ice cover up to 2.4 m thick lasting almost 11 months of the year. With a maximum depth of 50 m and little opportunity for wind-stirring, the lake waters are strongly layered. A brackish upper layer of about 10 m is underlain by about the same depth of more saline water; beneath from about 20 mlies a permanently stagnant bottom layer of ancient sea water- a memento of the island's emergence from the sea some 3000 years ago.

During the brief period of open water in summer temperatures rise 2—3° C in the upper 10 m layer. The unstirred brackish water beneath is permanently warmer, temperatures rising to 9.1°C at 20 m, the junction with the deepest layer. From this level downward the temperature falls to 6.5°-7° at the bottom. The anomalous heat is thought to be due to solar energy, which peretrates the surface ice in spring and warms the depths. Phytoplankton and zooplankton occur mainly in the upper 10 m. Diatoms, notably Cyclotella spp., predominate in summer, and microflagellates Rhodomonas and Cryptomonas spp. for the rest of the year. A layer of photosynthetic bacteria lives permanently on the boundary between brackish and highly saline water. Some 51 taxa of algae have been recorded from Garrow Lake, but only one crustacean species Limnocalanus macrura, and a single fish species, the four-horned sculpin Hyoxocephalus quadricornis.

Running-Water Communities. Craig and *McCart* (1975) divided northern Alaskan streams and small rivers into three categories; mountain streams, spring streams and tundra streams. Mountain streams are usually the longest, originating from springs on high ground and picking up ground water and tributaries as they descend. Most flow for four or five months of the year from May to October; some flow throughout the year. Their upper waters remain cool, seldom above 4—5°C in summer; lower reaches may be warmer in summer after crossing the plains, achieving 10—15°C.

Spring streams are generally shorter, typically forming the tributaries of mountain streams. Arising from perennial springs, they are usually

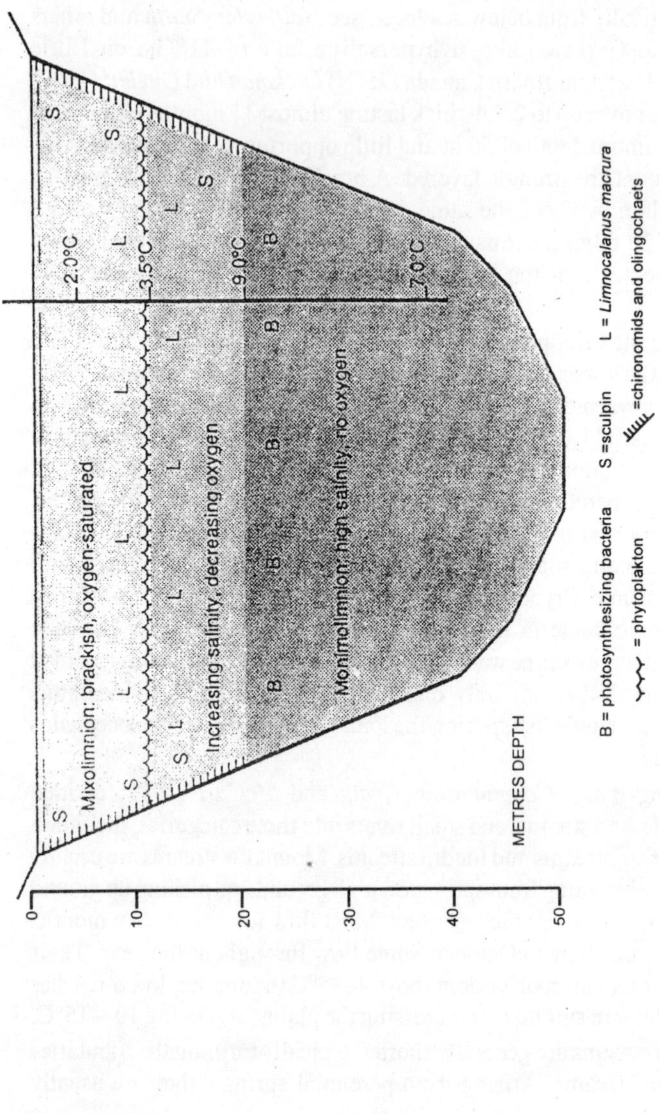

Fig. 2.3. Schematic diagram of life and environmental conditions in Garrow Lake, a meromietic saline lake of the high Arctic.

small, well established and stable, with high mineral content; many flow year-round. The spring water temperatures remain low and fairly constant throughout the year, seldom failing to freezing point in winter or rising above 8-10° in summer. Tundra streams flow in meandering channels through tundra vegetation, draining the peaty soils, picking up humic acids and acquiring a low pH as they go. Frozen solid in winter, they warm quickly in spring sunshine and may reach temperatures of 15-16° C by high summer, but are the first to slow down and freeze in autumn.

Of the three kinds, mountain streams are least productive, with the smallest standing crop of invertebrates and least variety of species. Tundra streams are richer in invertebrates by a factor of 10, spring streams richer still by a factor of 100. Mountain and spring streams support populations of arctic char Salvelinus alpinus; tundra streams support grayling Thymallus arcticus, which spawn in their sluggish waters.

Antarctic Aquatic Communities

Still-water communities. Antarctic freshwater ecosystems include permanently frozen lakes high among the inland mountains, seasonal inland or near-coastal lakes of the ice-free areas, some of which are highly saline, and fresh or partlysaline coastal lakes and ponds (*Heywood*, 1977, 1984). *Priddle* and *Heywood* (1980) regard antarctic lakes as forming an evolutionary series which has developed over the period of about 2000 years since the ice-sheet was maximal; this is in any case a convenient way of describing them.

Proglacil lakes. The simplest lakes lie on or in front of ice-sheets, formed by seasonal melting that may be enhanced by the presence of scree or windblown dust. In Antarctica many such lakes occur inland, some on shelf ice close to sea level, others high among mountains or nunataks. Of hundreds recorded from the air, only a very few have been visited even briefly by sledging parties, and little is known of their biology. They accumulate from annual melt-water off the mountains and ice-sheets; their temperatures remain close to freezing point during a superficial summer thaw, though some of the deeper ones may have a permanently unfrozen core. Nutrients are extremely limited, and the lakes support only thin populations of algae and bacteria.

Lakes formed in rock basins by retreating ice-sheets pass through several evolutionary phases. As a moraine-dammed valley is exposed, water flowing in seasonal torrents accumulates on the valley floor, forming a lake that lengthens and broadens as the ice face retreats. The presence of a lake shows the inflow of water, causing rock debris and finely-ground rock flour from the base of the melting ice-sheet to be deposited as sediment on the lake-bed. The surrounding catchment area at first contributes little but clear run-off, and the lake water remains oligotrophic for a long period. However, as vegetation and mineralized soils develop in the catchment, minerals, organic nutrients and soil microorganisms begin to enter the lake from this source. Lakes close to the sea acquire minerals faster than those inland, from wind-blown spray and from seals, penguins, gulls and skuas, which like to wash in fresh water.

Adamson and Pickard (1986) describe several kinds of freshwater lakes in the Vestfold Hills oasis area. Pelite and Chelnock lakes, respectively supraglacial and proglacial, are fed by melting ice cliffs; Crooked Lake is an open-valley lake fed by a through-flowing river and there are many closed-valley lakes reflecting the water balance prevailing over previous centuries; one, Thalatine Lake, has over 40 minor beach terraces reflecting some 1300 years of evaporation. Others, for example, Watts Lake, began as marine inlets but were isolated by isostatic uplift and washed free of salt water by melting land ice; there are also saline lakes of similar origin (see below). Many other antarctic lakes are known at these early stages of development. Few on mainland Antarctica gain substantial nutrients from the soils of their catchment, except around the coast where birds and seals become important agents of eutrophication (*Goldman*, 1970).

More advanced lakes are found in the maritime Antarctic. Long-term studies of 17 lakes on Signy Island (*Heywood et al., 1980;* see also *Hawes*, 1985) provide the most through coverage of a wide variety of lake types. *Heywood* (1984) summarize the ecology of three lakes of varying nutrient content, occupying valleys of a coastal lowland. These typify many other lakes of similar size and aspect throughout the maritime Antarctic (*Heywood*, 1987). For studies of similar lakes on the South Shetland Islands see *Paggi* (1987) and *Kieffer* and *Copes* (1987).

Formed in ice-cut cirques or shallow, steep-sided valleys, the Signy Island lakes are moraine-dammed and often rimmed by a rubble-covered shelf about 1 m below the surface; the shelves are swept clear of sediment by wind-induced turbulence, and fall away to a narrow, sediment by wind-induced turbulence, and fall away to a narrow, sediment-filled trough. There is no emergent vegetation. In an environment of heavy snowfall, where mean monthly temperatures are above freezing point in summer but down to —15°C in winter, the lakes are frozen over with 1-2 m of snow-covered ice for 8-11 months each year. Temperatures at the bottom, down to 15 m in the deepest, fall to about 1° C in winter. In summer when melting is well advanced, persistent winds stir the waters and the lakes become isothermal, with temperatures up to 6° C. During this period they receive varying quantities of nutrients and bacteria (*Ellis-Evans* and *Wynne-Williams*, 1985) and yeasts (*Ellis-Evans*, 1985a and b), washed in from their catchments.

Oligotrophic lakes. Moss Lake is typical of oligotrophic, high-level lakes, recently formed and remote from the sea. In a glacial cirque basin 48 m above sea level and 800 m from the shore, it has a surface area of 15000 m^2 and a mean depth of 3.4 m. Most water and ions enter the lake directly from precipitation or snow-melt. There is little leaching from the catchment area, which is small and covered with perennial ice, bare rock or scree, with hardly any mineral soil or vegetation. The waters are clear, and salinity and nutrient levels are very low.

Phytoplankton of diatoms and other green algae is poorly developed; chlorophyll a values of up to 8.0 μg l^{-1} were recorded, and annual production was estimated at 12.6 g C m^{-2} in a year (*Ellis-Evans*, 1981a). In compensation, these clear lakes often have a rich benthic flora of perennial mosses Calliergon, Drepanocladus spp.) and algae (for example Tolypothrix, Plectonema and Phormidium), both liberally covered with epiphytic blue-green and green algae. Growing slowly to form dense mats, some with strands several m long, these fix up to 6 g C m^{-2} annually. The calanoid copepod Pseudoboekella poppei is a planktonic browser, fed on in all stages of its development by the larger copepod Parabroteas sarsi. On the lake-bed cladocerans Macrothrix hirsuticorna, Aloma rectangula and Ilyocryptus brevidentatus and two ostracods Notiocypridopsis frigogena and Eucypris fontana browse or scavenge on the benthic mats, which contain a microfauna of protozoa, turbellaria, rotifers, tardigrades, nematodes, gastrotrichs and enchytraeid annelids (*Heywood* and others 1979, *Heywood*, 1984).

Table 2.2. Salinity and Nutients of thee Signy Island Lakes : S—Summe, W—Winter, Data from Heywood (1984)

	Moss	*Lake*	*Heywood*	*Lake*	*Amos*	*Lake*
	S	*W*	*S*	*W*	*S*	*W*
Chlorinity (mg 1–1)	23.0	49.0	35.0	56.0	37.1	94.7
Nitrite N (μg 1–1)	1.0	4.1	5.3	21.0	204.0	85.0
Nitrate N (μg 1–1)	21.0	50.0	39.0	128.0	321.0	721.0
Orthophosphate P (μg 1–1)	0.5	0.4	15.9	58.0	597.0	260.8
Silicate Si (μg 1–1)	143.3	267.0	174.0	368.0	191.6	656.9

Mesotophic lakes. Heywood Lake typifies older, more matue lakes close to the sea. It lies in two adjoining basins 4 m above sea level and

200 m fom the shore, with a suface area of 45000m^2 and a mean depth of 2.0m. An extensive catchment area with mineal soils, frozen in winter but water-logged in summer, supports swards of moss and lichens which contribute minerals to the water; the lake is also visited by seals in summer. Waters are clear under the ice in winter but turbid from organic and mineral particles when the ice has melted.

Salinity and nutrient values are very much higher those of Moss Lake, and the waters are markedly more productive. Chlorophyll a values up to 170 mg m^{-2} were recorded in spring and up to 40 mg m^{-2} in summer. Over 3g Cm^{-2} were fixed daily during the summer peak, and the annual rate of production was estimated at 173.0 g C m^2 (Light *et al.*,1981) or 139-270 g C m^2 (*Priddle et al.* 1986). Lakes that are rich in phytoplankton and other suspended matter tend to have correspondingly less benthic vegetation, presumably because of light limitation in summer. Bacteria were plentiful in the water column of Heywood Lake; *Hawes* (1985) provides evidence that they enhance algal photosynthesis in lakes where nutrients are low, by speeding the recycling of carbon, nitrogen and phosphates. Planktonic crustaceans include Pseudoboeckella poppei, Parabroteas sarsi and immature stages of the fairyshrimp Branchinecta gaini; mature stages tend to browse deeper on the benthos. There are fewer invertebrate species in the benthic algal mats, which are less developed than in Moss Lake.

Eutrophic Lakes. Amos Lake lies 10 m above sea level, adjacent to the shore on the windward side of the island; like many others in this situation, it is vastly enriched by marine influences. A small lake of surface area 6000 m and mean depth 1.7m, it has a relatively small surrounding catchment basin, but the area is a popular summer resort for seals and nesting giant petrels Macronectes giganteus. There is little vegetation, but excreta and moulted hair contribute organic material to the soils, and the water of Amos Lake are saline, turbid and nutrient-rich.

Well stirred by seals, Amos Lake was too marky for direct productivity comparisons with the other lakes. Productivity was concentrated close to the surface; chlorophyll a values were high in summer and a daily peak production of over 300 mg cm^{-2} was recorded, drecreasing rapidly below 1 m (*Heywood*, 1984). Pseudoboekella poppei, Parabroteas sarsi and Branchinecta gaini were present in the water column, but there was little or no benthic vegetation or associated microfauna. Bacterial counts were gererally high. Both aerobic and anaerobic bacterial decomposition contributed to nutrient recycling in lakes at all nutrient levels (Ellis-Evans, 1982; Hawes, 1985); the role of anaerobic bacteria is enhanced in winter when the water is static under its ice cover. Where nutrients are plentiful, productivity is high, production far outstrips decomposition, and organic sediments accumulate on the lake beds.

Saline Lakes. Lakes with densely saline waters are found in several of Antarctica's oasis areas. Their origins and histories are varied, but all occupy ground that was previously glaciated and many are ancient. Among the largest and most fully-studied lake systems, Lake Bonney in the Dry Valleys of South Victoria Land has probably existed for over 100,000 years (*Hendy et al.,* 1977), and a sediment core 2.8 m long from neighbouring Lake Fryxell is estimated from C-14 dating to represent over 50,000 years deposition (*Parker* and *Simmons*, 1985). Similar lakes are known also in smaller coastal oases at Bunger Hills, Vestfold Hills, Schirmacher, Soya and Thala Hills. The ecology of saline lakes has been reviewed by *Heywood* (1984) and *Vincent* (1988).

Saline lakes of the Vestfold Hills oasis string out along a valley, formerly a marine inlet, which rose and was cut off from the sea 5000-8000 years ago when the local land ice melted (*Kerry et al.,* 1977). Their salinities vary according to how long ago their waters were left to evaporate, and the amount of fresh water entering them annually; of the four main lakes, Deep Lake, the deepest (34 m) and most salty, has a mean salinity of approximately 280 ppt, roughly eight times that of sea water and similar in density to Dead Sea water. Deep Lake, and the slightly less salty Club Lake, seldom freeze over, though their surface temperatures drop almost to —20° C in winter. Wind-stirred in all but the deepest layers throughout winter, in summer they become thermally stratified, with surface temperatures over 10° C. Algae and bacteria are present in all the lakes at all depths; productivity is very low, and few herbivores or scavengers have been recorded. Metazoans are virtually absent except in some of the lakes where freshwater seeps in at the edges.

In higher latitudes, the saline lakes and ponds of South Victoria Land present a wide spectrum. Many are well above sea level and appear to owe their high salinity entirely to longterm accumulation and evaporation (for a discussion of this point see *Heywood*, 1984). Don Juan Pond, 122 m above sea level in Wright Valley and now only a few centimetres deep, is assumed to be the remnant of much larger freshwater lake of at least 10 m depth. Currently fed by a saline stream and limited snow-melt, its salinity, dominated by calcium chloride, is about 13 times that of sea water, and high enough to ensure that it seldom if ever freezes. The pond is virtually sterile except for algal mats which grow only at points about its edges where fresh water is available (*Harris et al.,* 1979; *Wright and Burton*, 1981).

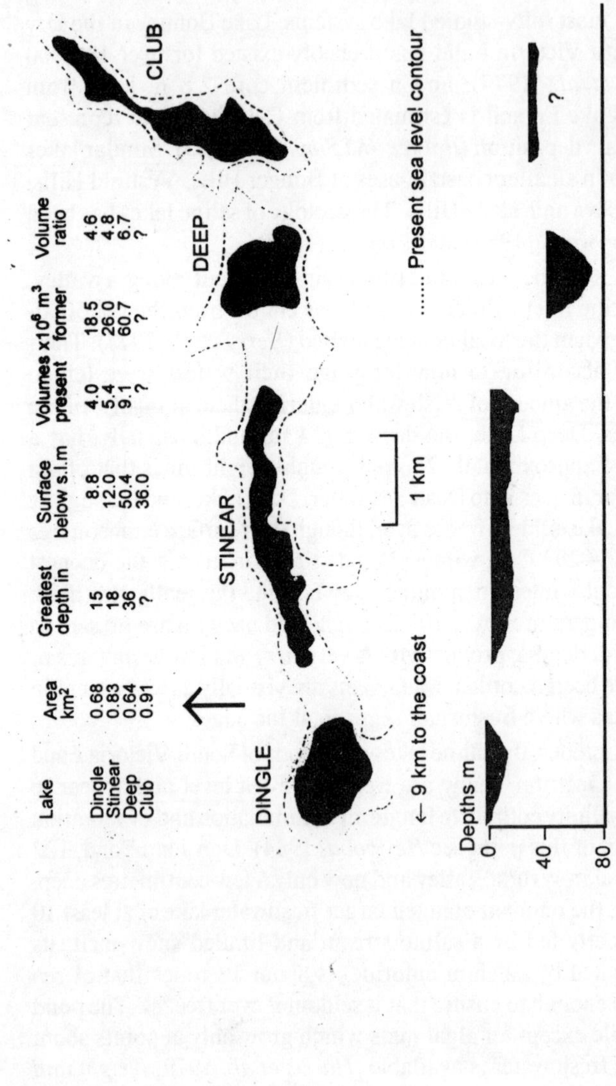

Fig. 2.4. The Vestflod Hils lakes system. Reduction in volume since the land uplifeted has resulted in salinities up to eight times that of seawater.

Lake Vanda, also in Wright Valley, is a highly-stratified lake some 5 km^2 in area and up to 70 m deep. The remnant of a larger lake that once filled the surrounding valley, it has a superficial layer of fresh or slighly saline water down to 50 m deep, replenished seasonally by glacial streams, notably Onyx River, and stirred by their turbulence. Beneath lies a core of ancient salty water with a concentration of 140 ppt. and a temperature of 25°C; the origin of this warmth is uncertain, but more likely to be solar than geothermal. The lake surface is permanently frozen to a depth of 2—4 m, with ice that thaws only around the edges in summer. Several other lakes in the areas share some or all of these characteristics.

The ice cover inhibits wind-induced turbulence, minimizes penetration of sunlight and keeps the temperatures of the surface waters almost constant. Algae are present in the upper layers; productivity is low even in summer, and probably restricted to a shallow near-surface layer beneath the ice. Oxygen produced by photosynthesis accumulates in surface waters, but the saline substratum is anoxic; nitrifying bacteria accumulate at the boundary between, forming a substrate where algae and heterotrophic bacteria also congregate, and photosynthesis is maximal. Sulphur bacteia may be present below the anoxic zone, reducing sulphate ions and liberating hydrogen sulphide. Benthos around the lake edge includes mats of blue-green algae and moss, often with a microfauna of rotifers, tardigrades and other scavengers.

In the productivity of Lake Vanda phosphorus is a limiting element (*Vincent and Vincent*, 1982) because of gravitational losses into the sediment and lack of turbulence to return it to general circulation. Phosphorus that diffuses upward from the bottom is absorbed by the accumulated bacteria and algal cells at the top of the anoxic layer; very little penetrates to the less saline layers above, which are thus limited to the very small amounts brought in by Onyx River. For a full discussion of nutrient cycling in this remarkable lake see *Vincent* (1988).

Running-Water Communities. Antarctica has many small seasonal streams, and a few large enough to be called rivers. Nearly all are coastal; those of the continent are fed mainly from melting glaciers, those of the maritime region mainly from melting snow. Usually dry throughout winter, they start with the onset of spring thaw. Unbuffered by variations in gradient, their flows often fluctuate widely from afternoon maxima to early morning minima. Their waters seldom have opportunities to spread and be warmed: temperatures are usually less than 5°C. Continental streams run for one to three months annually, those of the maritime Antarctic for four to six months or more. Many carry finely-divided glacial sediment.

Plankton in Antarctic streams is usually low, restricted to algae or other organisms washed from lakes or ponds along the route. Stream beds are sometimes more productive, those with clear water supporting films or mats of cyanobacteria (Phormidium, Nostoc. Oscillatoria) and epilithic algae (Binuclearia, Prasiola). Beds of continental streams dry out quickly after the brief summer flow; any ice present ablates, and the desiccated mat is subject to intense winter cold. Those of the maritime region remain moist for a longer season, and usually remain protected by ice or snow, if not by water, throughout winter. In consequence they support richer algal mats, often with well-developed filamentous species (for example Klebsormidium, Mougeotia) which are active for much of the year (*Vincent*, 1988). Though they appear green and contain abundant chlorophyll, productivity of these mats is generally low: much of their material is moribund, and persists only because of an absence of decomposers.

Though the periantarctic islands are well endowed with ponds, lakes and streams, comparatively little is known of their biology.

SUMMARY AND CONCLUSIONS

Though water is a solid for much of the polar year, and generally poor in minerals even when in liquid form, both snow and aquatic polar habitats support life. Melting coastal snow supports an ephemeral algal flora that stains it red or green. Polar ponds and lakes are limited in their energy uptake by snow-covered ice, which also inhibits wind-stirring for much of the year. Permanently frozen catchment areas limit the amount of minerals available, though there is usually a small intake from soils during the summer thaw. Because food chain are simple, minerals absorbed into primary production settle in sediments where, in the absence of decomposers and detritus feeders, they may be lost to circulation. Some polar lakes, especially deep ones close to the coast and those in snow-free areas, may be saline with strongly-developed layering. Productivity is generally low in both still-and running-water habitats, limited mainly by lack of nutrients.

Chapter 3

Streams and Valleys

Prelude In southeastern Australia, there is a river that flows for a distance of about 2000 km from the highlands of Victoria to Encounter Bay south of Adelaide. The aborigines who live nearby tell an interesting tale about the origin of this stream and its valley. They describe how a narrow crevice was opened by an earthquake, and how subsequently, whenever it rained, the crevice would develop a thin trickle of water. The tale does not end at that point, however, for it is necessary to account for the considerable width and graceful bends of the stream and its valley. A second earthquake, along with the best "fish story" of all time, is invoked to completely account for the characteristics of the stream. During the second quake, an immense fish squeezed upward into the cleft from somewhere deep within the earth. The trickle of water in the rift was quite inadequate for the great fish, and so with mighty strokes of its powerful tail it wriggled its way to the ocean, leaving behind the wide sinuous valley of the Murray River.

Actually, of course, the valley described above was eroded over a long period of time by the river that flows within it. The concept that, given sufficient time, even puny looking streams have such erosive powers would have been difficult for the aborigines to grasp. It was also a concept that was not understood by intellectuals in 16th century Europe. Most naturalists of that time believed valleys formed as a consequence of unknown catastrophic events. An exception was a Saxon professor of mineralogy named *Agricola* (1494-1555). *Agricola* taught his students that streams cut the valleys in which they flow and even were responsible for the development of fertile floodplains. Agricola's view was echoed much later in the writings of *James Hutton*, whose masterful reasoning is evident in this statement published in 1802 by his friend and advocate *James Playfair*:

Every river appears to consist of a main trunk fed from a variety of branches, each running in a valley proportioned to its size, and all of them together forming a system of valleys communicating with one another, and having such a nice adjustment of their declivities, that none of them join the principal valley, either on too high or too low a level, a circumstance which would be infinitely improbable if each of these valleys were not the work of the stream which flows in it.

Today, there is no disagreement with the concept that, except for relatively few fault troughs, most valleys are formed by streams. The process of valley formation begins when water flowing down a slope as

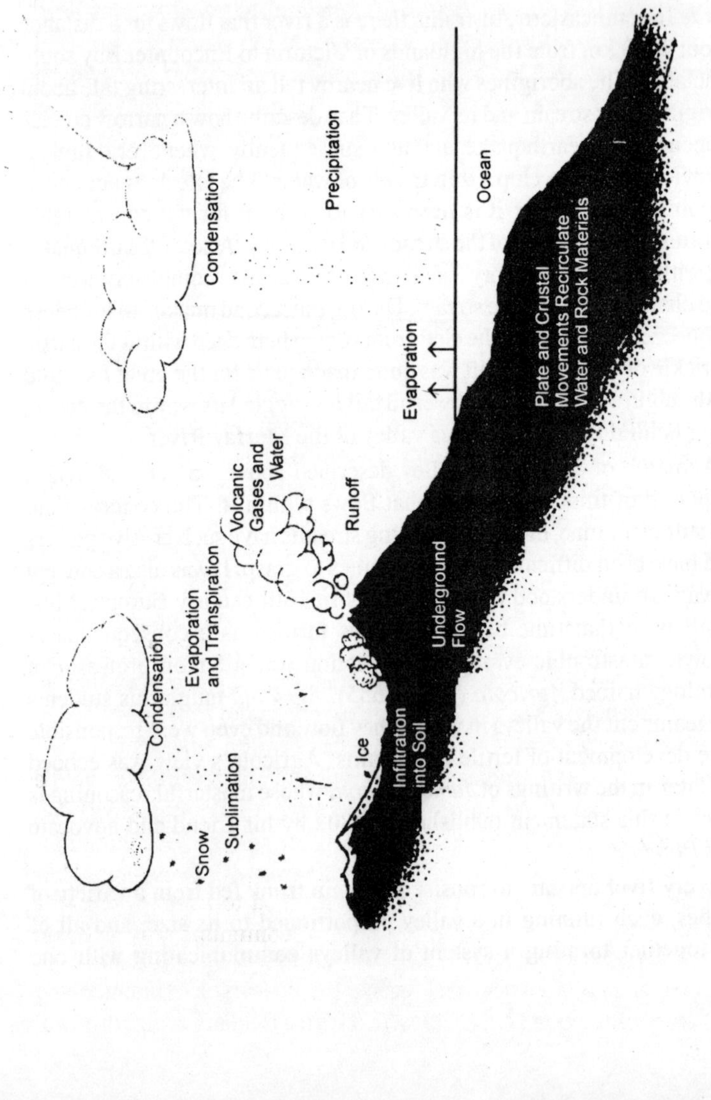

Fig. 3.1. The Hydrologic Cycle.

sheetwash is separated by surface irregularities into small channels that then develop into gullies. With further additions of water from rain or snow, gullies are deepened by the running water and widened by mass wasting until they begin to take on the appearance of small valleys. Headward erosion results in the lengthening of the older channels, while new ones are eroded on the slopes of the developing valleys. In their early stages of development, the streams are marked by many irregularities such as waterfalls and rapids. In time, however, the slopes of channels become more gentle, and the streams begin to widen their valleys by cutting laterally. Little by little, an areal pattern of broader primary streams and secondary tributaries begins to emerge. If we were to inform the tribe of aborigines mentioned earlier that the real factor behind the development of stream valleys was the sun, they would probably be as skeptical of our "sun story" as we are of their "fish story." Nev- ertheless, the sun is essential for the development of streams. The sun evaporates and lifts water that then falls from the atmosphere as rain or snow. Some of this water is returned to the atmosphere by evaporation or transpiration from plants. Another portion flows down slopes and in channels as runoff. A third portion percolates into the ground and emerges later as springs at lower altitudes. This water also ulti- mately enters the stream system. Thus streams are fed by water from runoff and springs. The rate at which water is supplied to the stream determines its discharge or volume of flow. Discharge in turn affects a stream's velocity, width, depth, and at least partially, the amount of sediment it can transport. In this chapter, we will define and examine the relations among these interacting variables and attempt to understand the many facets of stream behavior. Streams, after all, are not unimportant to us humans. Thye provide us with drinking water, electric power, water for crops, fertile floodplains, and convenient routes for highways. Properly managed, they help us dispose of the wast products of our cities. Most important, they have sculptured for us esthetically pleasing landscapes to which we can escape whenever our view of the world becomes disagreeable of too much concrete and too few trees.

Gravity: The Force Behind The Flow

Everyone knows that water flows from high places to lower ones. Gravity, of course, is the cause of the movement. Every molecule of water in a stream is attracted directly downward toward the earth's center by gravity, but the molecules are unable to move rapidly downward because they are supported by surrounding water molecules and the stream bed. Water molecules in a stream are therefore forced to move along parallel to the slope of the stream bed under the influence of a component of gravity. As was the case in our consideration of mass wasting, the proportion of the force of gravity acting on a water molecule depends on the steepness of the slope. If the slope is vertical (as in a waterfall), the water will be pulled directly downward by the full force of the gravity. As the angle of inclination of the slope from horizontal is reduced, the value of the component of gravity will also be lessened.

Fig. 3.2. Streams are fed by water from runoff as well as from underground water that emerges above or within the channel.

If the component of gravity acting on water molecules were unopposed in a stream, the water would quickly attain incredibly high rates of movement. Friction of the flowing water against the floor and walls of the channel, as well as internal friction among water molecules and between water molecules and suspended sediment, all serve to oppose the force of gravity. Because of these opposing forces, there is an upward limit to the velocity a stream can attain no matter how steep the slope over which it is flowing.

The slope of the stream channel between any two specified points (and along which the component of gravity operates) is called the *gradient.* Stream gradients are usually expressed as a ratio as follows:

$$\text{Gradient} = \frac{\text{Vertical Distance (in meters)}}{\text{Horizontal Distance (in meters)}}$$

One can determine the gradient of part of a stream by using data on a topographic map. To do this, one first locates two adjacent contour lines that cross the stream. Contour lines are simply lines connecting points of equal elevation. For example, depicts 180-meter and 190-meter contour lines crossing a stream at two points along, the path of the stream that are 2000 meters apart. If we assume the channel floor is parallel to the water surface, then the stream has fallen 10 meters vertically over the 2000-meter horizontal distance. The gradient of the stream in meters per km can be obtained by multiplying the stream in meters per km can be obtained by multiplying the gradient by the number of meters in a km. Thus 1000 × 0.005 equals 5 meters per km.

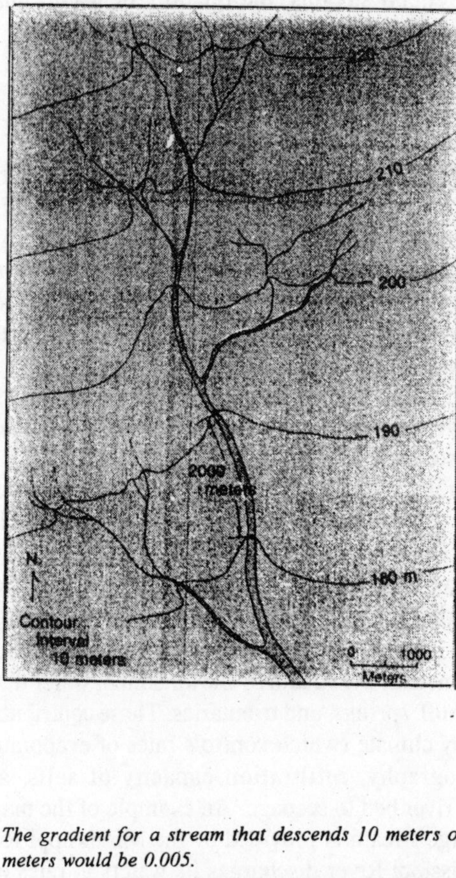

Fig. 3.3. The gradient for a stream that descends 10 meters over a distance of 2000 meters would be 0.005.

The Dynamics of Streams

Streams are highly complex systems affected by many interacting variables. As is often the case with natural systems, if any one of the variable is altered, changes are also produced in other dependent variables. The most important variables are discharge, velocity, gradient, sediment load, bed roughness, and cross-sectional area of the stream. As an example of the interdependence of variables, if the discharge of a stream were to be suddenly increased after a rain fall, then the stream's velocity will increase, water may rise in the channel so as to provide a larger cross-sectional area, and the load of solid particles carried by the stream may increase. A stream's characteristics will also change long the length of its course. In most perennial streams, the quantity of water, quantity of transported sediment, the velocity, and cross-sectional area increase downstream, whereas the gradient decreases.

Discharge

The amount of water passing through a given cross section of a stream in a given time is termed discharge. Discharge is usually expressed in terms of cubic meters of water per second. Thus, the quantity of discharge, by convention designated Q, is obtained by multiplying a stream's cross-sectional area in square meters (A) by the average velocity (V) in meters per second. The area of a stream's cross-sectional is derived from measurements of average width and depth. Velocity of a stream is measured with a special device called a *current meter*, and the average velocity is calculated from many current meter readings. After the cross-sectional area and average velocity of a stream have been calculated, it is a simple matter to determine discharge by use of the equation $Q = AN$. A stream with an average velocity of 0.5 meter per second and a cross-sectional area of 20 square meters would have a discharge of 10 cubic meters per second. The discharge equation indicates that a river with constant water volume would have to increase its velocity if its channel were restricted by either geologic features or artificial constructions.

A stream has no inherent ability to increase or decrease it discharge. Discharge is determined for the stream by the amount of water that enters the channel from runoff, springs, and tributaries. These contributions are in turn influenced by climate (which controls rates of evaporation and precipitation), topography, infiltration capacity of soils, and the susceptibility of the river bed to seepage. An example of the magnitude of discharge in a large stream is provided by the Mississippi River. At Vicksburg the Mississippi River discharges its waters at rates of about 57,000 cubic meters per second when in flood. Small streams vary in discharge from about 0,3 to 280 cubic meters per second.

Velocity

The *velocity* of a stream is the speed at which water moves down the channel in a direction perpendicular to the channel cross-section. Velocity is controlled by several factors, including the gradient of the stream, the volume of water flowing, how viscous the water is because of suspended particles, channel shape, and roughness of the channel bed. One can calculate the average velocity of a stream if its discharge and cross-sectional area are known from the relation V_{av}=Q/A. The average velocity may differ considerably from the actual velocity measured at a particular point in the channel. A stream is likely to be flowing fastest about a third of the distance down from its surface. Water would be moving a bit slower at the air-water interface because of friction with the overlying air and slowest all along the bottom and sides of the channel because of friction with the solid material in which the channel is eroded. A longitudinal segment of a stream between any two point is called a *reach*. If the section across which velocity is measured is in a straight reach, the greatest velocity will be toward the middle of the stream. Around curves, however, maximal velocity is shifted by the centrifugal component of force toward the outside of the bend. Indicates the distribution of velocity along straight and curved reaches of the stream.

Flow pattern

When water is moving slowly and smoothly, the paths taken by individual water molecules may be either straight or gently curved and are parallel to the paths of neighboring molecules. This type of flow is called *laminar*. It was first demonstrated in 1883 by *Osborne Reynolds*, who introduced a few drops dye to clear water flowing gently through a glass tube. The dye moved with the water in smooth, parallel lines. One can also produce this effect in a metal trough, which more closely resembles a straight reach of a river. If the velocity of flow in the trough is increased (by increasing either the gradient, or discharge), the flow lines of dye will become wavy and chaotic. Water immediately above the bottom of the channel is slowed by friction with the bottom and therefore moves slower than adjacent water masses, and the variance throws the water into a chaotic movement called *turbulent flow*. Such swirling eddying turbulence is the universal kind of flow in all natural streams. Turbulence is the result of high velocity and irregularities in the bed and banks of a stream. It is an important attribute of stream flow, for it enhances the ability of the stream to erode its bed and to keep particles suspended in the moving water mass.

Transportation and Erosion

The load

The dissolved and solid rock waste carried by a stream constitutes its *load*. A stream's load is derived from several possible sources. A part of the load is carried to the channel by sheetwash and mass wasting. Additional load is provided by the stream itself as it undercuts its banks and erodes its bed. At location where erosion by wind or ice is prevalent, these agencies may also contribute to the load carried by stream.

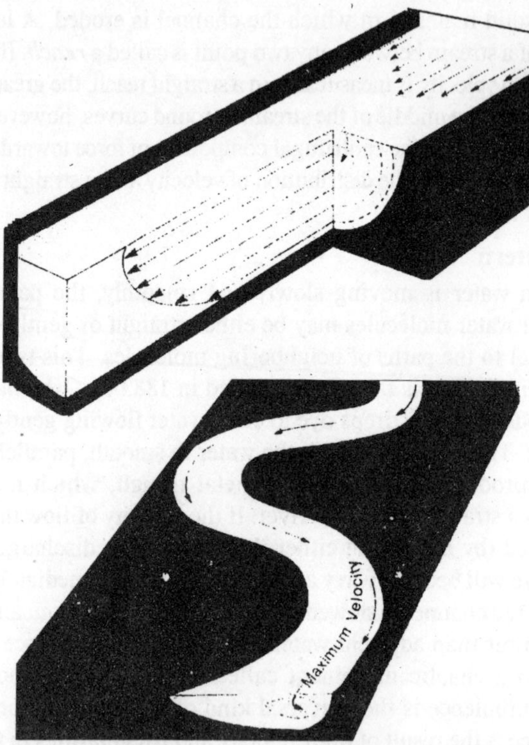

Fig. 3.4. Velocity distribution along a straight section of an idealized river. Upper right part of block (A) indicates relative surface velocities, and sides of block indicate minimal velocity near the bottom of the stream where velocity is decreased because of friction. Velocity increases upward except for a decrease near the surface where velocity is again reduced because of frictional drag. (B) Maximal surface velocity is generally at the center in straight sections of a stream and shifts toward the outer bank along curves in the river.

Dissolved load

It is easy to overlook the dissolved load carried by a stream. It is invisible and does not significantly affect a stream's behavior. Nevertheless, transportation of dissolved mineral matter is an imporatant function of rivers. It has been estimated that nearly 4000 metric tons of dissolved materials are carried to the ocean each year by streams. The most abundant components of this load are positive ions of calcium and sodium and negatively charged sulfate, chloride, and bicarbonate ions. These dissolved substances may precipitate as the thin mineral crust that forms on the inside of kettles. Soap does not lather well in mineral rich or "hard water" and will react to form calcium stearate. The latter compound is the bane of fastidious housekeepers, for it is the substance of which bathtub rings are composed. As one might guess, streams that flow across relatively soluble limestone terrains are particularly rich in dissolved mineral matter.

Solid matter

The solid grains in a stream are transported by suspension, saltation, and traction. Particles in *suspension* are carried along within the body of flowing water. They are kept from being deposited by upward-moving

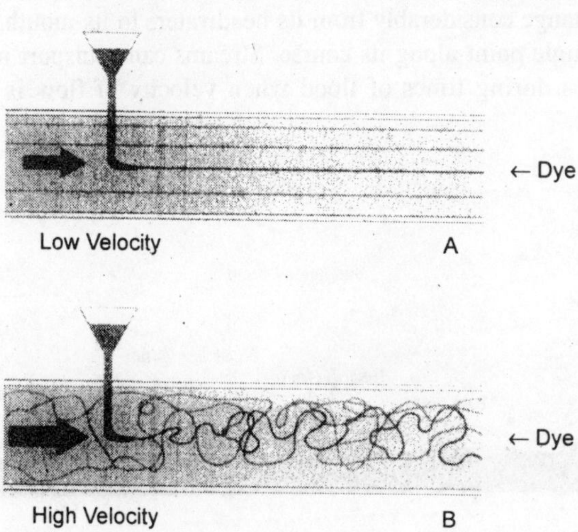

Fig. 3.5. In laminar flow (A), molecules move in parallel parths, and flow lines do not cross. Turbulence (B) is characterized by many irregular eddies superimposed on the general direction of flow.

turbulent eddies. Only relatively small grains, such as those in the silt and clay sizes, are able to resist the pull of gravity and remain in the *suspended load.* Except in extremely fast-flowing streams, sand particles do not remain suspended but collect on the surface of the stream bed where they move along in a series of leaps. The motions is termed *saltation*. Still larger sand grains, as well as granules, pebbles, and cobbles, are moved along by sliding and rolling motions. The process of transporting coarse sediment along the bottom of a stream, either by rolling or sliding, is called *traction*. All of the material carried by traction constitutes the stream's *bed load.* Because individual fragments in the bed load move only intermittently, the bed load moves down the channel more slowly than the water itself.

Precisely which range of particle sizes is transported by suspension, saltation, or traction is, within limits, dependent on velocity. Should the velocity of a rapidly flowing stream be decreased, the larger particles in the suspended load might become part of the saltation load, and particles formerly moving by saltation would continue their downstream progress by sliding and rolling.

Competence and capacity

The term *competence* is used to express the largest particle that a stream can transport under a given set of conditions. The competence of a river may change considerably from its headwaters to its mouth, and even at any single point along its course. Streams can transport much larger particles during times of flood when velocity of flow is at a

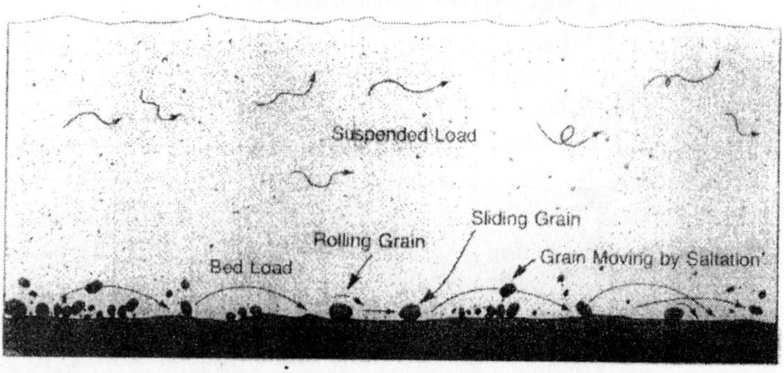

Fig. 3.6. Transportation of sediment by a stream. The particles being moved by saltation, rolling, and/or sliding constitute the bed load. Particles in the suspended load are carried above the stream bed within the body of flowing water.

maximum. In general, the diameter of a rock fragment that can be moved by the stream is proportional to the square of the velocity of flow. Thus, if the velocity is doubled, the stream can move particles four times as large as before. The explanation for this relationship is that each molecule of water not only strikes a grain of sediment twice as hard, but also twice as many molecules strike the grain during a given interval of time.

A second term used to describe sediment transport of a stream is capacity. *Capacity* refers to the maximal amount of material the stream can carry under a given set of conditions. Because there are limits to the amount of load that can be included within a given volume of water, it is evident that a stream's capacity will be markedly influenced by discharge.

Erosion by streams

Relation of velocity to erosion. Velocity is the most important factor in determining the rate of channel erosion by a stream. Erosion occurs whenever particles of sediment are lifted from or moved from the stream bed. Particles may be pushed forward by the force of the moving water

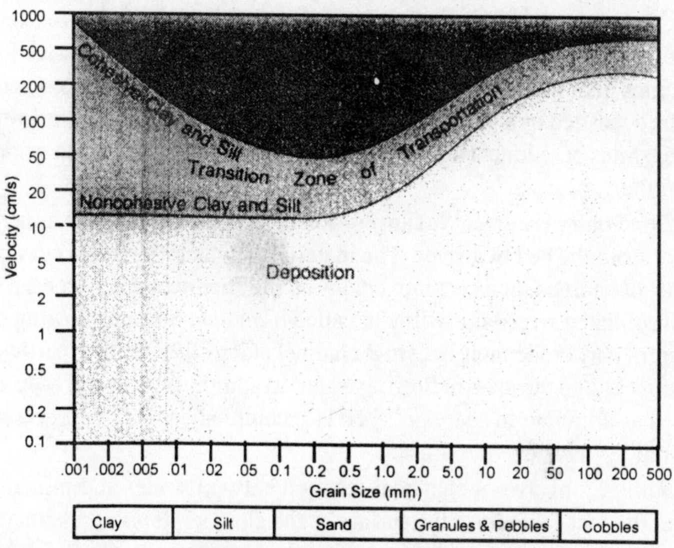

Fig. 3.7. Relation of average current velocity in water at least 1 meter deep to the size of mineral particles that can be eroded from a stream bed. For any given particle, the lower line is the velocity at which particles of that size will be deposited. The upper line is the velocity at which particles will be lifted from the bed. Between these two lines is the transitional zone of transportation in which suspended particles remain in suspension.

against their upstream sides. They may also be lifted because of the reduced pressure on their upper surfaces as water flows over them. The forces that attempt to lift grains at rest and bring them into the transported load are opposed by gravity as well as the natural cohesive force that tends to hold together small particles at rest. Of these two forces, gravity is clearly the most important, although cohesion does play an important role, at least for the finer clay-size particles. Once deposited on the stream bed, the flat clay particles tend to cling to the channel floor. Water, moving against the thin edges of the clay particles, has little surface to push against, and besides, it is flowing in the zone of lowest velocity. In general, if the channel surface is composed of clay, stream velocities must often reach over 500 cm/second before erosion can begin, whereas sand on the stream bed is readily transported by stream velocities of only 10 cm/second. Notice that velocities needed to initiate movement of particles are greater for clay than for coarse gravel because of the cohesiveness of clay. Intermediate particles are eroded at the lowest range of velocities.

Of course, once clay particles from a channel are lifted into the mass of flowing water, the particles remain in suspension even at very low velocities also indicates the velocity at which particles of various sizes will be deposited by a stream. For velocities in the region above the lower curve, grains of sediment already in motion will continue to be transported indefinitely.

Erosional Processes. Stream erosion is the removal rock and mineral matter from the bed of a river. The material in which the bed is cut may consist of bedrock, or as is more common, the stream bed may consist of unconsolidated river-laid sediment called *alluvium*. Streams flowing on alluvium may erode their beds and channel sidewalls by lifting particles of sediment into the mass of flowing water. In addition, erosion of bedrock as well as alluvium in a stream's bed is accomplished by such processes as solution, abrasion, and impact.

Solution involves a chemical reaction between water and minerals within the rocks that form the surface of the channel. It is process that is most prevalent in regions where streams flow across particularly soluble rocks like dolostone or limestone. The dissolution of rock forming the bed of the stream contributes to the dissolved load. The conribution from the bed, however, is relatively minor when compared with the much larger amount of dissolved material derived from chemical weathering across the entire drainage area and carried to the streams by underground water or sheetwash.

In contrast to the largely chemical affects of solution, *abrasion* refers to the mechanical wearing away of the channel as a result of the collision and grinding action of the sand grains and pebbles carried by the stream. Acting together, abrasion and solution may produce *abasin*-like depressions in the bedrock of streams. These smooth rounded cavities are called potholes. Most potholes are formed by the relentless circular motion of eddies and whirlpools that contain loose rock and mineral fragments as tools. Even without the "sandblast" effect of these grains, the force of churning water alone can produce potholes, although this requires more time.

Impact, an erosional process associated with wind action, is also important in stream erosion. It occurs whenever large particles carried by the stream are thrown forcibly against the sides and bottom of the bed. If the stream bed is cut in bedrock, the many continuous blows from these propelled particles knock off fragments of rock and thereby contribute to the solid particles comprising the stream's load. In addition, fragments of rock in transport are themselves eroded by impact and abrasion. The process contributes to the rounding of pebbles and cobbles.

Base level

Stream erosion, in combination with mass wasting, has done more to develop the landscapes of our continents than any other group of geologic processes. Every where we see the ravines, valleys, conyons, ridges, and floodplains that result in part from the activity of rivers. There are times when that activity is inspirational, as when streams topple over resistant ledges to form waterfalls. At other times, the activity of streams may be catastrophic, as when floods sweep away buildings and undermine bridges. But most of the work of streams goes on largely unnoticed, as the flowing water sculptures valleys and transports the material that once filled them to the ocean.

The degradational work of streams is truly immense. Each year, rivers carry an estimated 10 million metric tons of continental material to the oceans. This work, however, cannot continue indefinitely in a drainage basin that remains tectonically stable. Eventually a stream would cut its valley to sea level and would be uanble to accomplish further erosion. This lower limit of erosion is called *base level*.

The significance of base level was recognized in 1896 by the one-armed Civil War veteran and geologist *J.W. Powell*. While leading a perilous boat expedition down the unexplored gorges of the Colorado River, *Powell* was understandably impressed with the formidable erosive abilities of that great stream. "How long", he wondered, "could the river continue to actively cut downward?" The answer seemed readily apparent. Eventually, the stream would have eroded its bed nearly to sea level, and with little or no slope, would cease its geologic work. "We may consider the level of the sea," wrote *Powell*, "to be a grand base level, below which the dry lands cannot be eroded."

Powell also made studies of the mouths of tributaries entering the Colorado River and perceived that these confluences served as local base levels for each tributary. The tributary could cut its valley no deeper than the major stream into which it empties. Lakes, dams, and resistant rock formations may also form local base levels, which temporarily provide a vertical limit to the erosive powers of streams.

Streams and tectonics

If we recall the statement made earlier the rivers carry approximately 10 million tons of solid and dissolved material to the oceans each year, and further remember that this transfer has been in progress for over 3.6 billion years, then one might wonder why entire continents have not been reduced to what *Powell* described as "the grand base level." The reason, of course, is that the lands have not been static. They have opposed degradational agencies by rising to various heights above sea level during episodes of isostatic adjustment and/ or tectonic activity as a result of these uplifts, old streams flowing sluggishly across lowlands have been occasionally rejuvenated and additional streams formed to begin a new the erosional assault on the lands.

Plate tectonics, which has profoundly affected the development of major oceanic and continental features, has also played a role in opposing the leveling of the lands by mass wasting and flowing water. We have noted how mountain ranges are developed on the margins of converging lithospheric plates. These ranges in turn establish slopes that control the directions taken by running water. As an example, most of the South American continent is drained by rivers that flow eastward and empty into the Atlantic Ocean, and only a rather narrow zone west of the continental divide is drained by rivers that flow into the pacific. Thus, the mountains have controlled the locations and directions of streams and have themselves developed as a result of the convergence of the South American Plate with the Nazca Plate.

The Concept of a Graded Stream

If a stream of water begins to flow down a sloping surface, the water will cut a channel sufficiently large to contain the average or usual amount of water. In the early stages of development, the gradient of the stream is likely to be relatively steep, and the valley will develop a V-shaped cross-profile. The stream will work actively to erode its channel and eliminate the irregularities. As time passes, the gradient will be lessened while the load is steadily increased because of contributions from an expanding network of tributaries. Eventaully the stream attains a condition in which the supply of sediment fed into the stream approximately equals the stream's capacity to transport that load. Indeed, most of the river's available energy will be consumed in this transport, and rapid downcutting of the channel ceases. The stream is now said to have reached the graded condition. A graded stream is ideally a stream in equilibrium. Any change in the supply of sediment, velocity, or discharge will result in a displacement of equilibrium in a manner that will tend to absorb the effects of the change. For example, a graded stream that becomes underloaded

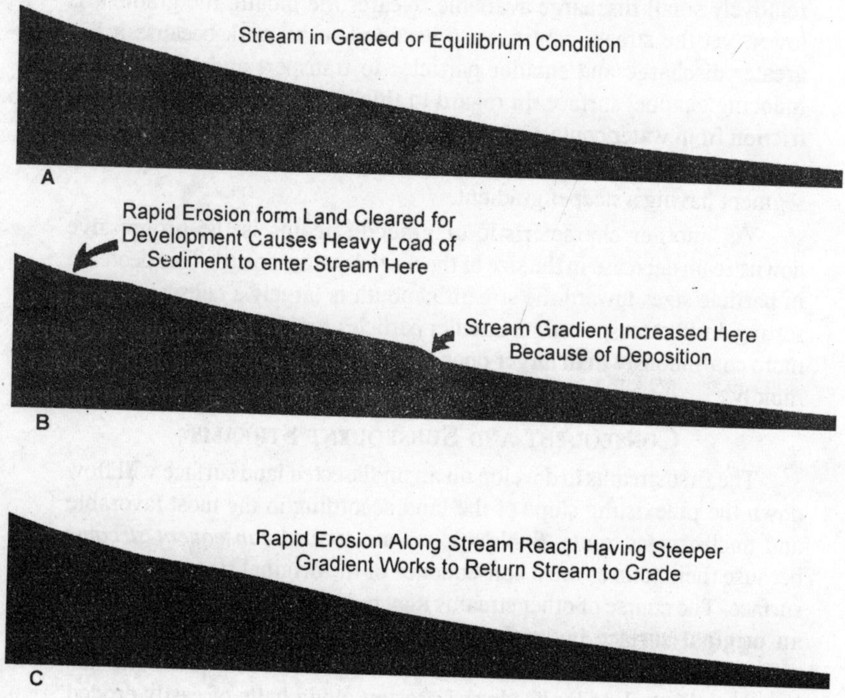

Fig. 3.8. A graded stream that becomes overloaded will initially deposit the portion of the load it cannot carry. The result is a bed build-up. At the down stream edge of the build-up, the steeper gradient will favour rapid erosin, and the stream will gradually remove the sediment and return to the graded condition.

(as when sediment-trapping dams are constructed in its tributaries or headwaters) will have energy to spare and will compensate by erosionally deepening its bed so as to flatten the gradient and decrease velocity. As an alternative, the stream might increase the number of bends (i.e. increase its sinuosity) and thereby lessen its gradient. Should a stream become overloaded, it may build up its bed intially by depositing the surplus load and thereby steepen its gradient, or it might increase overall gradient by reducing its sinuosity. In either case, the steepened gradient would result in increased velocity and capacity.

The overall result of these "cut and fill" events is that the stream develops a concave-upward profile of equilibrium. The profile, technically termed the *longitudinal profile*, can be constructed by connecting points of elevation along the length of the stream. The concave slope is a fundamental characteristic of graded streams. Near the headwaters, the gradient of the stream is steep and the river can do its work with the relatively small discharge available. Nearer the mouth, the gradient is lower, yet the stream continues to accomplish its work because it has greater discharge and smaller particles to transport and less friction-inducing channel surface. In regard to this last factor, the reduced total friction from water contact with the channel in lower reaches means the stream maintain a given velocity on a lesser gradient than can an upstream segment having a steeper gradient.

Yet another characteristic of graded streams is the progressive downstream decrease in the size of the particles transported. This decrease in particle sizes toward the stream's mouth is largely a consequence of sorting during transportation. Smaller particle are able to remain in motion more continuously than larger ones and so are moved downstream more rapidly.

Consequent and Subsequent Streams

The first streams to develop on an undissected land surface will flow down the preexisting slope of the land according to the most favorable and unobstructed route. Such streams are termed *consequent streams* because their courses are a consequence of the original slope of the land surface. The course of other streams may not be determined primarily by an original surface but rather by lithologic variations or structural differences. Such streams are called *subsequent*. Subsequent streams lengthen themselves by headward erosion along belts of easily eroded rock. As the process of head ward erosion proceeds, the head of the subsequent stream may ultimately extend into the drainage territory of rival streams that flow at slightly higher levels. When such connections

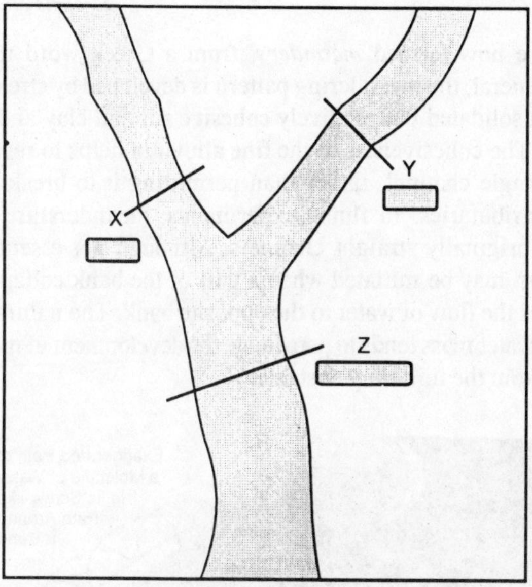

Fig. 3.9. The cross-sectional area of tributary X plus Y equals that the major stream Z. Yet the part of the channel surface in contact with flowing water (the wetted perimeter) of Z is less than the sum of X plus Y. Thus water flowing in Z experiences less frictional drag.

are completed, the flow of the higher-level stream will be diverted into the channel of the subsequent stream, thereby increasing its discharge and erosive powers. This "capture" of one stream by another is termed stream piracy and is a common place occurrence, especially in the early evolution of drainage systems.

Features Formed by Streams

Newly formed streams do not possess the valley flats and smooth gradients of older streams. As the river continues its work, however, gradients are reduced. The river will cease to cut downward as actively and begin to cut horizontally into the outside of bends. In the lower-velocity area that characterizes the inside of bends, deposition occurs. The process of cutting and filling is called *lateral planation* and is responsible for the relatively smooth areas bordering a stream. These areas are called *floodplains* because they are inundated during times when the river overflows its banks.

As the stream continues to widen its valley by lateral planation, the pattern of alternate left and right bends begins to assume some regularity.

The bends are now termed *meanders*, from a Greek word meaning "bends." In general, the meandering pattern is developed by streams that flow on unconsolidated but relatively cohesive silt and clay and on flat valley floors. The cohesiveness of the fine alluvium helps to restrict the stream to a single channel, rather than permitting it to break up into numerous distributaries. In flume experiments, meanders are readily formed from originally straight channels. Although not essential, the sinuous pattern may be initiated when a part of the bank collapses and thereby diverts the flow of water to the opposite bank. The natural spiral motion of the water mass tends to perpetuate the development of meanders downstream from the initiating obstacle.

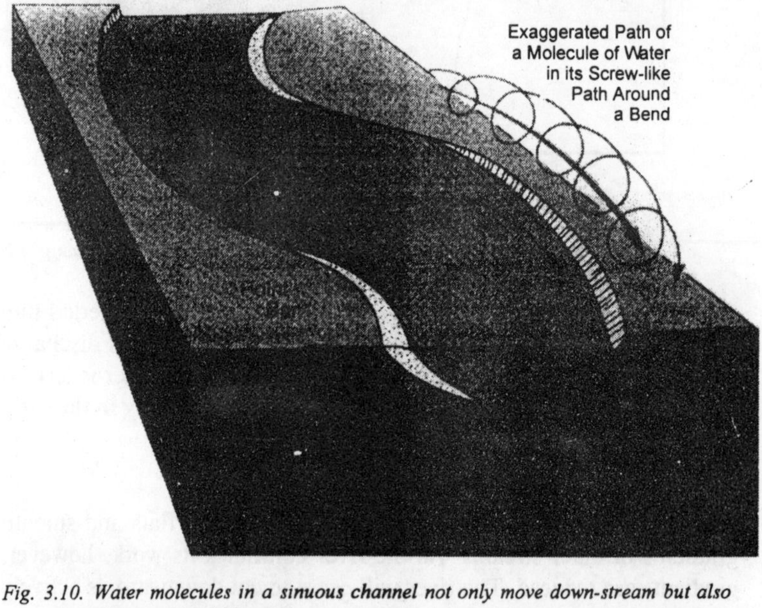

Fig. 3.10. Water molecules in a sinuous channel not only move down-stream but also follow a spiral-like path.

Most meandering streams traverse broad valley flats. Some, however, have steep valley walls and lack floodplains. The meander pattern in such streams was developed by the stream long ago when it was flowing on a valley flat. Subsequently, through regional uplift or some other geologic change, the river was caused to cut down into its formar floodplain but at the same time maintained its meander pattern. The result is meanders bounded by steep valley walls. Such meanders are said to be incised. When accompanied by other substantiating lines of evidence, incised meanders may be consided evidence for uplift of the earth's crust.

Not all streams or stream segments (reaches) develop a regular meandering pattern. Some divert flow into numerous shallow dividing and reuniting subchannels separated by transient islands and bars. Such streams are said to have a *braided pattern*. The braided pattern appears to develop in streams having highly variable discharge and readily erodible banks, composed of noncohesive materials such as sand and gravel. Because of the susceptibility of such bank material to erosion, the stream can easily divide into many small channels called *distributaries*. Sporadic decrease in discharge among the distributaries may cause local deposition in channels, resulting in blockage and further separation into subchannels.

The variability in discharge for some braided streams may be so extreme that water may be absent from the channel for weeks or months at a time. Such streams are termed *ephemeral*. Meandering streams, particularly smaller ones, may also be ephemeral and have discharge only during periods of rainfall. Ephemeral streams flow only in direct response to precipitation. *Intermittent streams* are those that are dry part of the year, contain water at other times, but that, unlike ephemeral streams, also receive water from underground supplies.

Features of floodplains

One may find a large number of secondary features formed along the valleys of meandering streams. These include point-bar deposits, cutoffs, oxbow lakes, and natural levees. *Point-bar* deposits are accumulations of sand and gravel along the inside of meander bends. These deposits develop as a consequence of the velocity being less around the inner margin of a bend, so that the stream deposits part of its load. Point-bars provide the frequent sandy havens for weary canoeists and vacationing bathers. On the outside bends of the meanders, the force of inertia tending to cause the water to flow in a straight line causes the water to impinge upon its bank, to "pile up," and to actively erode.

The cutting along the outside bends of meanders with accompanying filling along inside bends results in slow migration of the meanders in a downstream direction. The migration, if speeded up, might resemble the pattern produced where a snake had crossed an area of sand. Frequently, during the migration of meanders, two bends will come together to form a meander *cutoff*. The abandoned loop of the channel is left as a curved remnant on the floodplain. Because of its resemblance to the device placed over the shoulders of oxen to assist them in pulling wagons, these abandoned meanders have been dubbed *oxbow lakes*. With time, the oxbow lake may become filled with sediment and disappear.

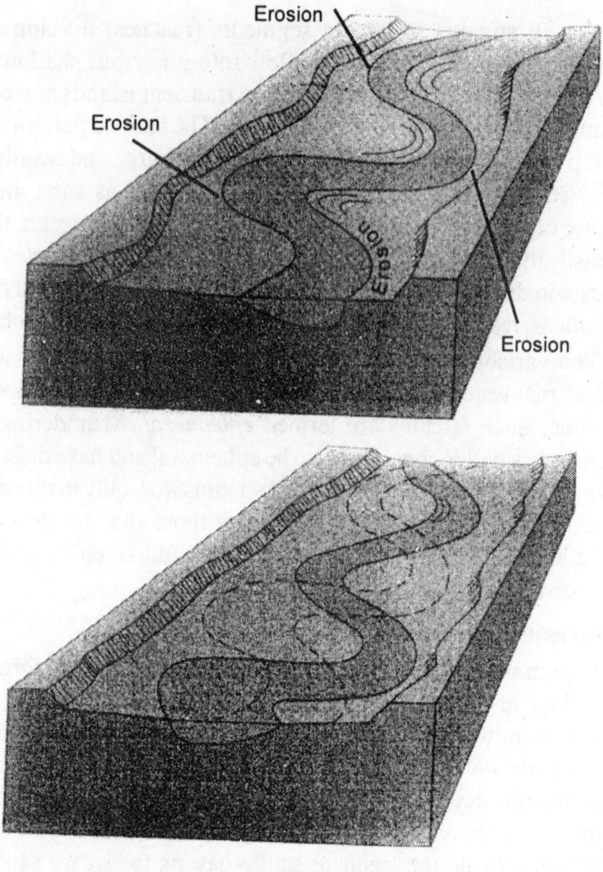

Fig. 3.11. Migration of meanders in a downstream direction. Dashed line in lower block marks the earlier channel location.

River floodplains are not completely level. Most floodplains have a raised crest or ridge adjacent to the channel. These ridges along the side of streams are called *natural levees*. They are formed during flood stages when the water overflows its banks, is suddenly slowed, and drops part of its load. Along parts of the lower Mississippi, the natural levee is the highest tract of land for miles around. Natural levees may prevent tributary streams entering the flood plain from emptying into the channel of the main stream. As a result, the tributary must follow a course parrallel to, and behind, the nautral, the natural levee until it comes upon a place

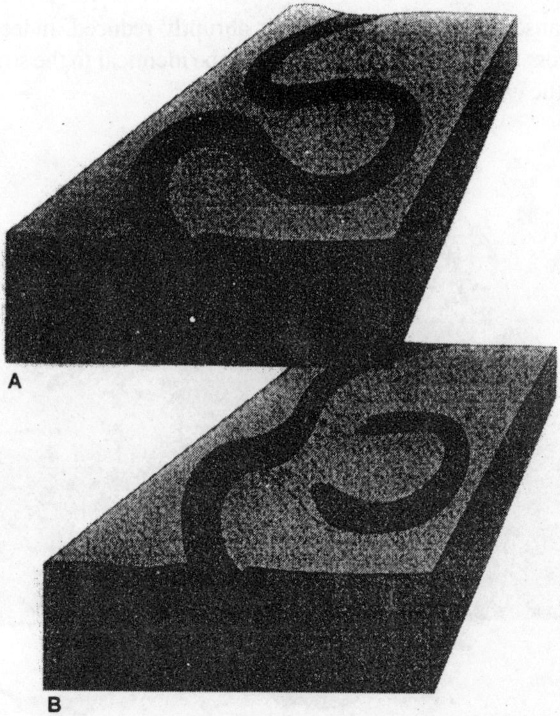

Fig. 3.12. Development of a meander cutoff and oxbow lake.

where it can enter the main channel. Such streams are called *Yazoo streams* after the river of that name in Mississippi.

Alluvial fans

Alluvial fans are cone-shaped deposits composed of river-transported silt, sand, and gravel. They are formed where streams emerge from a mountainous area and flow onto relatively level terrain. Stream velocity is reduced rather abruptly at such locations, largely because of widening of the channel and loss of water to the porous sediment beneath the stream bed. The stream is unable to carry its former load under these new conditions. Sediment is deposited within channels, causing water to spill over banks and form new channels, many of which disappear before reaching the foot of the fan because of water loss by rapid seepage. These events are repeated endlessly back and forth across the depositional area, eventually building the alluvial fans. It is somewhat surprising that deposition on the established fan occurs because water is lost to seepage, and not because the stream's gradient is abruptly reduced. Indeed, the gradient across the upper part of the fan may be identical to the stream's gradient in the valley upstream from the fan.

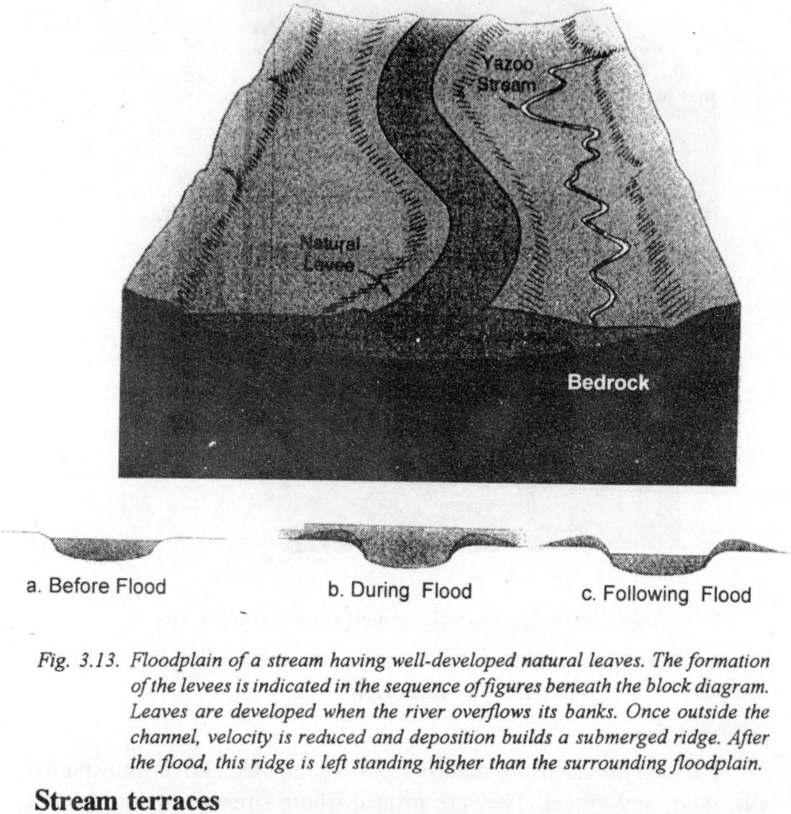

Fig. 3.13. Floodplain of a stream having well-developed natural leaves. The formation of the levees is indicated in the sequence of figures beneath the block diagram. Leaves are developed when the river overflows its banks. Once outside the channel, velocity is reduced and deposition builds a submerged ridge. After the flood, this ridge is left standing higher than the surrounding floodplain.

Stream terraces

A stream system is dynamic and constantly changing. In any given area at a given time, it may be expending most of its energy in transporting its load and have little energy remaining for erosion of its bed. At other times, a reduction in load may result in energy available for active downcutting. Elevation of the channel because of tectonic movements or isostatic uplift, increases in discharge, or lowering of sea level are other factors that might cause a stream to begin eroding its bed. During the downcutting, areas of previously deposited alluvium of the flood plain are removed, leaving the undissected flat remnants temporarily undisturbed. These level remnants located along the margins of the valley are called *stream terraces*. They may persist until eroded by the stream as it meanders endlessly back and forth across the valley. Occasionally old terraces are buried under more recent alluvium when conditions cause the river to cease active downcutting and begin a depositional phase. Such buried terraces are of particular interest to archaeologists seeking the level floodplain surfaces on which ancient peoples may have built their villages.

Deltas

Accumulations of sediment deposited by streams where they enter a large body of water like a lake or sea are called *deltas*. On encountering the body of standing water, the stream's velocity and transportive powers are quickly reduced, and deposition occurs. Sediment accumulating in the channel reduces the gradient, blocks the channel, and causes the flow to be diverted and divided into new channels. The branches leading outward from the main channel are called *distributaries*. The system of branching distributaries is similar to that seen upstream, except that the pattern is reversed. Several environmental conditions will favor the development of deltas. An abundant supply of sediment, as one might guess, is the most important condition. In addition, delta formation is enhanced by shallow depth of water, tectonic stability, and lack of strong waves or currents in the area of delta growth.

One of the most distinctive sedimentologic features of deltas is cross-stratification. This feature begins to form as soon as the river enters the sea or lake and drops the coarser components of its load nearest the landward part of the delta. Usually sediment is swept over the initial pile-up, coming to rest as seaward sloping layers. These layers constitute the *foreset beds*. They make up the major portion of simple deltas. Finer sediments carried to the deltaic area by the stream remain in suspension longer and are swept out farther into the basin. These nearly horizontal (or only gently dipping) layers constitute the *bottomset beds*. They are covered by foreset beds as the delta progrades seaward. Above the foreset beds, *topset beds* may develop as deposition occurs on top of the advancing foreset beds. These same features, when found in sedimentary rocks, allow geologists to recognize ancient deltas. Of course, the depositional sequence is frequently interrupted by shifting of distributary channels or erosion by waves, and this is why perfect examples of cross-bedding are not found everywhere in excavations of deltaic sediments.

Because of the fertility of their soils and the convenience of their coastal locations, modern deltas have always been centers of commerce and agriculture. Most of the agricultural lands of Egypt, for example, are located on the delta and floodplains of the Nile. The fertile fields of the Mekong Delta are a vital food source for the people of Cambodia and Vietnam.

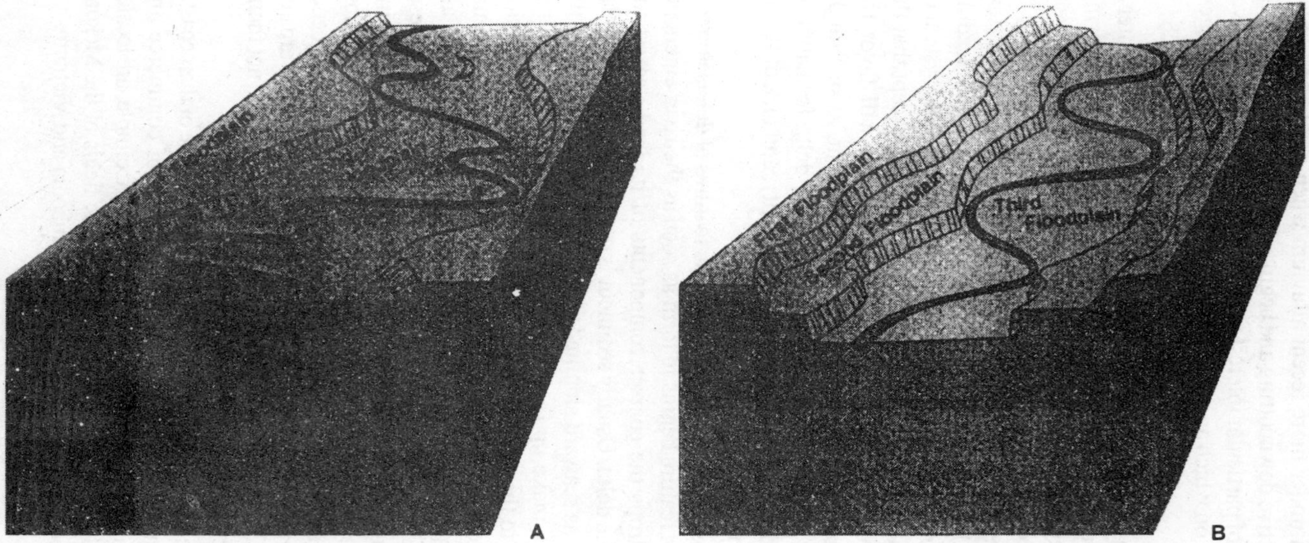

Fig. 3.14. Development of terraces by periodic uplift. In block (A) uplift has caused the stream to cut into its former floodplain and gradually develop a new floodplain. With another pulse of uplift, the process is repeated (B), and yet a lower floodplain is produced. Remnants of the former floodplains form the terraces that border the valley.

Ancient deltas are nearly as important as their present-day counterparts but for different reasons. Deltas of bygone geologic epochs are found on the continents at many locations around the world, and a few lie beneath parts of the continental shelves. Experience has shown that ancient deltas are favorable locations for the origin and accumulation of oil and gas. The intertonguing of coarse fluvial sediment with impermeable clay frequently produces ideal geologic situations for the entrapment of petroleum and natural gas. In addition, major coal beds occur in association with the sediments of ancient deltas.

Waterfalls

Among the most aesthetically pleasing and spectacular features of streams are waterfalls. *Waterfall* is a place in the stream where water descends vertically to a lower level. Waterfalls are usually a consequence of either bedrock characteristics or glaciation. Most commonly, waterfalls develop in places where the stream flows across an outcrop of a particularly resistant stratum that is underlain by one or more layers of more easily erodable rock. Downstream from the outcrop of hard rock, the less resistant layer is more rapidly eroded, resulting in an abrupt drop in the elevation of the stream bed.

Erosion at the upper edge of the waterfall will proceed rapidly as water rushes over the rock surfaces and excavates the fragmented debris at the base of the fall. As a result, the water fall itself gradually recedes upstream. Eventually, most water falls may degenerate into rapids and disappear altogether.

Niagara Falls, located between Lake Erie and Lake Ontario, developed when the retreating ice of the last glacial age uncovered an escarpment formed by southwardly tilted resistant dolostone. Weak shales beneath the dolomite strata are continously under mined in the pool beneath the falls, and this erosion contributes to the southward retreat of the falls. Indeed, the falls at Niagara are receding at an average rate of about 1 meter per year and will eventually reach Lake Erie. That event, however, will not occur for several thousand years and need not enter the honeymoon plans of prospective newlyweds.

Water falls in the eastern United States are abundant where eastward-flowing streams pass from highlands composed of igneous and metamorphic rocks onto coastal plain sediments, which are easily eroded. Even our colonial ancestors noted the general alignment of waterfalls at the contact between the two different kinds of rock and named this line the "fall line". Water wheels located at waterfalls along the fall zone powered colonial flour mills.

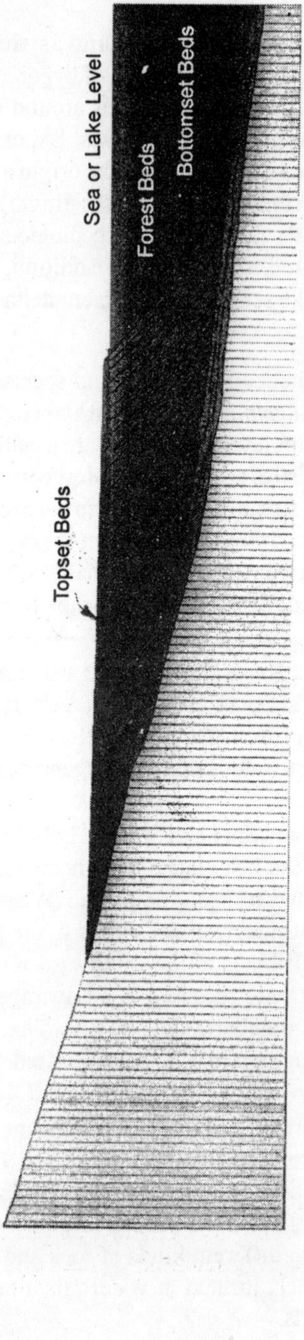

Fig. 3.15. The ideal arrangement of beds in a data. Relatively coarse material is deposited initially to form the inclined layers or foreset beds. Somewater finer sediment is swept farther toward the basin and deposited as bottomset beds. Forest beds may prograde over these bottomeset beds. The stream deposits the topset beds on top of the foreset beds.

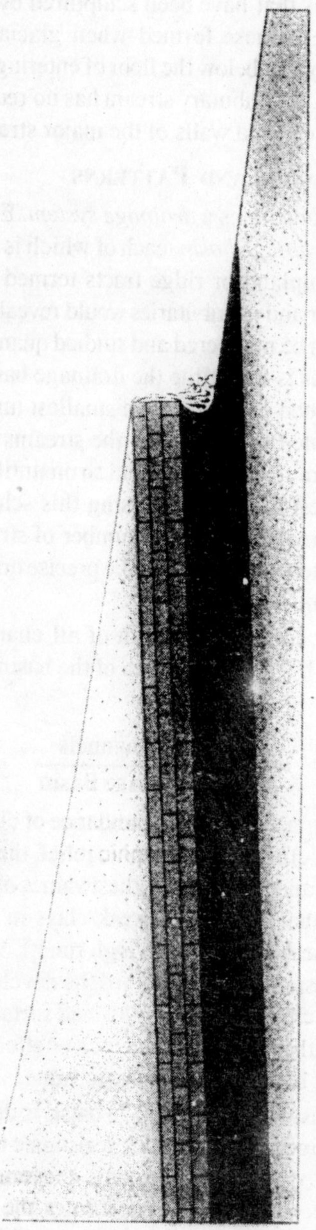

Fig. 3.16. Where an outcrop of relatively resistant rock is underlain by less resistant rock, the weaker rock may be rapidly eroded by the stream and the more resistant layer undercut. If the resistant rock callapses and leaves a vertical face, water will plunge over the crest as a waterfall.

Not all waterfalls are formed directly as a result of undermining by streams. In mountainous regions that have been sculptured by glaciers, waterfalls are common. Many of these formed when glacial erosion deepened the floor of major valleys far below the floor of entering tributary valleys. After the ice has melted, the tributary stream has no recourse but to plummet down the steeply excavated walls of the major stream.

Drainage Basins and Patterns

A river and its tributaries constitutes a *drainage system*. Every such system drains an area called a *drainage basin*, each of which is separated from other drainage basins by upland or ridge tracts termed *drainage divides*. A tracing of a major river and its tributaries would reveal a definite heirarchy of channels, which can be numbered and studied quantitatively. The first step in such an analysis is to outline the drainage basin and to number the tributaries as indicated on figure. The smallest unbranched headwater channels are designated as *first order*; the streams receiving water from first order streams are *second order*, and so on until the main trunk stream receives the highest designation. Using this scheme, it is possible to ascertain average stream length and number of streams in a drainage basin and drainage system area and to make precise quantitative comparisons among different drainage systems.

Carried a step further, the cumulative length of all channels in a drainage system can be divided by the surface area of the basin to obtain the drainage density. Thus

$$\text{Drainage Density} = \frac{\text{Length of Channels}}{\text{Area of Drainage Basin}}$$

Drainage density, of course, measures the abundance of channels in a given basin. It is influenced by climate, topographic relief, the nature of material exposed at the surface, and time. The highest values of drainage density are found in badlands that develop on weak clays in semi-arid regions. In such areas, low permeability results in high runoff. Vegetative cover is minimal, and hence erosion proceeds toward the development of extreme gullying and numerous channels. Where the land surface is more resistant to erosion because of either more resistant rock or effective plant cover, the drainage density will have a lower numeric value.

The arrangement of streams with in a drainage baisn is determined by such factors as intial slopes, inequalities in rock resistance to erosion, whether strata are level or tilted, and even tectonic movements. The particular plan or design of the river system constitutes the *drainage pattern*. By the study of drainage patterns, it is often possible to infer some of the characteristics of the structural geology of an area as well as events in geologic history. For example, if the rocks underlying an area are esssentially homogeneous or if they consist of flat-lying strata, the stream network will be characterized by an irregular branching of tributary streams. The overall drainage pattern is called *dendritic* (from the Greek *dendron*, tree) and rather resembles the branching of a tree. By contrast, *trellis patterns* consist of a system of nearly parallel streams, usually aligned between the outcrops of folded rocks that are relatively resistant to erosion. Patterns of this type are well displayed in the drainage systems of parts of the Appalachian Mountains where the drainage divides are formed by elongate ridges of resistant sandstones. Trellis drainage may also be controlled by aligned deposits of glacial debris or wind-blown sediment, but this is less common in the United States.

In landscapes having trellis drainage patterns, the main streams often make nearly right-angle bends where they cross the drainage divides. In addition, tributary streams tend to enter main streams at approximate right angles. Two *intriguing* features that are occasionally found in regions of trellis drainage are windgaps and watergaps. *Watergaps* are gorgelike stream valleys cut directly through a well defined mountain ridge. Most water gaps can be attributed to the erosional activities of a stream that had established its course long ago in rocks having one type of structure and that gradually eroded its way down to an underlying sequence of rocks having quite different sturcture. The stream responsible for cutting the watergap is said to have been superposed (contraction of superimposed) on the underlying structure. Because the stream had already established its course in the overlying alluvium, it is able to continue in this course cutting across resistant and nonresistant strata indiscriminately. Watergaps characterize orogenic resions where tectonic ridges rise across the paths of rivers.

If the river has sufficient energy to maintain its course across the ridge rising in its path, it may erode a watergap. Streams that have been able to maintain their direction of flow across active tectonic ridges as described here are called *antecedent*. The name signifies that they are older (antecedent to) than the structures thay cut.

Occasionally a stream flowing through a watergap may be diverted into the more rapidly deepening channel of one of the longitudinal streams that flow across softer rocks. This event constitutes stream piracy and leaves the watergap without water. The notch cut into the ridge is now called a *windgap*, although the action of wind has had nothing to do with its origin.

A third type of drainage pattern is that which develops around dome mountain uplifts or on the sides of volcanic cones. Because streams flow away from a high central area in all directions, the overall pattern is designated as *radial.* Drainage on exposed igneous stocks and laccoliths is also often radial in pattern.

Streams located around domal uplifts, where alternating layers of strata outcrop in a circular plan around the central mass, frequently develop an *annular drainage pattern*. As was the case with trellis drainage, the pattern of channels is structurally controlled. Streams flow across the outcrop of softer rocks and between stream divides composed of more resistant rock.

Floods

Nearly every year the news media report a disastrous flood somewhere in the world. A flood is any relatively high streamflow that spills out of its channel onto the valley floor. Everyone knows that floods develop whenever there is heavy runoff due to the persistence or intensity of rain, rapid melting of snow, or alteration of land surfaces, which increases runoff. The channel of the stream is shaped primarily by its usual amount of discharge, and therefore when it receives an extraordinary volume of water, the surplus can only spill over the banks and flow out onto the floodplain. Floodplains act as safety devices for streams in that they provide a place for the release of water the channel cannot hold. This simple fact is sometimes overlooked by overzealous but uninformed developers of housing tracts.

A river will have only a moderate discharge on most days of the year. Perhaps a few days each year, there may be enough water to fill the channel bank full but not sufficient to cause flooding. For most streams, actual flooding rarely occurs more frequently than about once every 2 or 3 years on the average. Streams do have relatively high temporary water storage capacity, and it takes a heavy rainfall or sequence of rains to cause flooding. In order to plan for the exceptional floods, scientists examine river flow charts for as many past years as there are records available. Using statistics, it is possible to calculate the probability of future flooding in specific streams. The method will not permit one to predict the precise date of a major flood but will indicate the probability of a flood of a certain size within a certain interval of years. For example, when geologists (and insurance adjusters) speak of a "10-year flood," they are referring to a flood having a certain discharge that has a *probability* of occurring once during a 10 year period. In general, 2-year floods are rather modest in size. Ten-year floods can cause serious damage to

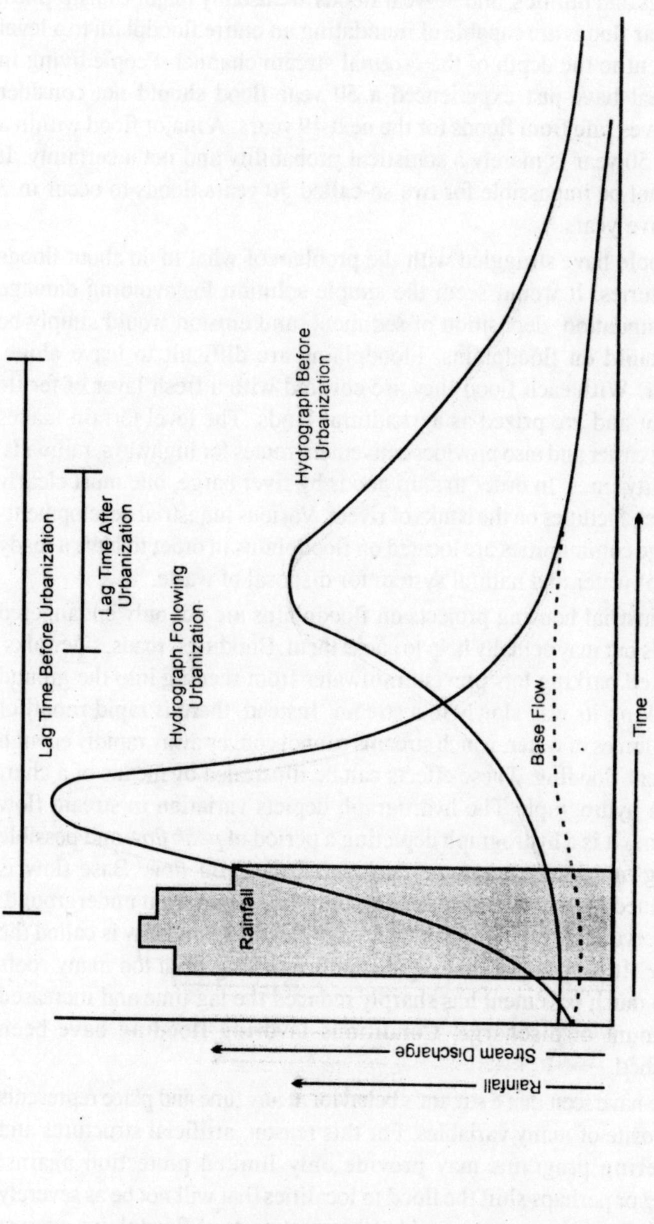

Fig. 3.17. Two hypothetic hydrograph curves illustrating the effect of urbanization and leg time between heavy rainfall and peak discharge.

buildings and utilities, and 50-year floods are usually major catastrophes. Fifty-year floods are capable of inundating an entire floodplain to a level equivalent to the depth of the original stream channel. People living in areas that have just experienced a 50 year flood should not consider themselves safe from floods for the next 49 years. A major flood within a span of 50 year is merely a statistical probability and not a certainty. It would not be impossible for two so-called 50 years floods to occur in 2 successive years.

People have struggled with the problem of what to do about floods for centuries. It would seem the simple solution for avoiding damage from inundation, deposition of sediment, and erosion would simply be not to build on floodplains. Floodplains are difficult to leave alone, however. With each flood they are covered with a fresh layer of fertile sediment and are prized as agricultural lands. The level terrain makes farming easier and also provides convenient routes for highways, railroads, and utility lines. In order to ship goods by river barge, one must clearly have dock facilities on the banks of rivers. Various industrial developments and large communities are located on floodplains in order to have a ready source of water and natural system for disposal of waste.

Industrial housing projects on floodplains are not only endangered by floods but may actually help to cause them. Buildings, roads, sidewalks, and paved parking lots prevent rainwater from seeping into the ground and making its way slowly to a stream. Instead, there is rapid runoff of huge volumes of water, which streams cannot convey away rapidly enough to prevent flooding. These effects can be illustrated by means of a chart called a hydrograph. The hydrograph depicts variation in stream flow with time. It is a hydrograph depicting a period of *peak flow* and possible flooding and low-water stage designated the *base flow.* Base flow is maintained largely by water flowing into the stream from underground. The interval between a time of heavy rainfall and peak flow is called the *lag time.* It is apparent that rapid runoff resulting from too many roofs and too much pavement has sharply reduced the lag time and increased the amount of discharge. Conditions favoring flooding have been established.

We have seen that a stream's behavior at any time and place represents a composite of many variables. For this reason, artificial structures and engineering programs may provide only limited protection against flooding or perhaps shift the flood to localities that will not be as severely affected. Sometimes it is possible to protect parts of floodplains against the more frequent low-magnitude floods, although complete protection against a 50- or 100-year flood would be a monumental and uneconomic feat of engineering. Such protection would be more costly than the financial resources of the public could bear. There are, however, practices that may reduce the loss of property and lives from flooding. For example, artificial levees and dikes may be emplaced to help hold the water in its channel. Before such structures are emplaced, however, they should be carefully evaluated, for they may contribute to flooding upstream. Channels may be artificially straightened so as to speed up the flow and move water out quickly before it can spill over the banks. Here too there is a danger, for by speeding the flow of water, locations downstream may be flooded.

Fortunately, one need not always resort to dikes and levees. There are many nonstructural measures that are also helpful, including zoning to prevent the construction of homes and other nonessential buildings on frequently flooded tracts. Ideally, valley flats should be used for agriculture, recreation, game reserves, and human activities that do not endanger the lives and property of large numbers of people. Where unavoidable, buildings erected on the floodplain should be specially constructed to resist flood damage, and flood insurance should become a requirement of all who dwell on floodplains. Flood warning systems have already been established by the U.S. Weather Bureau for major rivers of the United States, and flash flood warning systems activated by automatic devices are currently being emplaced in streams subject to sudden overflow. Finally, measures can be taken to reduce the flood hazard at its source by retarding excess runoff through terracing and planting.

In many flood-prone regions, dams have been constructed in order to store water and allow it to move downstream in a regulated manner. Dams, however, are not always as effective in flood control as we would like them to be. It is true that dams do relieve flooding by containing some of the water, but they also collect the sediment that was carried by the river. The water released by the dam lacks a load of sediment and therefore quickly erodes the channel downstream from the dam in order to acquire a new load. Unfortunately, the discharge is relatively small because of the water retained behind the dam, and so the river drops its load as soon as there is a decrease in velocity. The deposition builds up the channel downstream, raising the level of the bed so that even modest flows may spill over the banks. Someone once remarked, "nature can be perverse." The validity of that phrase seems evident whenever humans attempt to tamper with a complex natural system like a river.

The Debatable Concept of Cyclic Landscape Evolution

In the late 1890s, *William Morris Davis*, an eminent American geomorphologist, proposed a conceptual scheme of landscape changes in humid climates. *Davis* postulated that the principal factors in the development of a landscape are the *processes* of erosion (running water, moving ice, gravity) acting on land surfaces, the underlying *structure* of the bedrock, and the length of *time* over which the various processes have operated. He went no to propose that, beginning with a nearly flat initial surface (as for example, a newly emerged section of continental shelf), the landscape would pass through a cycle of changes designated "youthful," "mature," and "old age." Landscapes in youth would lack valley flats and would be separated by poorly drained interstream tracts composed of the initial surface. As stream erosion and mass wasting progressed, valley flats would develop, drainage density increase, the major stream would attain a graded condition, and divides would be converted to ridges and slopes. The landscape would be considered "mature." In "old age," according to the *Davis* conceptual scheme, valleys would be expanded to several times the width of the meander belt. Lakes, swamps, and marshes would develop on the floodplain, and there would remain only a few resistant remnants of divides. *Davis* referred to this low-lying surface as a *peneplain* and considered it the terminal stage in the cycle of erosion. Elevation of that surface would result in a repetition of the stages, and this is why *Davis* employed the term "cycle" in naming his hypothesis.

The *Davis* geomorphic cycle is a theoretic scheme that he developed by observing natural landscapes having the general appearance of one or another of his conceptual stages. A complete cycle has never been actually observed (an impossible task) or experimentally reproduced. Critics of his theory argue that any particular segment of the earth's crust will not remain fixed in position long enough for an entire cycle of changes to occur. Nor are influential factors like climate and bedrock likely to remain unchanged over the long episodes of erosion.

Davis used the terms "youth," "maturity," and "old age" to describe streams also. He defined "youthful streams" as those that had deep V-shaped valleys. "Mature streams" had flat broad valleys with floodplains at least as wide as the meander belt, and "old age streams" were slow-moving, widely meandering streams flowing over floodplains several times wider than the width of the meander belt. Unfortunately, these anthropomorphic terms are misleading, for a single stream may have youthful characteristics in its headwaters and mature or old-age characteristics in a lower segment of the longitudinal profile. Nevertheless, if the terms are divorced from any time significance, they are useful and expedient in designating stream valleys of a particular morphology.

Although many flaws can be found in the idea of *cyclic* landscape evolution, all geomorphologists would agree that valleys and the landscapes they occupy do change with time. Recently, the term *sequential evolution* has come into favor. The new term can be used to describe the unidirectional evolution of one landscape into another if uninterrupted by tectonic or climatic events. That landscapes do indeed evolve sequentially is indicated by small-scale experiments as well as observations of real landscapes.

Chapter 4

Underground Water

Prelude There has always been a sense of mystery associated with our thinking about water underground. Ancient peoples were certain that great rivers flowed unseen beneath their fields. The spring that formed where underground water flowed out onto the land were thought to be gifts of benevolent gods. Some believed these spring waters could cure the sick and give strength to the feeble. In desert communities, the survival of entire populations was dependent on success in finding underground water. The enormous importance of a supply of underground water to the ancient tribes of Israel is documented in the bible by frequent references to the digging of wells and to the many battles fought to protect them. The well was the focal point of the community. Around it, information was transmitted and historic personal relationships established.

Early Greek philosophers, including Homer, Thales, and plato, believed that underground water was really derived from the oceans. According to their conception, water was transmitted inland in subterranean channels and then purified of salt and other contaminants as it ascended through the crevices and voids of rocks and soil. A far more valid hypothesis of the origin of underground water was provided somewhat later in history by the Roman architect Vitruvius. Vitruvius correctly argued that an appreciable part of the water from rainfall percolates downward through soil and rock, flows along through whatever fractures and openings are available in the subsurface, and emerges at distant locations as springs. Vitruvius had a sound understanding of the hydrologic cycle. He recognized that the atmospheric return of water to the continents was more plausible than the underground return proposed by his Greek predecessors.

Of all the water that falls as rain or is derived from melting snow, about one-third runs off at the surface as sheetwash and in stream. A similar amount evaporates or is used by plants, and the remainder infiltrates into the regolith and rocks beneath, percolating downward until there are no longer any air-filled openings, and then rising in level toward the surface as additional water is added. This underground water that nearly fills all openings in rock or sediment is called *groundwater* by geologists. It has been estimated that groundwater supplies about one-fifth of the total water needs of the United States.

Several factors influence the amount of water that will become part of the groundwater reservoir for a particular region. The more important of these factors are the amount of precipitation, the volume of openings in the subsurface materials, the slope of the land surface, and the nature of the vegetative cover at the surface. Once the water has percolated into the subsurface, it is capable of movement toward outlets such as wells and springs, can accomplish certain kinds of geologic work, can be cleansed of disease-causing organisms, and can contribute to the hot waters and vapors emitted by geysers and hot springs. In this chapter, we will examine the movements, benefits, hazards, and characteristics of groundwater. Initially, it will be necessary to understand the subsurface distribution of underground water and the factors that influence its movement. This understanding will provide a basis for a discussion of gravity and artesian springs, the formation of cav- erns, and the uses and misuses of underground water supplies.

The Sources of Groundwater

Most of the water found underground is derived from rain or snow. Such water is called *meteoric*. Actually, only about 25 per cent of meteoric water finds its way into the underground water system. A larger part is carried away as runoff, evaporated, or utilized by plants. Of course, some meteoric water stored in lakes or flowing in streams may step downward and become groundwater. In order for such seepage to occur, however, the river or lake bed must be above the level of the subsurface zone in which all openings are filled with water. Streams whose waters contribute to the groundwater supply are called *influent*. A larger number of streams receive part of their discharge from groundwater and are thus *effluent* with respect to groundwater. The water in many lakes, ponds, and bogs is also effluent in origin.

Whenever sediment is deposited in water, water will necessarily fill all the open spaces between grains. Water trapped in sedimentary rocks in this way is termed *connate water*. Often connate water is salty, either because it was originally sea water or because of the mineral matter that has been dissolved in it over long intervals of geologic time. Petroleum engineers are quite familiar with connate water, for it is frequently encountered during well drilling operations.

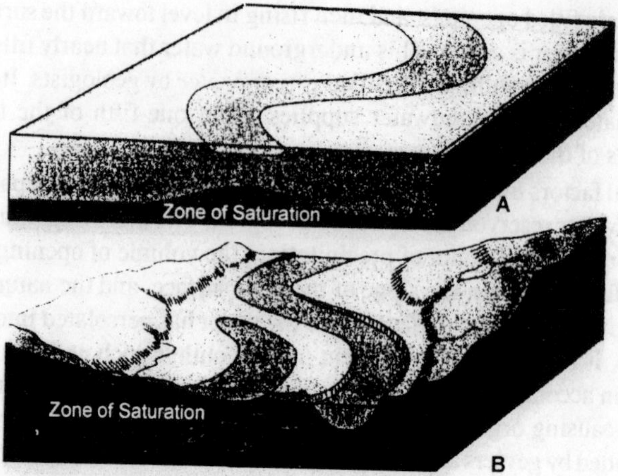

Fig. 4.1. An influent stream (A) contributes stream water to the groundwater supply. Streams that receive part of their water from underground sources are termed effluent (B).

Magmatic or *juvenile water* is produced directly by igneous activity. Along with recirulated meteoric water, it is most visible to us as a component of the vapors emitted from volcanoes. Deeply buried magmatic bodies also contribute magmatic water to the surrounding rocks. It is likely that at least a part of the water emitted by some thermal springs is magmatic. In terms of its immediate usefulness to mankind, magmatic water is not as important as meteoric water. Historically, however, it is of immense importance, for the planet's entire hydrosphere has a magmatic source.

Rock Properties Affecting Groundwater Supplies

Aquifers and aquicludes

A body of rock or sediment through which water can move and that yields sufficient water for domestic or industrial use is termed an *aquifer*. Examples of aquifers include unconsolidated sands and gravels, sandstone strata, partly dissolved or cavernous limestones, and nearly any other rock type that is highly fractured. Geologists employ the term *aquiclude* for rocks that do not permit passage of significant quantities of groundwater. By far the most common aquiclude is clay. Clay-rich rocks like shale may actually contain considerable amounts of water, but that water cannot flow freely through the microscopic pores between clay particles.

The quantity of water that can be obtained from wells drilled into aquifers depends in part on the amount and characteristics of the void spaces in the water-bearing rock, as well as the manner in which these voids are interconnected. The hydrologic terms used to describe these two attributes of aquifers are porosity and permeability.

Porosity

Porosity is defined as the total volume of open spaces, pores, or voids in a rock or sediment expressed as a percentage. The spaces may be fractures, cavities dissolved in rock by water, or simply openings fortuitously formed between grains as they were deposited. In a clastic sediment or sedimentary rock, porosity will be markedly influenced by sorting. Sorting is a measure of the uniformity of the sizes of particles in sediment or rock. In well-sorted sandstones, for example, the grains are mostly about the same size or fall within the narrow range of sand-size particles. There are fewer of the tiniest clay and slit-sized particles to fill the spaces between the larger grains. Poorly sorted sandstones contain a complete range of particles from clay-size to sand-size. Therefore, what might have been pore space in a rock having better sorting is occupied by fine particles in a poorly sorted rock. Therefore, poor sorting generally correlates with relatively lower porosity.

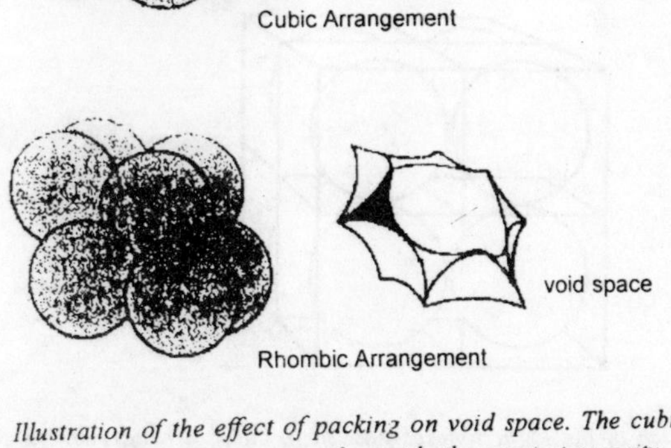

Fig. 4.2. Illustration of the effect of packing on void space. The cubic arrangement of grains is the most open and provide the greatest porosity. In addition, the minimal cross-sectional area of the pore is greater in cubic packing. In natural materials like sand, the grains would not be perfect shpheres, they would not be of identical size, nor would they be so precisely arranged.

Another factor that influences the porosity of an aquifer is the manner in which the grains are packed together. If that packing is relatively open, there will be a greater volume of space available for water storage. The shape of grains and the presence of cementing materials like calcium carbonate or silica can also influence porosity. One factor that does not directly affect porosity is grain size. Given an aggregate of larger spherical grains packed in open arrangement, and a second aggregate of smaller but similarly shaped and packed grains, both would have identical porosities. A simple calculation shows this relation is valid. The volume of a spherical grain is:

$$V_{sg} = \frac{\pi}{6} d^3$$

where V_{sg} is the volume of the spherical grain and *d* the diameter. Assume that one has arranged eight spherical grains. The edge of the cube that circumscribes the eight spherical grains is twice the diameter of a single grain, and the volume of the cube is $(2d)^3$, or $8d^3$. The ratio of the volume of the eight uniform spherical grains to the volume of the circumscribed cube, V_c, is:

$$\frac{V_s}{V_c} = \frac{8\frac{\pi}{6}d^3}{8d^3} = \frac{\pi}{6} \text{ or } \frac{3.14}{6} \text{ or } 0.52$$

Thus, the solid spherical grains occupy 52 per cent of the volume of the circumscribed cube, and void spaces occupy the remaining 48 per cent. Reducing the grain size will not diminish the porosity because grain size cancels out. If, however, the grains were packed more closely, porosity might be reduced to a value of 26 per cent.

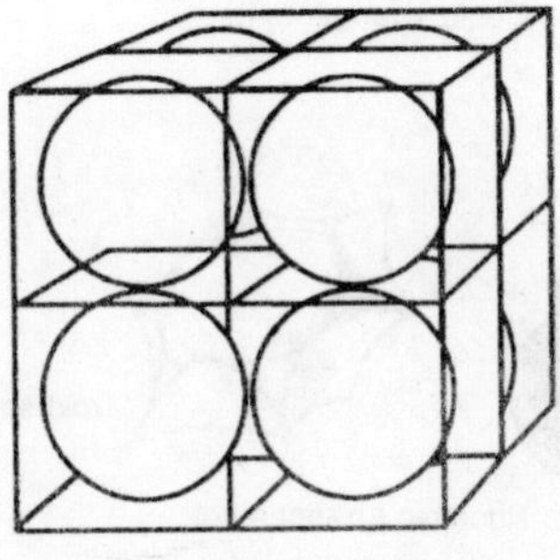

Fig. 4.3. Each of the eight spheres packed in cubic arrangement occupies 52 per cent of the volume of the cube in which it rests. Porosity is therefore 48 per cent. Because of variation in particle size, packing and particle shape, natural materials will not attain so great a porosity.

A rock, of course, is not composed of perfectly spherical grains arranged in the most open manner, and only rarely are sedimentary rocks found with porosity as high as 48 per cent. Porosities from 5 to 15 per cent are considered average in rocks, although higher porosities occur in unconsolidated sediments.

Permeability

Permeability is a term used by geologist to express the relative ease with which water moves through the spaces or interstices in a rock or sediment. These spaces must be interconnected if a rock is to have permeability. It is possible to measure permeability by subjecting a piece of rock to a given water pressure and recording the amount of water that passes through the rock in a measured interval of time. When this is done for materials having a range of grain sizes, it is apparent that the flow rate is greatest in coarser materials. Unlike porosity, permeability increases as the grain size increases. The reason for this in that the size of voids or interstices also increases in a sediment composed of larger grains. Grain surfaces retard flow, and there is more total surface area to do this in fine-grained sediment than in coarse-grained material. In fine silts and clays, the film of water adhering to each particle is in continuous contact with the film of adjacent grains, and there is less low-friction "throat area" for the uninhibited passage of fluid. Rocks composed of clay may have considerbly more porosity than sands, but because of their smaller interstices and the consequently higher frictional resitance to flow, clayey materials have much lower permeability than sands. Unconsolidated and well-sorted gravels, as well as cavernous limestones, are among the most permeable of earth materials. Also, some rocks are porous but not permeable. This is usually because the pores in the rock are not interconnected.

The Occurrence of Water Underground

Underground water zones

Unless trapped above impermeable layers of rock, meteoric water will percolate steadily downward into the earth under the pull of gravity. Eventually, however, the water will reach a depth at which the great pressures of overburden have closed most of the open spaces and the rock has become impermeable. Continued additions of water will then fill all pore spaces above the impermeable zone, and the surface of the saturated zone will rise toward ground level as more water is added. The situation resembles what would occur if a tub were filled with gravel and then a shower of water added. The water would percolate down to the bottom of the tub and then gradually rise as it filled up the spaces between the gravel. If the shower of water were stopped before the tub was filled, one could reach down through the gravel and find the level of the free water surface. In nature, that surface could be located by digging a hole into the ground until one reached a depth where water began to flow into the hole. After a period of time, the surface of the water in the well would stand at the level of the free water surface in the rock. The subsurface zone below that level is appropriately called the *zone of saturation.* Above the zone of saturation is the *vadose zone* or *zone of aeration*, so called because some of the pores are filled with air as the meteoric water infiltrates downward. If additional wells are dug nearby and the elevation of the free water surface is recorded in each well, then it would be possible to use that information to map the underground surface at the top of the zone of saturation. This upper surface of the saturated zone is called the *water table.*

Fig. 4.4. A simple experiment that indicates the manner in which the zone of saturation and water table develop.

Just above the water table, moisture may be pulled up into the vadose zone as result of capillary attraction. This irregular zone of water is called the *capillary fringe.* In general, the capillary fringe is thicker in finer-grained materials than coarse clastic sediment. One can observe capillary attraction when a glass tube is inserted into a glass of water. Water will

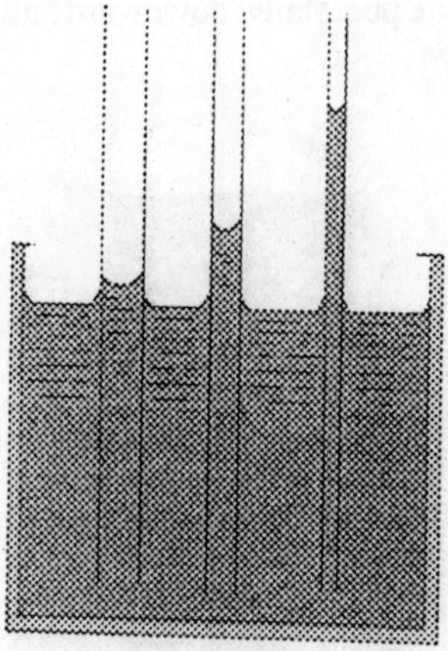

Fig. 4.5. Capillarity can be demonstrated by suspending glass tubes in water. Water rises in the glass tube because the concave surface layer or molecules, in contracting, draws the water upward with it by molecular attraction. The height of rise varies inversely with the diameter of the tube. It is for this reason that the capillary fringe is thicker in sand than in a coarse gravel.

appear to oppose gravity and move upward in the tube. Capillary attraction is the result of surface tension, or the tendency of a water surface to act like a stretched rubber membrane. Surface tension is caused by the mutual attraction of water molecules for one another. In a tubelike crevice or pore, water molecules are attracted laterally to the minerals adjacent to the pore and downward to other molecules, so that a membranelike concave surface is produced. The attempt by surface tension to flatten the concavity tends to draw the water up the tube. As soon as the weight of the raised column of water equals the force resulting from surface tension, water will cease to rise in the tube.

The configuration of the water table

The water table is not a static surface but will vary in elevation and slope according to the configuration of the overlying topography, the permeability of the rocks and sediments, and the amount and frequency of rainfall. If a hilly terrain is underlain by homogeneous permeable earth materials, and if rainfall is relatively frequent, the configuration of the water table will roughly approximate the surface contours of hills and valleys. In the event rain would fall continuously for a time, the zone of saturation would gradually extend upward to the surface of the ground, and water would flow into the lower lying areas. On the other hand, if there were no rain for a long time, the water table would slowly flatten as the water in the saturated zone percolated downward and flowed laterally toward nearby stream valleys.

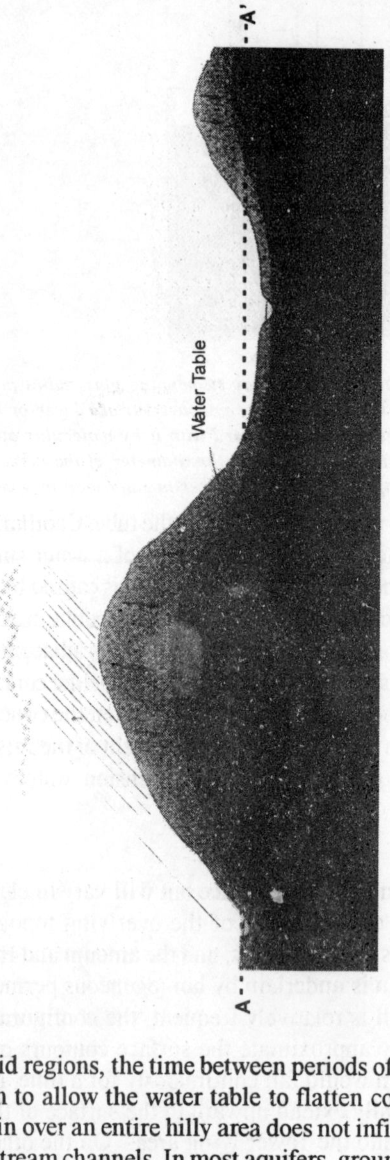

Fig. 4.6. In a hilly area underlain by uniformly permeable material, the configuration of the water tube will be subdued reflection of surface topography, provided rainfall is frequent. The flow of groundwater through such permeable homogenous material is indicated by the arrow.

In humid regions, the time between periods of rainfall is usually not long enough to allow the water table to flatten completely. Also, water falling as rain over an entire hilly area does not infiltrate rapidly and rush to adjacent stream channels. In most aquifers, groundwater can only move slowly through the tortuous interstitial spaces, and before it can reach an outlet, more rain falls, causing a "pile up" of water in the divides farthest from the streams. It is for this reason that the water table rises under hills and descends beneath valleys so as to take the form of a subdued reflection of surface topography. It is a "subdued" reflection because the vertical distance from ground surface to the water table is greater along the divides than along the valleys.

Although most areas are underlain by a body of groundwater having only one water table, there are also some places where localized impermeable beds occur at a shallow depth below the surface and prevent the further downward percolation of water toward the main water table. Water may collect on top of the impermeable strata to produce a local secondary water table above the main one. Such features are appropriately called perched water tables. Glaciated areas and areas where there are frequent intertonguings of sandstones and shales are likely to have perched water tables.The quantity of water available from the limited saturated zone beneath a perched water table may be considerably less than beneath the main water table. When large quantities of groundwater are needed, it is usually advisable to drill wells through the perched water table and penetrate the main water table.

Groundwater Movement

Patterns of flow

The energy required for the movement of water molecules through rock or sediment is supplied by gravity. Water responds to the pull of gravity by attempting "to seek its own level." This is why groundwater percolates from higher parts of the water table to lower parts and often out onto the surface as springs. Part of the groundwater beneath divides flows directly down the slope of the water table. An even greater part, however, moves slowly toward a nearby stream along curved paths of flow. Along these paths, water may be carried deep into bedrock before ascending toward the stream channel. These flow patterns replenish and replace the deeper realms of groundwater and prevent their stagnation. Water moving in this manner will dissolve and transport soluble matter and provide cements for formerly unconsolidated sediments.

The curved flow paths for groundwater are apparently the result of the fluid attempting to move toward points of least hydraulic head. Along any horizontal line, such as A-A', the water is under greater hydraulic head beneath a divide than beneath a stream, and so it moves toward the stream. The flow patterns of groudwater have been duplicated in laboratory models in which dye has been injected at various points so as to trace the path of water molecules. These experiments indicate that, in general, the rate of movement of water molecules along shallow path is greater than in the deeper arcs.

Rates of flow

Two factors that influence the rate at which water in the zone of saturation will flow are the permeability of the aquifer and the slope of the water table. *Hydraulic gradient* is the term used to express the slope of the water table. Rather like the gradient of a stream, the hydraulic gradient is equal to the vertical distance between two points on the water table (*b*) divided by the horizontal distance between these two points (*l*). The vertical measurement is termed the *hydraulic head*. One can quickly determine the hydraulic head by subtracting the elevation of the free-standing water surface in valley wells from similar measurements obtained in wells dug high on divides. For example, if the water in an upland well stood at an elevation of 550 meters above sea level, and at 500 meters above sea level in a nearby valley well, then the hydraulic head (*b*) would be 50 meters. If the wells were 1000 meters apart, then the hydraulic gradient would be 50 meters divided by 1000 meters or 0.05.

The relation between rate of groundwater flow, hydraulic gradient, and permeability was worked out in the 1860s by *Henry Darcy*, an engineer for the city of Dijon, France. *Darcy* made observations of the height of water in wells and attempted to relate these observations to the permeability of the aquifer and the movement of water from well to well. He also conducted laboratory experiments on the flow of water through a pipe filled with sand of various grain sizes. He observed that the flow rate was fastest for the most permeable (coarsest) sediment. Further, he was able to show that, for an aquifer of a certain permeability, the rate of flow from one location to another was directly proportional to the hydraulic head and inversely proportional to the horizontal distance the water travels. Thus, as the slope of the water table increases, so also does the rate of flow. In addition, the direction of maximal rate of flow will be in the direction of the steepest slope of the water table, that is, the direction of greatest hydraulic gradient. This important relationship is known as *Darcy's Law.*

In most aquifers, the velocity of groundwater flow rarely exceeds 1 or 2 meters per day, although the range of velocities recorded have included rates as fast as a 100 meters per day and as slow as only a few cm per year. Several methods have been used to obtain velocity measurements. Some involve the injection of dyes or radioactive indicators in wells higher on the water table and the detection of these tracers in distant wells. In another interesting technique, wells having metal casings are wired together to form an electrical circuit. A highly conductive soluble compound is poured into the upland well, which on arrival at the downslope well causes a short circuit between the metal well casing and an electrode. The short circuit is automatically recorded by a clocklike device. The velocity of groundwater movement is obtained by dividing the distance traveled by the groundwater (with its tracer) by the time required for the transfer of the trace material form the first to the second well. Thus, if two wells were 400 meters apart, and the tracer required 200 days to reach the second well, groundwater would be moving toward the second well at the rapid rate of 2 meters per day.

Wells and Springs

It is always a delight and somehow surprising to see water flowing out from a ledge of rock or spouting from a pipe sunk deep into the earth. These are, however, rather ordinary occurrences of groundwater emerging at the earth's surface as springs and wells. In general, wells and springs are classified into two groups. Those that are fed by water flowing through unconfined aquifers are called *ordinary wells* and *springs.* If, however, the groundwater is confined to an aquifer by impermeable rock layers, the groundwater system is called *artesian.*

Ordinary wells

As indicated earlier, if a hole is dug to a depth below the water table and encounters permeable materials at that depth, groundwater will flow into the hole. The hole has become a water well. The presence of permeable sediment or rock is important, for without good permeability water will not flow into the hole rapidly enough to replace that which is with drawn. Also important is the necessity of digging a well deep enough. The water table rises during periods of high rainfall and falls during the dryer season (or drought years). Clearly, the well should penetrate considerably below the elevation of the water table at it its lowest predicted elevation. There is another reason for drilling a well to a depth appreciably below the water table. When water is pumped from a well, a conical depression in the water table forms in the area surrounding the born hole. This *cone of depression* may eventually reach to the intake level of the well, causing it to go "dry". Much to the consternation of neighboring users of groundwater, the decline in the water table around large cones of depression may also cause nearby wells to become dry. In the past, exceptionally wide and deep cones of depression developed around wells that supply the large quantities of water needed for irrigation and industry, and attempts to reestablish former levels of groundwater have been unsuccessful, even when pumping was discontinued. Fortunately, for most domestic wells, the cone of depression rarely subsides deeply enough to cause significant problems.

Ordinary or gravity springs

A spring is a natural flow of groundwater that has emerged onto the surface of the earth. The quantity of water emerging in this way may be only a trickle, or it may be a gushing flow that may proceed over the surface as a stream. As indicated in ordinary or gravity springs may develop at points where the water table intersects the ground surface along the sides of a valley. Springs may also be localized by impermeable strata, bedding planes, fractures, faults, or coverings of debris from slumping or landslides. Some springs are associated with perched water tables and emerge above impermeable layers of rock exposed along hillsides.

Artesian wells and springs

In some wells groundwater encountered at depth is under sufficient hydraulic pressure that it is able to rise above the level of the aquifer containing it and may even flow out at the surface. These wells and springs are given the name *artesian* after the Old Roman province of Artesium in France. An artesian system is the result of the simultaneous occurrence of three geologic conditions. First of all, there must be an inclined aquifer. One or more dipping layers of sandstone or other coarse sediment, layers of gravel in old alluvial fans, or cavernous limestones may be suitable inclined aquifers. Secondly, the aquifer must be enclosed by impermeable beds (aquicludes), which serve to prevent the escape of water from the aquifer to the surface. The third condition needed for an artesian system is that the elevation of the intake area is sufficiently high that enough hydraulic pressure will be developed to force the water in wells upward above the level of the aquifer. The pressure that forces the water to rise in the well is caused mainly by the weight of the water coming down toward the well site from the higher collecting area. If the artesian system were free-flowing, then water would gush upward at the well site to the level of water in the upland intake area. That surface to which water in an aquifer would rise by hydrostatic pressure is called the *potentiometric surface*. Water does not rise to the potentiometric surface in natural artesian systems, however, because of the Frictional loss of energy as it percolates through the aquifer. Nevertheless, to qualify as an artesian system, there must be sufficient head (and hydraulic pressure) to overcome friction.

Perhaps the best known artesian system in the United States is that developed in the plains surrounding the Black Hills of South Dakota. Water enters the Dakota Sandstone where the formation is exposed in the

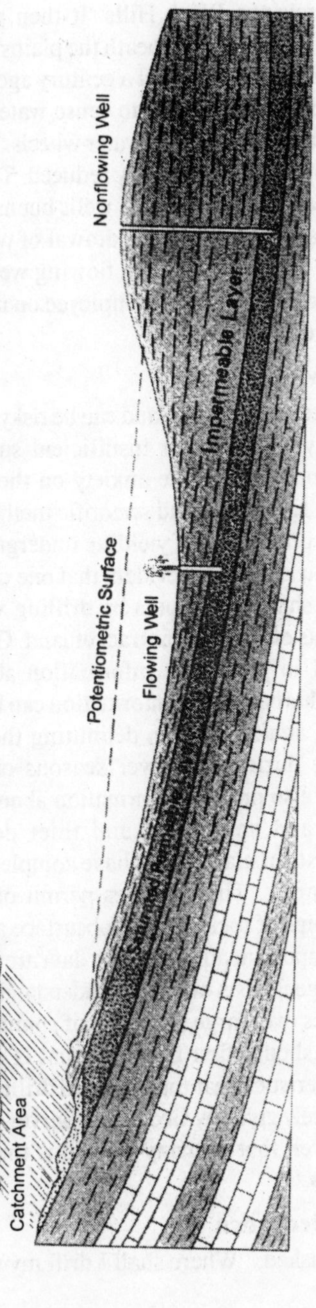

Fig. 4.7. Typical conditions for the occurrence of an artesian well.

outcrops that encircle the Black Hills. It then percolates through the sandstone and laterally outward beneath the plains. Overlying shale strata provide the impermeable cover. Half a century ago, hydraulic pressure in this confined system was sufficient to cause water from wells to gush a few meters into the air and even turn water wheels. There are now so many wells, however, that pressure is greatly reduced. The weight of overlying sediment has "squeezed" water toward wells but has not compensated for the lessening of head caused by with- drawal of water from over 10,000 wells in the region. Today, the yield in flowing wells is only a fraction of earlier amounts, and pumps must be employed on many wells from which water formerly flowed freely.

Where to dig a well

Drilling for water on a tract of land can be risky business, and whether an abundant, barely sufficient, or insufficient supply of water will be obtained is cause for considerable anxiety on the part of a landowner. There are, however, reasonable and scientific methods useful in finding a site having the best probability of yielding underground water. From the discussion of the water table, it is evident that one would be more likely to encounter water at shallower depths by drilling wells along the lower slopes and valley flats of a particular tract of land. Government geologists are usually helpful in providing information about wells drilled in neighboring sites. This backlog of information can be useful in predicting the depth of known aquifers and in delimiting the vertical drop in the ground water table during the dryer seasons of the year. Geologic reconnaissance can also provide information about the juxtaposition of potential aquifers and aquicludes and thier depth and dip. Also, government geologists in many states have completed seismic reflection studies over broad areas. These studies permit one to reconstruct the structural relationships of rocks in the subsurface and occasionally map the distribution of important aquifers. The data are analyzed with the aid of computers so that geologists can better understand, predict, and manage groundwater supplies over large segments of counties and states. Before drilling a well, one should first find out what is already known about groundwater characteristics near the proposed drilling site. In most cases, this information is freely given by Geological Survey scientists. One should bear in mind, however, that in many areas it is impossible to provide a guarantee of success.

Beware of the water witch

Many people if asked, "Where shall I drill my well?" would receive the prompt reply, "Don't ask me, hire a water witch." A water witch, or dowser, is a person who claims to have the occult power of locating the site for a well by walking across the ground while holding a forked stick horizontally. When the butt end of the stick or "divining rod" is attracted downward, the well site has been located. It has been estimated that over 25,000 water witches are currently working in the United States. The majority are not charlatans, but sincere men and women of good character and benevolent intentions who sometimes do not even charge for their services. Indeed, they are often successful in finding what prove to be good sites for wells. The reason for their success may be related to their long-standing knowledge of groundwater occurrence in the local area, the ability to apply common sense geologic interpretations, the acquired knowledge they have about the water table being closer to the surface in valleys than on hilltops, and recognition that certain kinds of vegetation are clues to underlying aquifers. Of course, the principal reason dowsers find water in humid regions is that groundwater occurs ubiquitously below the surface, so that if a reasonably deep well is drilled, the probability of success is good.

There is, of course, no known scientific basis for the alleged powers of the water witch. Studies conducted in Australia in the early 1900s indicated that there were twice as many dry holes among the well sites selected by dowsers than locations based on geologic information. The United States Geological Survey also examined the question in great detail. In 1917, *O.E. Meinzer*, speaking on behalf of the Survey, concluded, "It is difficult to see how for practical purposes the entire matter could be more thoroughly discredited, and it should be obvious to everycne that further tests by the United States Geological Survey of this so-called 'witching' for water, oil, or other minerals would be a misuse of public funds."

The Use and Misuse of Groundwater

Depletion

As is the case with most geologic resources, the supply of groundwater can be easily depleted. The groundwater that has been rapidly withdrawn during the past several decades required centuries to accumulate. In some regions, groundwater accumulated thousands of years ago at a time when precipitation was considerably greater than it is presently. In order to prevent wells from going dry and insure a supply of groundwater, communities have resorted to various techniques for artificially replenishing aquifers. In some instances, such artificial recharge involves water spreading, that is, covering flat surface areas with shallow ponds from which water can infiltrate into underlying aquifers. In other cases, water may be pumped down into the aquifers during seasons when surface water is readily available. Finally, after realizing the limitations of particular groundwater reservoirs, governments can enact regulations that sensibly limit the number of wells and the withdrawal rates so that all users can obtain a fair share of the water supply.

Contamination

Groundwater derived from sandstone or sandy sediments is famous for its purity. Contaminating particles adhere to the surfaces of the myriads of mineral grains and become trapped in interstitial spaces. Of course, there are limits to the filtering capacity of even sandy materials, and the ultimate purity of water from a well may depend on the volume of the pollutants being added to the underground reservoir and the distance over which the groundwater has traveled. Natural filtration is usually not effective for many dissolved chemical pollutants that may spoil groundwater. Also, not all aquifers are composed of granular materials. Large open conduits such as those in cavernous limestones, basalts containing lava tunnels, and dense rocks with large joints provide little filtration.

Whenever sewage or chemical wastes are dumped into excavations or topographic depressions, there is a strong possibility that groundwater supplies may become contaminated due to the downward percolation of contaminants into the zone of saturation. This is particularly true if the area for dumping is underlain by highly permeable materials. Not infrequently one discovers places where refuse has been dumped into pits that lead directly into cavernous conduits that supply water for nearby towns. Salty water from oil fields and gasoline from rusted storage tanks of neighborhood gasoline stations may similarly contaminate a community's primary source of water.

Most of us assume that water that falls as rain and seeps directly into porous rocks would probably be relatively free of contaminants. In recent years, however, it has been shown that rainwater may be tainted even before it reaches the ground. When compounds such as sulphur dioxide, hydrogen sulfide, and nitrogen oxide are emitted by power plants, smelters, factories, and automobiles, they rise into the atmosphere and combine with water vapor to form sulfuric and nitric acid aerosols. These microscopic drops are carried by wind and suspended in the atmosphere until meteorologic conditions return them to the earth's surface as acidic rain or snow. *Acid rain* greatly increases rates of chemical weathering and contributes significantly to the dissolution of limestones and other rocks. Of more immediate importance, acid rain seeps into highly permeable

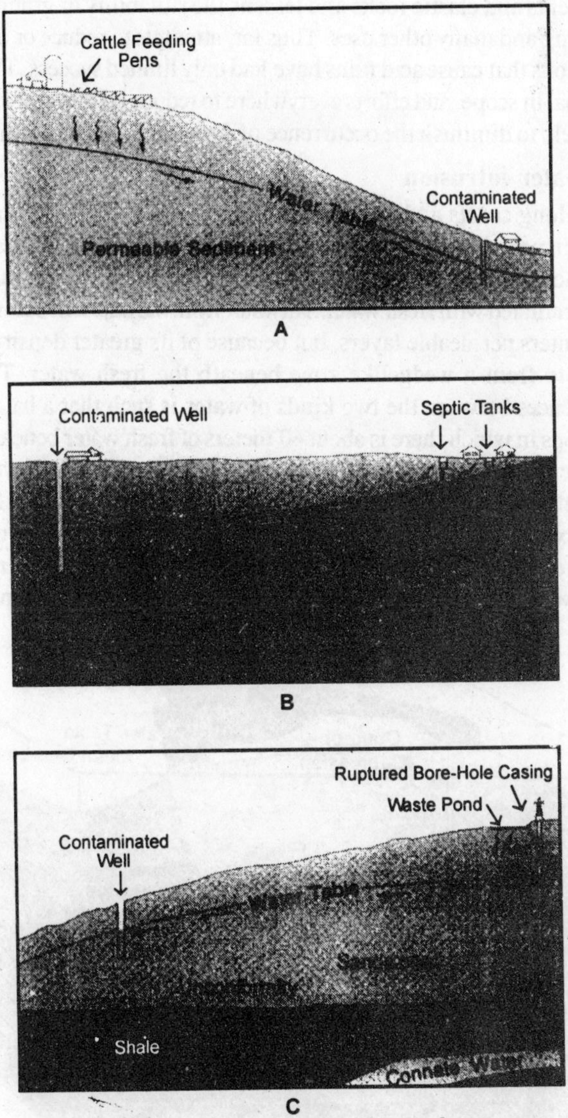

Fig. 4.8. Well pollution. (A) Seepage of pollutants from feeding pens results in contamination of nearby wells located downslope. (B) Septic tanks provide the contamination that moves toward a well because of the inclination of an impermeable shale stratum. (C) Contamination of groundwater from a waste pond and ruptured casing of an oil well.

sediments and clastic rocks and lessens the suitability of groundwater for drinking and many other uses. Thus far, attempts to reduce or detoxify the emissions that cause acid rains have had only limited success. The problem is global in scope, and efforts everywhere to reduce all forms of air pollution will help to diminish the occurrence of dangerously acidic rainfall.

Saltwater intrusion

Along coasts and on small islands, two kinds of water compete for space in permeable sediments and rocks. Meteoric water derived from rain and snow infiltrate in the manner already described and gradually builds a zone saturated with fresh water.Saltwater from the adjacent ocean, however, also enters permeable layers, but because of its greater density, the brine tends to from a wedgelike zone beneath the fresh water. The density differences between the two kinds of water is such that a balanced state develops in which there is about 40 meters of fresh water beneath sea level for every 1 meter of elevation of the water table above sea level. Thus, if the water table is 5 meters above sea level at a given location, fresh water may extend to a depth of 200 meters below sea level. If the water table, however, is lowered by only 5 meters as a result of drawiang too much water from wells, then the top of the saltwater zone may rise and contaminate wells.

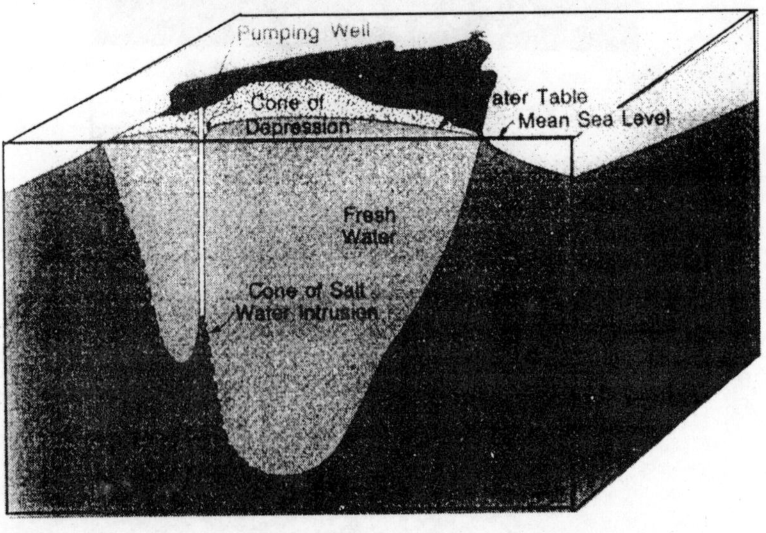

Fig. 4.9.Fresh groundwater floating on salty groundwater. Vertical scale of area below sea level is one-half that of area above sea level. Note that a cone of saltwater intrusion is developed by pumping a body of fresh water floating on saltwater.

One locality where saltwater incursions have been a major problem is on Long Island. The aquifers beneath Long Island consist of coarse highly permeable glacial sediments underlain by unconsolidated sediments that dip gently toward the Atlantic. These beds receive their water from rainfall, and for a time they supplied all the water needs for the island. As the population of the island grew, however, the number of wells put down increased. Withdrawal of groundwater became particularly rapid in the industrialized western part of the island. Inevitably, the fresh water-to-saltwater interface moved upward until saltwater entered the deeper wells. Today, water for the western part of the island must be supplied by pipes from the mainland. In the central and eastern parts of Long Island, the groundwater supply is still used, partly because conservation practices have inhibited the further intrusion of saltwater.

Subsidence

An important environmental consequence of heavy withdrawal of groundwater (and also petroleum) is subsidence of the ground surface above the reservoir rocks. Fluid withdrawals from loose fine-grained materials lead to volume reductions and in artesian systems reduce the pressure with which the aquifer formerly resisted compression. Perhaps the most famous subsidence problems are found in Mexico City, where local sinking due to groundwater withdrawal has exceeded 7.5 meters. In places, the steel casings of wells now protrude above ground level and houses are entered through second-story windows. For some areas of the city, the rate of subsidence has been recently reduced by careful control of groundwater withdrawal.

Venice, Italy, is another city plagued with subsidence resulting both from groundwater depletion and the compaction of loose sediments beneath heavy structures. The city has subsided over 3 meters since it was founded 1500 years ago. Within the last few years, efforts to recharge the aquifers beneath the city, and to regulate withdrawal of water from wells, have reduced the rate of subsidence appreciably.

Advantages of a groundwater system

One should not let the problems that are sometimes associated with dependency on groundwater supplies bias one's thinking about this valuable resource. The use of groundwater has far more advantages than disadvantages. Many a weary farmer on a hot summer day will agree that probably the best beverage on this planet is a cup of water freshly drawn from a well. In fact, groundwater has a justified reputation for its uniformly cool temperature and purity. Groundwater has other benefits even in areas where there is a supply of surface water. Often it can be reached within a few hundred meters of where it is to be used, and thus long pipelines from water purification centers are not needed. In its natural subsurface reservoirs, groundwater is protected from costly losses due to evaporation. Also, although the amount of water drawn from wells may be limited, the yield is generally more uniform than from relatively small streams that may periodically become dry. As indicated in the preceding pages, groundwater can become contaminated, and so one cannot assume a priori that all well water is free of impurities. It is also true, as noted earlier, that aquifers composed of medium or fine-grained sand or sandstone have a remarkable ability for trapping pathologic microorganisms and unpleasant suspended particles. Where care is taken to protect groundwater from contamination, it can usually be used with little or no expensive treatment.

Groundwater in Soluble Rocks

Except in those areas where water flows rapidly through caverns or lava tunnels, groundwater moves too slowly to cause appreciable mechanical erosion or to transport coarse particles. On a less perceptible scale, however, groundwater does accomplish geologic work by dissolving minerals, transporting the soluble matter, and precipitating that material as cements in granular sediments and as depositional features in caverns and other underground openings.

As described in the discussion of chemical weathering, limestones, dolostones, marbles, and evaporites are particularly susceptible to solution by water that contains carbon dioxide. Limestone taken into solution may later be precipitated by either removing carbon dioxide (through agitation, photosynthesis, or heating) or by evaporating part of the water. Evaporation would increase the concentration of dissolved matter to the point where there would be more in solution than the dimin- ished volume of water could retain. The "surplus" calcium carbonate would come out of solution and be deposited. The basic equation for the relation between water, carbon dioxide, and limestone is as follows:

$$\underset{\text{calcium carbonate}}{CaCO_3} + \underset{\text{water}}{H_2O} + \underset{\text{carbon dioxide}}{CO_2} \rightleftharpoons \underset{\text{calcium bicarbonate}}{Ca(HCO_3)_2}$$

Notice that the addition of carbon dioxide to the left side of the equation enhances solution. A loss of carbon dioxide from the bicarbonate on the right side results in precipitation of calcium carbonate.

Solution of limestones occurs at the most rapid rate near the surface. Here, recently fallen rainwater still retains the carbon dioxide absorbed from the atmosphere, and there are further additions of the potent gas from organic materials in soil. Also, the water itself is not yet saturated with lime and is capable of causing dissolution. The water flows along bedding planes, joints, and fractures and begins to widen them by solution. Surface collapse often occurs where large openings may be dissolved out of the limestone. Such depressions are called *sinkholes*. Sinkholes may also develop where the ceiling of large solution cavities or parts of caverns collapse. Often sinkholes are connected to subterranean solution channels so that water is drained from them. Many sinkholes, however, become phugged with caly and debris, so that they from lakes and ponds. Although some sinkholes are as much as 1000 meters in diameter, on the average they are less than about 30 meters across. The progressive collapse of the roof of a cavern may produce a linear series of sinkholes, and these may coalesce to form a steep-walled trough called a *solution valley*. Solution valleys are recognized by their peculiar right-angle bends, which tend to follow the original joint pattern in the limestone bedrock. Here and there along a solution valley, the stream may pass beneath a segment of the original cavern roof that has not yet collapsed and thus form a natural bridge. In other places, a considerable length of uncollapsed cavern may receive the flow of the surface stream. Such so-called *disappearing streams* may emerge elsewhere.

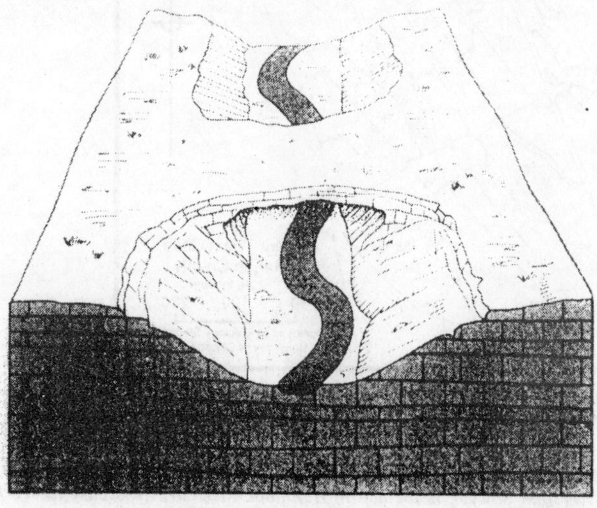

Fig. 4.10. Collapse of a significant portion of the roof of a cavern has produced this natural bridge and solution valley.

Caverns are, of course, the most intriguing of all solution features. Each year thousands of people visit caverns in order to observe the fascinating rock formations and examine organisms strangely adapted to life in perpetual darkness. The development of caverns is almost inevitable in humid areas underlain by thick and extensive limestones. Caverns may be large or small, may have a simple or complex labyrinthic plan, may extend vertically as well as horizontally, and may have passages developed along multiple levels. Subterranean streams course through some caverns, whereas in other caverns streams are lacking. The rectilinear pattern of

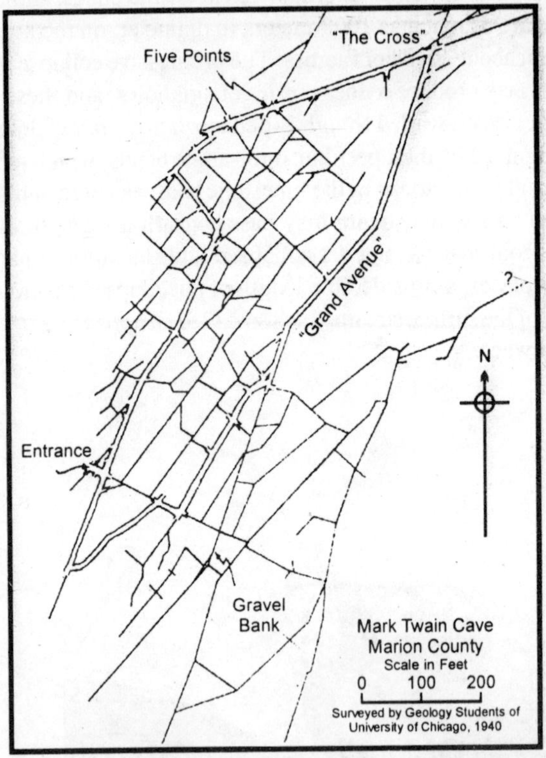

Fig. 4.11. Mark Twain Cave. This cave, made famous because of its description in the novel Tom Sawyer, is located in Hannibal, Missouri. It is easy to see how Tom Sawyer and Becky Thatcher may have become lost in the labyrinthine passages, the locations of which are determined by three or more intersecting sets of joints.

passages in some caverns indicates that they developed as water moved through an established system of joints whereas others appear to have no relationship to joints.

The depositional features of caverns are well known. There are the downward-extending iciclelike *stalactites*, as well as *stalagmites*, which grow in conic form upward from the floor of the cavern. The construction of a stalactite begins with a drop of lime-saturated water temporarily adhering to the cavern roof. With the loss of carbon dioxide, calcium carbonate comes out of solution to form a thin layer around the drop. As more water flows down through the center and along the sides of the original layer, the stalactite grows by successive additions of calcium carbonate. Stalagmites are formed by drops of water that fall from the ceiling of the cavern and strike the floor, where both agitation and evaporation contribute to the build-up of calcium carbonate. *Colunms* develop when stalactites and stalagmites eventually grow together. Features such as stalactites, stalagmites, and columns are composed of a rather dense banded variety of limestone called cave traverse.

Aside from their aesthetic value, features like stalactites help geologists unravel the history of cavern development. Clearly, such features must have formed when the cavern was above the water table and filled with air. Yet, in most caverns, the walls and ceilings are lined with crystals that could only have developed beneath water and hence beneath the water table. These observations indicate that the formation of most caverns began in the zone of saturation but that the cavernous areas were subsequently drained as a result of a lowering of the water table. In the central part of the United States, the lowering of the water table was most commonly in response to slight regional uplift, which raised the water-filled caverns slightly above the zone of saturation, causing a lowering of the water table and draining of the caverns. Following uplift, stalactites and other cave features began to develop within the vacated subterranean chambers.

Calcium carbonate is not the only deposit found abundantly in caves. Clay is another common material. Much of this clay was present in the original limestone as an impurity and, being relatively insoluble, was left as a residual deposit after the limestone was dissolved. Additional amounts of clay are brought to the cave by water percolating downward from the surface and some carried in by streams that drain into subterranean passages.

People have been exploring caves throughout history. The ancient Assyrians, motivated by tales of gem minerals and precious metals to be found in caves, explored caves in the valley of the Tigris River. Their explorations were unsuccessful. Limestone caverns are not likely places in which to find such riches. The Greek philosopher Seneca left an account of cave exploration by some of his contemporaries who were also in search of mineral wealth. "These men," wrote Seneca, "dared to descend to a region where the whole of nature is reversed. The land hung above their heads and the winds whistled hollowly in the shadows. In the depths, frightful rivers led nowhere into the perpetual and alien night. After accomplishing so much, they now live in fear for having tempted the fires of hell."

Long before the classical Greek period, prehistoric people used caves as havens from inclement weather and shelter that could be defended against predatory animals and hostile tribes. The tools, arms, adorments, religious artifacts, and even the skeletons of these ancient cave dwellers are well known to archaelogists. Often paleontologists join the archaeologists in their subterranean digs, for cave may contain skeletal remains of Ice Age bears, pigs, sloths, and a host of other contemporaries of our early ancestors.

Without doubt, caves will continue to stimulate the imagination, not only of scientists, but of anyone likely to enjoy the mystery and excitement that comes as one moves cautiously through uncharted passageways. In the French Alps and Pyrenees, explorers have mapped cave segments more than a km from the surface and thrilled to the discovery of magnificent subterranean waterfalls and lakes. The less adventuresome can enjoy conducted tours through the better known caverns of the world. Mammoth Cave in Kentucky is one such cavern that has an interconnected series of passages extending over a total distance of 34 km. In New Mexico, Carlsbad Cavern boasts a single chamber that is an astonishing 1200 meters long, 200 meters wide, and 100 meters high.

Karst topography

Karst is a term applied to topography formed in regions of limestone or dolomite bedrock by the vigorous solution work of groundwater. One recognizes karst topography by the presence of large numbers of sinkholes, solution valleys, disappearing streams, and caverns. The development of karst topography is enhanced by the presence of welljointed carbonates (or evaporites) near the surface, abundant rainfall, and sufficient relief to insure continuous movement of groundwater that will carry away dissolved matter. The term karst comes from a limestone plateau in Yugoslavia where solution features are well developed. Similar topography can be found in Kentucky, Tennessee, Indiana, northern Florida, and Puerto Rico.

Hot Springs and Geysers

To qualify as a *hot spring,* water emerging from the subsurface must be at least as warm as the body temperature of a human. Most hot springs are found in regions where there has been geologically recent igneous activity. In such regions, rocks immediately below the surface may still retain part of their original heat. Indeed, that heat may be retained for centuries because of the insulating effect of overlying layers. Groundwater that comes in contact with the hot rocks is heated and sometimes even mixed with hot magmatic water before finding its way to the surface and emerging as a hot spring.

Geysers are special kinds of hot springs that discharge intermittently in the form of a tall column or fountain of water and steam. The essential component of a geyser is one or more tubular conduits extending from the surface into a zone of hot rocks. Water that percolates downward through the conduits is heated above the boiling point but is temporarily prevented from boiling because of the weight of the overlying water column. Eventually, water at some level in the tube reaches a temperature where it boils at the higher pressure. Steam is rapidly generated and lifts the water above it until it flows out at the surface. The deeper superheated water, suddenly freed of the weight of overlying water, flashes into steam and blasts upward toward the surface. After the eruption has dissipated, water flows back down through the tube system, and is heated for another eruptive cycle. The cycles may be irregular or rather regular, as is the case for Old Faithful in Yellowstone Park. Until recently, this famous geyser erupted about every 65 minutes (with a range of 30 to 90 minutes), but presently the interval between eruptions is closer to 80 minutes.

In these times of concern over meeting our energy needs, increasing attention is being given to utilizing the steam produced in hot spring areas to generate power. In order to tap this resource, wells are drilled into moist hot rocks. The steam released into the well is fed into turbines that generate electricity. The energy produced in this way is relatively inexpensive, has no radiation hazards, and does not add pollutants to the atmosphere. Unfortunately, there are only a few sites around the world favorable for the development of geothermal power at reasonable costs. Even in these favored locations, corrosive solutions destroy pipes and equipment and may even endanger plant and animal life if not properly managed. One way to handle the disposal problem is to pump the waste water back underground where it will be heated for a second cycle of use.

Locations where hot igneous rocks exist close enough to the earth's surface to be used in generating geothermal power are unfortunately relatively uncommon. Suitable conditions exist at locations in California, Nevada, New Mexico, Wyoming, Utah, Montana, Italy, Alaska, New Zealand, Mexico, Iceland, Japan, and the U.S.S.R. The 80 wells of the geothermal facility at the geysers in Sonoma Country, California, generate enough power to serve the electricity demands of at least a million people. Plans are underway to expand this facility. The geothermal plant at Lardarello, Itally, has been producing electricity from natural steam since 1904, and is thus the oldest facility of this type. In Reykjavik, Iceland, geothermal steam is not only used to generate electricity, but it is pumped into buildings for heating and used to warm greenhouses that produce tropical fruits and vegetables.

Concretions and Geodes

Among the minor features associated with ground water deposition are accumulations of mineral matter called *concretions.* Concretions may be ellipsoid, discoid, or variously shaped and may range in size from a few mm to 1 or 2 meters. Most concretions are composed of calcite or silica, although one also frequently finds hematite, limonite, siderite (iron carbonate), and pyrite concretions. Concretions developed in a rock after it has been deposited are usually the result of localized chemical precipitations of dissolved substances from groundwater. Often precipitation starts around a mineral or fossil particle that differs chemically from the enclosing rock. Concretions formed within sedimentary rocks in this way may retain relic laminations and textural features of the original rock. Other concretions are merely local concentrations of the cementing material in a clastic sedimentary rock and therefore are similar in composition to the host rock. Concretions may differ in composition from the rock in which they have formed. Chert nodules in limestone or dolostone are common examples.

Not all concretions develop in rocks after deposition. Some apparently form on the floor of lakes or seas as sediments are being deposited. Concretions that form in this way do not contain relic features of the rocks that enclose them.

Although the odd shapes of concretions are intriguing, most people find geodes more interesting because of their beauty. *Geodes* are hollow crystal-lined roughly spherical bodies varying from 1 or 2 cm to as many as 60 cm in diameter. They are most characteristic of certain limestone strata, although they are also known to occur in shales. In addition to their roughly globular shapes and hollow interiors, geodes usually have a thin clay film between their outer wall and the enclosing host rock. Beneath the layer of inwardly projecting crystals is a layer of banded silica (chalcedony).

The origin of geodes appears to involve three stages. In the initial stage an opening is created in the host rock, perhaps by decay of an organism. This initial cavity, at least in marine sediments, is likely to be filled with saline connate water. In stage two, a jellylike film of silica is precipitated onto the inner walls of the cavity. The film acts as a membrane, allowing molecules of fresh water from the surrounding rock to migrate into the cavity. This adds water volume to the cavity and causes pressure against the surrounding rock. The evidence for this pressure is apparent in many geodes that show cracks and displacements resulting from expansion. Stage two ends when the salt concentration inside and outside of the developing geode has been equalized, and the gel solidifies as the chalcedony lining. In stage three, silica-bearing solutions enter the hollow interior through expansion cracks and precipitate the eye-catching array of inwardly directed quartz crystals.

Chapter 5

GLACIERS

Prelude If one were to leave the main highways and explore the back roads of the northern United States, Canada, and northern Europe, it would be possible to find large boulders of granitic rock lying at random about the countryside. One would surmise that these boulders were far from home, for they lie on quite different soil and sedimentary rocks; and exposures of similar igneous rocks; are not found nearby. Such displaced boulders and cobbles are called *erratics*. They give us cause to wonder about what gargantuan process could have transported and dumped them onto the hills and fields where they now rest.

Two centuries ago scientists would have explained erratics as having been carried by enormous currents of water and mud during the devastation accompanying the great biblical deluge. Indeed, these same scientists referred to the bouldery deposits as *diluvium*, a Latin word meaning deluge. *Charles lyell*, the eminent British geologist, was not entirely satisfied with this explanation of erratics. He noticed that they did not occur in the southern parts of Europe, that they were scratched and grooved like rocks scoured by alpine glaciers, and that they were not rounded as are rocks transported by water. *Lyell* argued, therefore, that the erratics were in some way associated with accumulations of snow and ice. He had observed large amounts of rock debris frozen into the icebergs that formed at the coastal terminations of glaciers. This led him to reason that during the biblical flood, similar boulder-laden icebergs had drifted across the inundated European continent. *Lyell* believed that, as the ice melted, boulders and cobbles were dropped randomly onto the submerged hills and valleys of Europe.

Lyell proposed his imaginative theory in 1833. Although most geologists accepted his ideas, a few found it hard to imagine the enormous rise in sea level required to float icebergs over Europe's high plateaus and mountains. Also, at some localities in Europe, the huge erratics lay directly on bedrock surfaces that appeared to have been scratched and polished by moving ice. Some scientists, therefore, continued the search for an alternative to the diluvian-iceberg theory.

An alternative theory was proposed in Switzerland, and its development began with studies made by a Swiss director of salt mines named *Jean de Charpentier. Charpentier* was fascinated by glaciers and explored them whenever he had the opportunity. Initially, he was not concerned with an explanation of erratics but rather used bouldery deposits as evidence that alpine glaciers once extended well beyond their present limits. In 1836, *Charpentier* brought a young friend and colleague, named *Louis Agassiz*, to his home in Bex, Switzerland, in order to show him the field evidence favoring his idea. *Agassiz* was a shrewd and discerning scientist. On every side he saw indications of the way glaciers moved, witnessed the way they had altered the landscape, and observed their distinctive markings and deposits. He not only became convinced that *Charpentier* was correct about the former greater extent of alpine glaciers but also was able to visualize how erratics were carried across the plains and lowlands of northern Europe. Erratics were transported, said the energetic *Agassiz*, by a blanket of ice so thick and so vast that nearly half of Europe was buried beneath it.

It is not unusual in science for revolutionary new ideas to be greeted with skepticism. This is precisely what occurred when, in 1837, *Agassiz* presented his theory to the Swiss Society of Natural History. A few prominent members of the Society suggested that *Agassiz* would be best advised to give more attention to his study of fossil fishes and less to stories of gigantic ice sheets. Nevertheless, Agassiz's theory was based on objective and observable criteria. Soon others were able to see the evidence as well, and the ranks of believers in a "Great ice Age" slowly began to swell. Even *Charles Lyell* eventually accepted *Agassiz's* ideas and indicated his support in a lecture he presented to the Geological Society of London in 1840. By the 1860s, many of the most ardent diluvialists had been converted, and the glacial theory was firmly established.

There were, however, many questions associated with the new theory that still had to be answered. What caused the build-up of the enormous continental glaciers? After having advanced over the northern parts of Europe and North America, why then did they subsequently recede? Was there cause for concern that the ice might return and devastate cities and farms? In order to formulate theories that might be useful in answering these questions, geologists went to the Alps, Alaska, Greenland, and Antarctica to learn what they could about how glaciers are formed, how they are able to flow, and the manner in which they so magnificently sculpture our most spectacular landscapes. In this chapter, we will review some of their findings.

GLACIERS: THEIR MAGNITUDE AND ORIGIN

A *glacier* is a large mass of land ice derived from snow, having definite limits, and moving slowly under the influence of gravity. At the present time, about 10 per cent of the earth's land area is covered by glaciers, and, as *Agassiz* correctly suggested, in the recent past that figure was about three times higher. Present-day coverage of glacial ice is sufficient to convince most geologists that we are presently living in temporary warmer interval within an ice age whose end is not in sight. We would not have to convince an Eskimo of the validity of that concept, but a sunbather in Florida might be more skeptical. Perhaps, that skepticism might be lessened on learning that glaciers cover about 14.5 million km^2 of our continents. Of this amount, 12.5 million km^2 are accounted for by the Antarctic ice sheet and 1.7 million km^2 by glaciers in Greenland. The remaining glaciated areas consist mostly of smaller ice caps on polar islands, glaciers along the perimeter of Alaska and Scandinavia, and the mountain glaciers of the Yukon, Alps, and Himalayas.

There are two conditions that are necessary for the growth and development of glaciers. Temperatures must be below freezing at least part of the time, and there must be snowfall in sufficient amounts to exceed losses that normally occur through melting and evaporation. These conditions are most prevalent in high latitudes, high elevations, or both. Glaciers will expand or contract depending on either seasonal or long-term climatic changes. Certainly during the climatic changes of the recent Ice Age, glaciers covered lowlands more extensively, and extended much lower into mountain valleys than they do today.

Because of the impressive ice sheet that covers Antarctica, one might guess that temperatures well below freezing are conducive to glacial development. Actually, extremely low temperatures are not necessary. In fact, glaciers are more likely to form when temperatures are only slightly below freezing, because under such conditions air can hold more moisture than at lower temperatures. Although snowfall is meager in the frigid Antarctic, the ice has been accumulating there for millions of years.

If the 24 million km^3 of ice covering various parts of the earth were to melt, sea level around the world would rise by about 100 meters. New York City, all of New Jersey, Florida, Louisiana, and vast areas of our eastern states and interior California would be covered by shallow seas. Landlocked midwesterners might travel relatively short distances to enjoy the surf. Of course, one should not hurry to purchase "ocean front" property in inland places like Missouri, for such melting and marine encroachments would take place very slowly over a period of several thousand years.

Ice from Snow

The first step in the formation of a glacier is the accumulation of snow as a permanent snow field. Flakes of freshly fallen snow are, of course, noted for their delicate hexagonal form and intricate growth pattern. After the flakes lie at the surface for a period of time, or if they are buried by additional snow, they begin to lose their delicate form as a result of sublimation, partial melting, and refreezing of the water near the center of the flake. (*sublimation* is a process whereby water molecules pass from the solid state to the vapor state and back to solid without passing through the liquid state.) The conversion to ice is enhanced by the weight of overlying snow. Eventually, most of the water once distributed as ice throughout the snowflake is concerntrated as a granule. The material has now ceased to be snow and is in the form of granular ice called *firn*. The pellets of firn are really poorly formed hexagonal crystals or ice. Under the pressure of overlying ice and snow, these crystals begin a transformation into solid ice. Most of the air is gradually expelled from the mass as the ice pellets are packed tightly together. Melting occurs at contacts between grains (so-called "pressure points"), and the molecules of water are added elsewhere to growing ice crystals. As the process continues, adjacent crystals intergrow, and the mass becomes solid crystalline ice with a texture similar to, but coarser than, the texture of a coarse-grained gneiss. If snowfall is rapid, the transformation from snow to solid ice may occur in as little time as 5 years. On the frigid surfaces of Antarctica, the process may take thousands of years.

Kinds of Glaciers

One way in which glaciers are classified is based on their relation to surface topography. Great ice sheets, for example, may cover large parts of continents, burying mountains and plateaus indiscriminately. The size and shape of such glaciers is not dependent on the configuration of the ground surface. Glaciers that are confined by the mountain divides and valley sides constitute a second category of glaciers.

Glaciers not constrained by topography

Ice sheets and *icecaps* are great domal masses of ice that differ primarily in size. Icecaps are generally smaller than ice sheets and rarely exceed 50,000 km^2. The ice in both types of glaciers flows outward from a central area of maximal ice accumulation much like thin pancake batter poured on

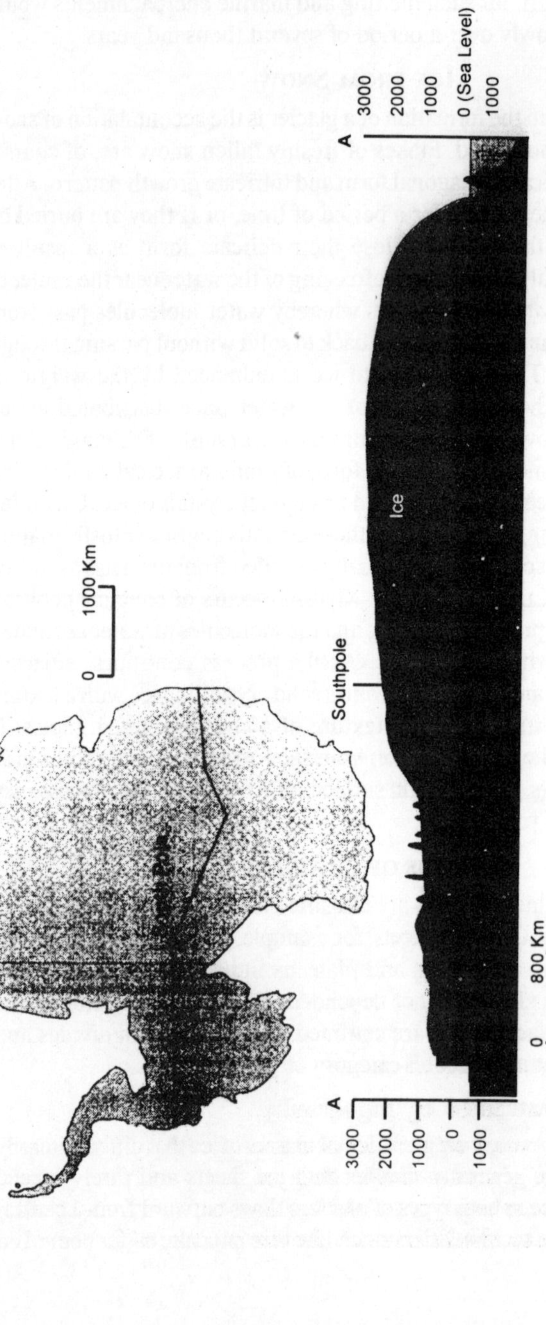

Fig. 5.1. The Antarctic ice sheet in cross-section. Line of section A-A' is indicated on index map. Vertical scale is exaggerated.

a skillet. In cross-section, the maximal elevation is near the center of the ice sheet, and from that point the ice slopes away gently in all directions until it reaches the periphery where there is a marked steepening of slope.

Today icecaps are developed on Iceland, Baffin Island, and in the Canadian Arctic archipelago. As for the larger ice sheets, the only two that remain today cover most of Greenland and Antarctica. The Antarctic ice sheet attains a height of over 4200 meters above sea level and in places is over 3000 meters thick. Buried beneath this thick blanket are hills, plateaus, and impressive mountain ranges. Here and there one of the higher parts of the mountains protrudes through the glacial ice as an isolated peak called a *nunatak*. Around the margins of both Greenland and Antarctica, the moving ice reaches the ocean, where it may extend seaward as floating pack ice or break off into huge icebergs.

Glaciers constrained by topography

Glaciers that owe their size and shape to the characteristics of the landscape differ in many ways from ice caps and ice sheets. The most obvious difference is that they are smaller. In addition, they do not have the low domal shape of ice caps, and their direction of flow is not radial but down the existing slope of the valley. Typically, glaciers constrained by topography develop in high mountainous regions. They are initiated in lofty catchment areas where snowfall is sufficiently heavy and frequent to accumulate as a snowfield. The snowfield is the nourishment area for the ice that moves down the slope as a valley glacier. Although valley glaciers exist today that are over 100 km in length, most are less than 30 km long. In the Rocky Mountains, a variety of valley glacier called a cliff or cirque glacier is common. Typically, they are seen as relatively small patches of white nestling against steep cliffs.

Where valley glaciers emerge from a mountain range, they spread out across the unconfined mountain front as *piedmont glaciers.* Not uncommonly, several adjacent piedmont glaciers merge to form a compound peidmont glacier. Today, such glaciers are particularly numerous in Alaska. During the recent ice age, however, piedmont glaciers moved sluggishly across vast areas of the High plains along the eastern margin of the Rocky Mountains.

Cold and warm glaciers

The above classification based on overall form and relation to topography is not the only way glaciers are classified. Another scheme recognizes two categories of glaciers, according to their temperature. There are, for example, *polar* or *dry-base glaciers* in which the entire thickness of the ice is well below the pressure-melting temperature. The pressure melting temperature is the temperature at which melting occurs under a given pressure. In general, when the pressure on ice is increased, the melting point of ice is decreased. We take advantage of this phenomenon when we squeeze snow into a snowball. The water melted in the snowball by applying pressure is refrozen when we release the pressure. In polar glaciers, the temperature of the ice even at the base is below the pressure-melting temperature. Therefore, melting does not occur, and the basal ice is usually frozen firmly to the rock beneath. Although some water has been detected beneath parts of the east Antarica ice sheet, it is primarily a polar or "dry base" glacier. Even at great depth, the ice in Antarctica is colder than -23°C.

The second category in the thermal classfication of glaciers can be termed *temperate* or *wet base glaciers*. The ice in these glaciers is sufficiently close to the pressure melting point that ice and water frequently coexist. Lubricated by the water, ice in temperate glaciers flow more readily, and erosional processes are enhanced. Many of the Alpine and North American glaciers are of the temperate kind.

It is sometimes impossible to designate a particular glacier as either polar dry-base or temperate wet-base. Therefore, the term *intermediate glacier* has been suggested for glaciers that alternate seasonally between the wet-base and dry-base condition or that vary in these characteristics in different parts of the ice mass.

Glacier Dynamics

The glacial balance

Glaciers that maintain their size and shape over a long period of time are said to be in balance. In such glaciers, the amount of frozen water that is added is balanced by the amount being lost through melting, sublimation, and evaporation. In a valley glacier, the area in which there is a net gain in snow and ice usually is found in the upper reaches of the valley, in what is designated the *accumulation zone*. Accumulation generally decreases toward the snout of the glacier until one passes into the area where there is a net loss of ice due primarily to melting. This lower end is called the *ablation* zone. From the snout, ablation (glacial melting) decreases upglacier. An imaginary line called the *line of equilibrium* separates the ablation and accumulation zones and itself represents that part of the glacier in which gains approximately balance losses. The line of equilibrium will shift along the glacier, depending on whether it is advancing or retreating. The snout of a glacier will maintain itself at about the same

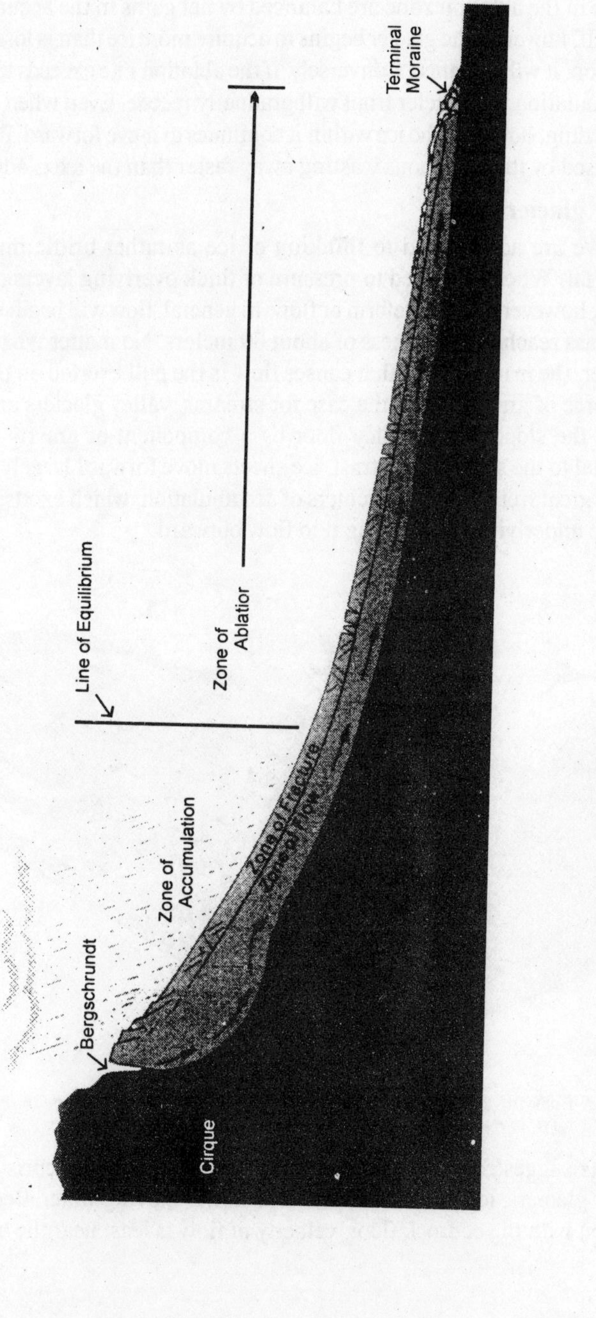

Fig. 5.2. The ones of accumulation, ablation, and line of equilibrium as ideally developed in a valley glacier.

position as long as the glacier is in equilibrium, that is, as long as net losses in the ablation zone are balanced by net gains in the accumulation zone. If, however, the glacier begins to acquire more ice than is lost through ablation, it will advance. Conversely, if the ablation rate exceeds the rate of accumulation, the glacier front will gradually recede. Even when a glacier is receding, however, the ice within it continues to move forward. Recession is caused by the terminous wasting away faster than the ice is advancing.

How glaciers move

We are accustomed to thinking of ice as rather brittle unyielding material. When subjected to pressure of thick overlying layers of frozen waste, however, ice will deform or flow. In general, flow will begin when the ice mass reaches a thickness of about 60 meters. No matter what kind of glacier, the prime mover that causes flow is the pull exerted on the ice by the force of gravity. As is the case for streams, valley glaciers are drawn down the slope of the valley floor by a component of gravity directed parallel to the slope. In contrast, ice sheets move forward largely because of the great weight near the centers of accumulation, which exerts pressure on the underlying ice, causing it to flow outward.

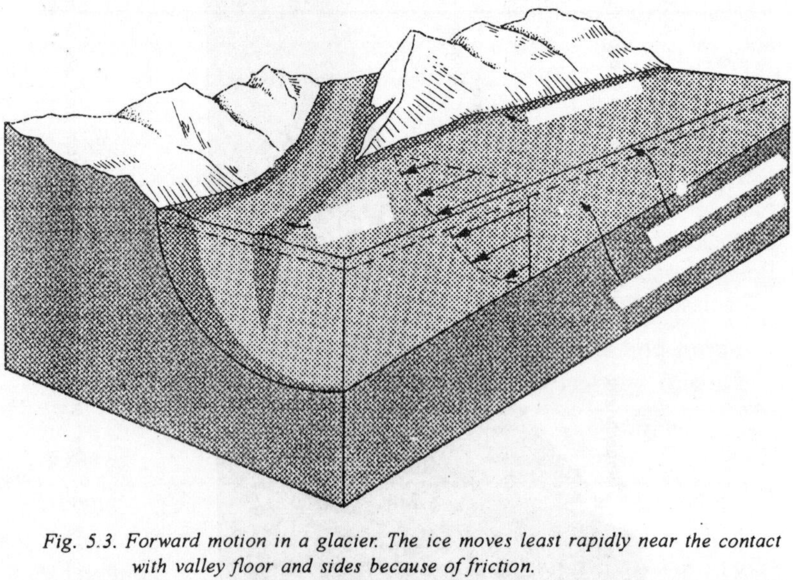

Fig. 5.3. Forward motion in a glacier. The ice moves least rapidly near the contact with valley floor and sides because of friction.

As suggested by the even pattern of ribbons of dark debris seen on valley glaciers, ice flows laminarly like slowly moving water. Because of friction with the bedrock floor, velocity of flow is least near the base of a valley glacier and increases from the base toward the top, except for the uppermost 60 meters. Ice in this top layer is under insufficient pressure to flow and is carried along as a brittle slab by the flowing ice below. This upper brittle portion of the glacier is designated as the *zone of fracture* in order to distinguish it from the underlying *zone of flow*. As implied by its name, the zone of fracture is often characterized by chaotic fracturing and the development of deep crevasses. In plane the center of a valley glacier moves along more rapidly than the flanks where there is friction with the valley side. *Agassiz* and *Charpentier* were well aware of this phenomenon and had measured the surface velocity of the ice by placing stakes across the surface of a glacier and recording their progress from year to year. With the exception of sudden the most rapid movements called surges, the most rapid movement measured in alpine glaciers is about 75 meters per year.

The actual flowage of ice in a glacier represents an adjustment to the pressures acting on the ice, and these pressures are in turn affected by the thickness of the mass and the slope of its surface. Meltwater trapped within the glacier and variations in temperature also influence how fast the ice moves.

Several mechanisms are involved in the movement of glaciers. What appears as plastic flowage is the result of mutual displacements of ice crystals relative to one another and displacements within crystals along sheets of atoms. Such displacements produce ice crystals that on microscopic examination appear to have been bent.

Other mechanisms for movement include granulation of one portion of the ice mass as it moves against another. Partial and temporary melting may also enhance the movement of the glacier, provided temperatures within the ice are not exceptionally low. For example, ice flowing across bedrock obstacles will experience higher pressure on the "upstream" side of the obstacle than on the "down- stream" side. As a result, partial melting will occur on the "upstream" side and the meltwater will flow around the obstacle and freeze again on the "downstream" side. Elsewhere, water produced in this way (or by melting from other causes) may form thin layers of liquid that provide a low friction horizon along which overlying ice may slide at increased speed.

Not all of the movement in a glacier is the result of melt-freeze or plastic flow. Whenever stress on the ice mass exceeds its ability to respond with displacements within and between the crystals, rupture surfaces will develop in much the same way as do faults in rocks. Such rupturing and associated fracturing is mostly confined to the upper 30 to 60 meters of the glacier.

In addition to the movement of glaciers by actual flowage of the ice mass, glaciers progress by simply sliding along the underlying ground surface. Glaciologists refer to such movements as *basal slip*. Basal slip is most prevalent in valley glaciers of temperate regions.

The rates at which valley glaciers flow vary widely. Some move rapidly, others slowly, some erratically, and some with a constant rate throughout the year. A characteristic of many glaciers is a *surging behavior* in which a glacier having a slow and uniform flow periodically surges forward at higher velocity. Glaciers in the United States and the Himalayas are known to have sprinted forward on occasion at rates of over 300 meters per day. The movement is usually uneven and "jerky" and is accompanied by a shivering motion of the ground and loud cracking noises. Most surging in glaciers appears to be associated with the accumulation of excess water at the base of the ice mass. Such meltwater occurs in temperate glaciers whenever a thickening of the ice lowers the pressure-melting temperature sufficiently to produce a layer of water.

THE WORK OF GLACIERS

Because most of us live far away from regions undergoing active glaciation, we may fail to appreciate the awesome power of glaciers. Glacial sculpturing on a grand scale has greatly enhanced the beauty of the Rocky Mountains, the Alps, the Himalayas, and coastal regions of Alaska Greenland, and Scandinavia. Across northern Europe and North America, glaciers of the past have scraped away topographic obstructions and molded hummocky lowlands. Vast amounts of fertile soils have been stripped from bedrock in some regions, whereas in others immense tonnages of rock debris have been spread across the land. The highly productive soils of the United States corn belt are partly composed of fertile soils transported into the region by continental glaciers.

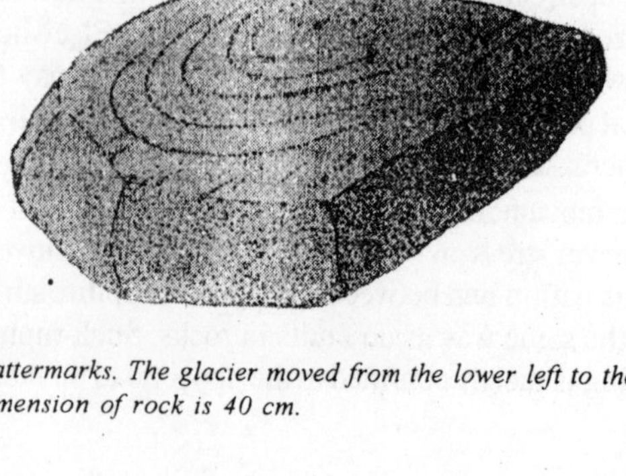

Fig. 5.4. Chattermarks. The glacier moved from the lower left to the upper right. Long dimension of rock is 40 cm.

Erosion by glaciers

Erosion by glaciers is different from fluvial erosion. Flowing ice can carry more and larger rock tools with which to gouge and wear away bedrock than can rivers. Glaciers need not be moving as rapidly as water to accomplish their work, nor do they always flow over the lowest ground available. The processes of glacial erosion include *abrasion, quarrying,* and *avalanching.* These processes vary greatly among glaciers, and a process that is highly effective in valley glaciers may be of less importance in an ice sheet.

Abrasion

Abrasion refers to the wearing, grinding, and rubbing away of solid rock by moving glacial ice armed with angular rock fragments. The debris within the ice acts somewhat like the teeth of rasp in producing scratches and grooves in the rocover which the glacier moves. The Finer scratches are termed *glacial striations,* whereas coarser lineations are dubbed *glacial grooves.* Boulders impinging on bedrock as the glacier inches forward may crack the bedrock into curved fractures called *chatter marks.* The concave sides of these marks face the direction toward which the ice flows. Geologists attempting to ascertain movements of former glaciers are delighted when they find well-preserved glacial striations and chatter marks. In addition to scratches produced by rock fragments in the ice, pulverized rock (rock flour) along the sides and bottom of a glacier acts as a fine abrasive in producing polished bedrock surfaces. Regardless of whether bedrock is being scratched, gouged, or polished, the abrasion process is most effective if the glacier is actively moving and also if there is sufficient melting to continuously expose new rock tools along the sole of the glacier.

Glacial quarrying

Glacial quarrying (glacial plucking) is the process by which a glacier extracts and carries away pieces of the bedrock over which it is moving. Quarrying is accomplished in several ways. The weight of a huge mass of ice pushing against an obstacle may itself be sufficient to dislodge rock masses provided the pressure required does not exceed that at which ice deforms. Also, the passing of the glacier over bedrock results in a pulling or tensional force on the ground surface, which may open incipient fractures and facilitate lifting pieces of rock into the mass of moving ice. Meltwater beneath the glacier seeps into fractures in the underlying bedrock and may then freeze solidly. The resulting expansion opens the fractures more widely and may cause new breaks that free chunks of bedrock from the parent mass. As movements continues, these blocks of rock, frozen solidly into the ice, are pulled out and carried away.

Avalanching

As used by glaciologists, the term *avalanching* is the sudden and rapid movement of snow and rock debris down mountain slopes and onto the surface of a valley glacier. The avalanching process is enhanced by the fact that abrasion and quarrying occur actively on the sides as well as the bottom of the glacier filling a valley. As a result, the valley sides are undercut and this leads to loss of support for loose material lying on the valley slopes. Inevitably, the unconsolidated debris slides or falls onto the ice surface and is then moved along as if on a conveyer belt. From a distance, the debris appears in the form of graceful dark bands, which parallel the valley sides. These bands of dirt and rock flow with the ice and serve as indicators of direction of movement.

Erosional features

Anyone who has visited the higher ranges of the Sierra Nevada, the Rocky Mountains, or the Alps is certain to be impressed by their rugged grandeur. Indeed, the effects of glacial erosion are most spectacular in mountains. On every side one finds magnificent U-shaped valleys, elegant waterfalls cascading from hanging valleys, truncated spurs, cirques, aretes and cols, and placid tarns.

Valley glaciers, of course, occupy valleys eroded by streams. In mountainous regions, stream valleys characteristically have a V- shape cross-section caused by the fact that the stream itself can only cut within its channel and depends on mass wasting to establish the slope of the valley side. In the glaciers that occupy those valley, however, ice is in contact with, and can erode, rock at the base of the valley and well up onto the valley sides. As a result, glaciers sculpture a valley shape that has a parabolic crosssection and often impressively steep walls.

Glaciers not only change the cross-sectional appearance of the valleys they occupy but also straighten the valley by wearing away the bends. The result is a straight, fast, and direct route of escape for the ice. Thus glaciated valleys tend to be much less sinuous than stream valleys. The movement of ice down the valley truncates ridges that once existed between stream bends, so that steep cliffs or *truncated spurs* occur between tributary valleys.

Another distinctive feature of glaciated mountainous regions are *hanging valleys*. They are the result of the fact that tributary glaciers erode at a slower rate than does the main glacier. As a result, the floors of

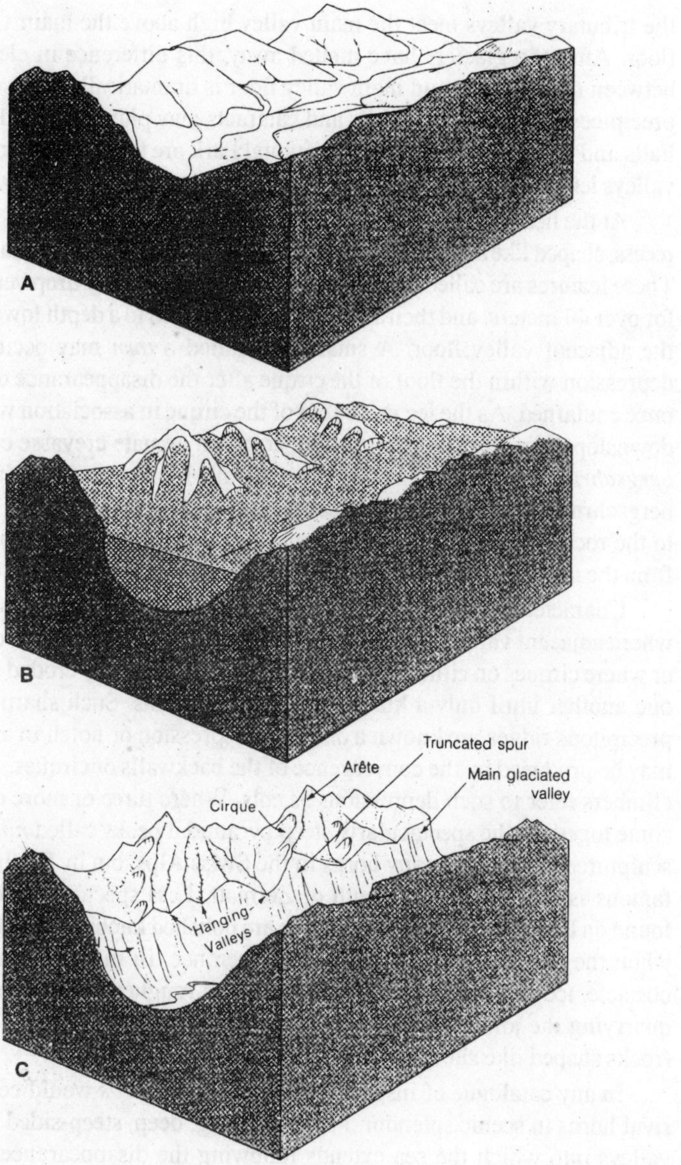

Fig. 5.5. Landforms produced by glacial erosion in mountainous regions. (A) Before glaciation. (B) During glaciation. (C) After glaciation.

the tributary valleys meet the main valley high above the main valley's floor. After the glaciers have melted away, this difference in elevation between the tributary and main valley floor is dramatically exposed as a precipice over which waterfalls and cataracts may plummet. Bridal Veil Falls and other falls in Yosemite National Park are the result of hanging valleys left after the glacier retreated.

At the head of a glaciated valley, one frequently finds a steep-walled recess, shaped like a half bowl and excavated primarily by glacial quarrying. These features are called *cirques*. The walls of cirques may drop vertically for over 40 meters, and their floors are often gouged to a depth lower than the adjacent valley floor. A small lake called a *tarn* may occupy the depression within the floor of the cirque after the disappearance of ice it once contained. As the ice moves out of the cirque in association with the downslope movement of the entire glacier, an arcuate crevasse called a *bergschrund* develops next to the back wall. Meltwater flows into the bergschrund and freezes in bedrock fractures, thereby anchoring the ice to the rock. When the ice moves again, large pieces of rock are plucked from the mountainside, thus deepening and further sculpturing the cirque.

Characteristically in glaciated mountainous regions one finds places where adjacent valley glaciers have sharply reduced the width of divides or where cirques on either side of a mountain are gradually eroded toward one another until only a knife-edge divide remains. Such sharp-edged precipitous ridges are known a *aretes*. A depression or notch in an arete may be produced by the convergence of the backwalls of cirques. Alpine climbers refer to such depressions as cols. Where three or more cirques come together, the spectacularly steep pyramidal peaks called *horns* are sculptured. There are many horns in the Swiss Alps, but by far the most famous is the Matterhorn south of Zermatt. Less spectacular features found on the floors of glaciated valleys are polished knobs of rock formed when the ice rode over a bedrock protuberance. In moving across the obstacle, ice smoothed the upstream side and roughened the lee side by quarrying the jointed rock. These features are called *roche moutonnee* (rocks shaped like sheep).

In any catalogue of inspirational landforms, *fjords* would certainly rival horns in scenic splendor. Fjords are long, deep, steep-sided glacial valleys into which the sea extends following the disappearance of the glacier. They are sculptured by thick glaciers with steeply sloping surfaces, which flow down from the mountains into the sea and are able to erode their valleys to a depth below sea level. Today, the depth of water in some fjords is even deeper than when they were filled with ice, because of the rise in sea level following the last ice age recession. In many of the famous Norwegian fjords, water depths exceed 1200 meters.

The erosional features produced by ice sheets are less spectacular than those carved by mountain glaciers. Ice sheets tend to make rounded rather than rugged topographic forms. They often produce impressive glacial lineations and grooves even in very dense igneous and metamorphic rocks. Grooves have been found in areas covered by the Scandinavian ice sheet that are over 2 meters deep and extend for distances of more than 100 meters. Such features provide striking evidence of the direction taken by that great mass of ice and of its enormous abrasive powers.

Another way in which ice sheets erosionally modify landscapes is by scouring and deepening topographic depressions. Preglacial stream valleys oriented parallel to the direction of the ice movement are particularly susceptible to this erosion. In such valleys, there are fewer barriers to movement, and the ice itself is thicker and hence more effective in erosion. After the ice has receded, the elongate basins fill with water to form picturesque lakes, notable examples of which are the Finger Lakes of New York.

Transportation by glaciers

The work potential of glaciers differs from that of stream in that there is practically no limit to the size or amount of material that can be carried by glacier as suspended load. The competency and capacity of glaciers are truly enormous. Indeed, parts of some glaciers contain more rock debris than ice itself. In general, the size of rock fragments carried by a glacier diminishes with increased distance of transport. This condition is a consequence of the crushing and wearing away of rock debris as the ice advances. Nevertheless, chunks of particularly durable rock like quartzite and granite may be transported for hundreds of km without being destroyed. As an example, erratics whose origin was Ontario, Canada, were carried by Ice Age glaciers as much as 1000 km into Missouri, and boulders from Finland are now scattered across the German countryside.

Valley glaciers and ice sheets differ somewhat in the distribution of the load of rock debris they transport. Ice sheets, for example, carry very little load on the surface of the ice. Their surface is above the majority of mountain tops, and so landslides do not operate to provide a surface load. In general, ice sheets also carry a smaller volume of debris per unit volume of ice than do valley glaciers and that load is carried primarily near the bottom of the sheet or pushed along at the front.

In the case of valley glaciers, avalanching and mass wasting contribute to the accumulation of a significant amount of debris on top of the ice. The larger blocks of rock slowly work their way downward through the ice so that the load becomes generally coarser near the base of the glacier. Debris from previous years may appear as superimposed layers in downstream cross-sections of the glacier. Rock on the ice that does not work its way downward is transported along the upper brittle layer in conveyer-belt fashion and is eventually dumped at the snout of the glacier.

Deposition by glaciers

Glacial sediment. Glaciers drop their laod of coarse and fine sediment either directly from the moving ice mass or indirectly through meltwater. As one might expect, sediment deposited by streams of meltwater is likely to be better sorted than debris dropped directly from glacial ice. The general term for all deposits resulting from glaciers is *drift*. The term originated in the decade before the glacial theory was announced by *Agassiz* and alludes to the erroneous idea that all glacial sediment "drifted" to present locations within floating ice or during surging biblical floods. As used today, the term embraces all debris carried and deposited by glaciers, glacial meltwater, or even icebergs derived from glaciers.

Because of differences in origin, it is useful to distinguish two kinds of drift, namely, stratified and unstratified drift. Nonstratified drift is more appropriately called till, a term originally used by nineteenth-century Scots to describe the rocky clayey soils of northern Britain. Till is a poorly sorted jumble of rock and mineral fragments in a range of size and without a discernible arrangement of those particles. There is no trace of the kind of winnowing and sorting of particle sizes that characterizes sediments deposited by water, and therefore till is believed to have been dropped directly from a glacier without appreciable reworking by meltwater.

Stratified drift is glacial sediment deposited and reworked by water and/or by wind. Stratified drift deposited by meltwater streams is described as outwash or *glaciofluvial* in recognition of its origin and its similarity to ordinary stream deposits. Glaciofluvial deposits are better sorted than till and often exhibit distinct sand and gravel layers. Cross-bedding may also be well developed.

Glaciolacustrine is a term used to designate stratified drift that accumulates in lakes. Many glaciolacustrine deposits have distinctive lamination. Sediment accumulating during the warmer summer months when water is stirred by waves forms a layer that is somewhat lighter and coarser than a darker, thinner layer deposited during the winter when the lake is frozen over. The regularly repeated pairs of layers or *varves* record the years during which a particular glacial lake existed. Each pair of light and dark bands or layers represents one year's accumulation. Counting the number of varves tells us how long the lake was there.

The final category of stratified drift is designated *glacioeolian* in recognition of its wind-blow derivation. *Loess*, which is wind-blow dust, is the most common glacioeolian sediment. Of course, not all loess is associated with glaciation, but in many area it appears to have been derived from the floodplains of meltwater-swollen streams.

Depositional features

Moraine is probably the first term that comes to mind in preparing a list of the depositional features of glaciers. It is a term used by eighteenth -century Swiss peasants for ridges of rock debris found near the margins of glaciers. Today, geologists define moraines as accumulations of drift deposited directly by glaciers. The more easily recognizable types are ground moraines, terminal moraines, and lateral moraines.

Ground moraine consists of a broad blanket of till in which there are not discernible ridges of glacial clastics. The material comprising ground moraine is deposited largely from the voluminous detritus carried near the bottom of the glacier, as well as sediment that has melted downward during ablation. Ground moraine may completely cover earlier topographic features and typically takes the form of broad undulating plains. Vast areas of the northern United States are mantled by the ground moraine of Ice Age continental glaciers.

Terminal moraines are accumulations of till along the lobate front of the glacier. They are produced by the conveyor-belt action of the moving ice, which brings rock fragments to the snout of the glacier even when it is in a state of equilibrium and not actively advancing. When the ice does progress forward, however, the glacier may push terminal morainal deposits forward in much the same way as a bulldozer might. if the amount of flow and melting in a glacier are in balance, the snout of the glacier will not

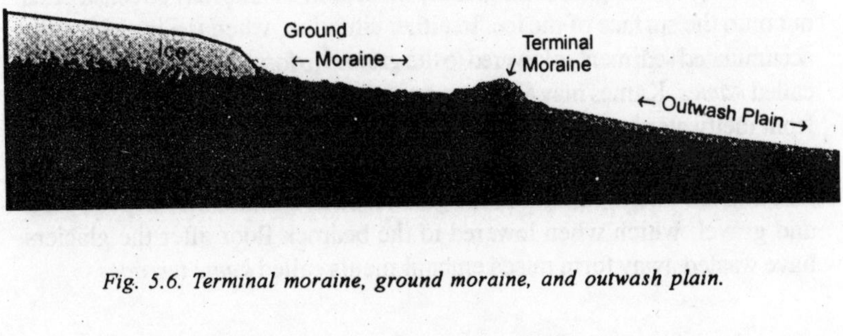

Fig. 5.6. Terminal moraine, ground moraine, and outwash plain.

advance, and the end moraine may become irregular and hummocky. Glaciers that retreat slowly and in increments may leave behind a succession of distinctive cresent-shaped terminal deposists called *recessional moranies*. By contrast, when glaciers recede continuously, they deposit a layer of debris that is indistinguishable from ground moraine.

Rock debris that has fallen from mountainsides onto the margins of valley glaciers is carreid along and eventually deposited as ribbons of till called *lateral moraines*. Long after glaciers have disappeared, these lateral moraines remain as ridges along margins of valleys. When glaciers from two adjoining valleys come together, neighboring lateral moraines coalesce and form a *medial moraine*. Out beyond the terminus of a glacier, one frequently finds an apron of large rock fragments, gravel, sand, and clayey materials. This irregular blanket of debris constitutes the *outwash plain*.

Its constituent particles are transported outward from the glacier by streams of meltwater, which are so choked with sediment that they frequently assume a braided pattern. In the outwash plain, material previously deposited as ground moraine may be reworked into deposits of stratified drift.

In Canada and Maine, one may sometimes encounter long sinuous ribbons of sand and gravel and wonder why someone went to all the trouble of preparing a raised railroad bed without ever adding the rails. These features, however, are definitely not railroad beds but rather winding ridges of stratified drift called *eskers*. Eskers mark the locations of former subglacial streams that flowed through the ice near the margins of the glacier. Whenever the velocity of such a stream was checked because of loss of water, rerouting, obstacles, or lack of sufficient gradient, the streams dropped their load of sediment within their tunnels. After the glacier had wasted away, there remained a winding ridge of glaciofluvial material. Some eskers extend for over 10 km and reach heights of 15 to 30 meters.

The upper surface of a glacier is likely to hold numerous random depressions into which surface meltwater may wash sand and gravel. Also, along the margins of the glacier, small alluvial fans may be constructed out onto the surface of the ice. In either situation, when the ice melts, the accumulated sediment is lowered to the ground to form the irregular mounds called *kames*. Kames may also form near the front of the glacier as sediment from meltwater is rapidly deposited.

In valley glaciers, streams of meltwater may develop between a valley side and the lateral margin of the glacier. Such streams also deposit sand and gravel, which when lowered to the bedrock floor after the glaciers have wasted away form raised embankments called *kame terraces*.

One kind of depositional feature that is not built up above the general ground level, but rather forms a depression, is called a *kettle*. One can readily imagine that the load of debris carried by a glacier is not likely to be uniformly distributed throughout the ice. Here and there, a large mass of ice may exist that contains relatively less debris than adjoining areas. When the glacier melts away, there will be less material lowered to the

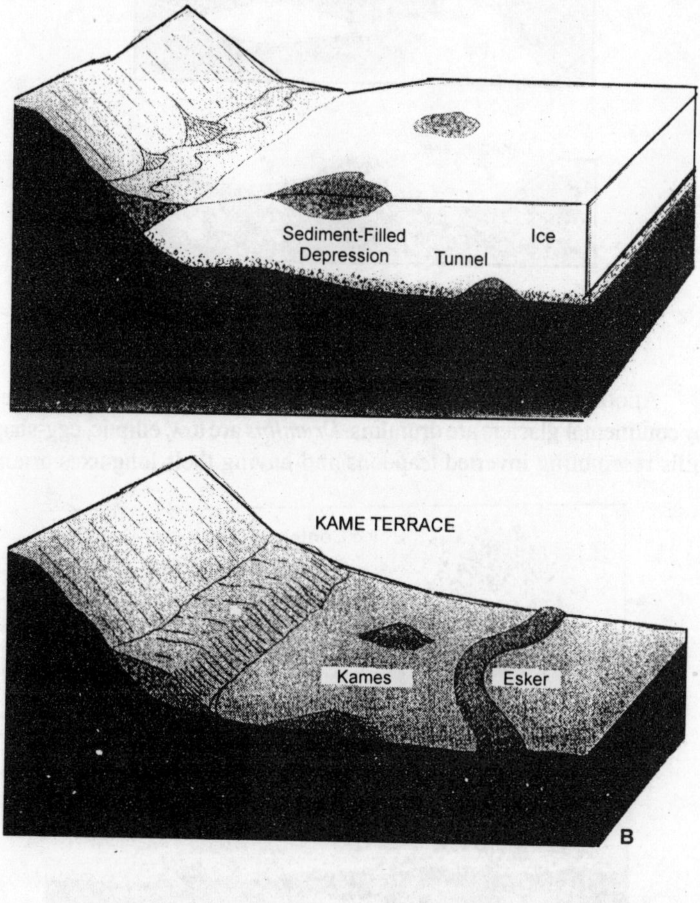

Fig. 5.7. The formation of kames and eskers.

ground at the site of the lesser load. The result will be a small basin or kettle, which may subsequently be filled with water to form a *kettle lake*. Kettles may also develop from the melting of large blocks of ice that were buried in till. Where excessive rock material existed in scattered parts of the glacier, not kettles but *knobs* may form upon melting, thereby giving rise to kettle and knob topography.

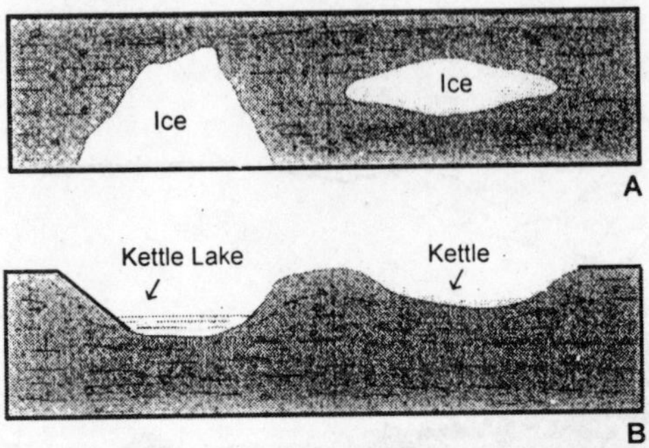

Fig. 5.8. Formation of kettles. (A) Cross-section of drift containing buried masses of ice. Upon melting (B), depressions are formed at the surface by the lost volume of ice.

Another feature particularly characteristic of regions once covered by continental glaciers are drumlins. *Drumlins* are low, elliptic, egg-shaped hills resembling inverted teapoons and having their long axes oriented

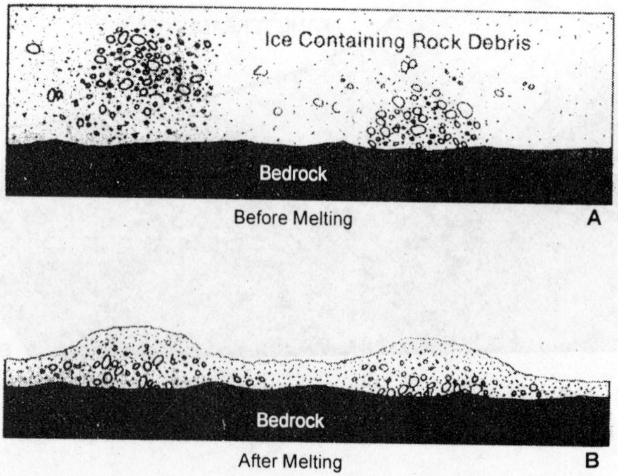

Fig. 5.9. Formation of knobs by melting of ice in which there are local concentrations of debris.

parallel to the direction of glacial movement. They are rarely more than about 50 meters in height, generally occur in large numbers within a given area, and have steeper slopes on the side from which the glaciers came. As for how they are formed, most offer evidence of a depositional orgin followed by erosional modification of the deposited material. Clearly, their streamlined shaped and the parallel orientation of their long axes indicate drumlins were shaped by moving ice. Because of its role in American history, *Bunker Hill* in Boston is probably the most famous drumlin in the United States.

The Pleistocene Ice Age

The development of vast continental ice sheets has occurred several times in the geologic past, but those ice sheets of the Pleistocene Epoch are the most recent and hence have the clearest records. You will recall from the discussion of the geologic time scale that the Pleistocene Epoch is the older of the two final epochs of the Cenozoic Era. The Pleistocene is believed to have begun about 1.5 million years ago and ended 8000 or 10,000 years ago with the onset of the Holocene or Recent Epoch.

Although justifiably associated with continental glaciation, the interval of geologic time designated Pleistocene did not begin with the first advance of the ice nor end with the final recession of European and American glaciers. The low temperatures and abundant precipitation that favor ice-age conditions occurred at different times in different places around the globe. Glacial conditions existed in Alaska and Antarctica long before the ice began its march upon the United States and Europe. Thus, by definition, the beginning of the Pleistocene was synchronous around the world, but the advent of ice-age conditions was not.

When the continental glaciers did begin their advance, they ultimately covered about 30 per cent of the earth's land area with over 40 million cubic miles of snow and ice. In North America alone, the ice sheet extended nearly 6400 km across the entire breadth of Canada. Such an extensive coverage of ice had profound effects, not only on the glaciated terrains themselves but also on lands far from the ice fronts. Climatic zones in the Northern Hemisphere were shifted southward, and arctic conditions prevailed across northern Europe and the United States. Mountains and uplands in Eurasia and North America were sculptured by spectacular mountain glaciers. While the snow and ice was accumulating in higher latitudes, rainfall increased in the lower latitudes, with generally beneficial effects on plant and animal life. Even as recently as 10,000 years ago, presently aid regions in north and eastern Africa were well watered, fertile, and populated by nomadic tribes.

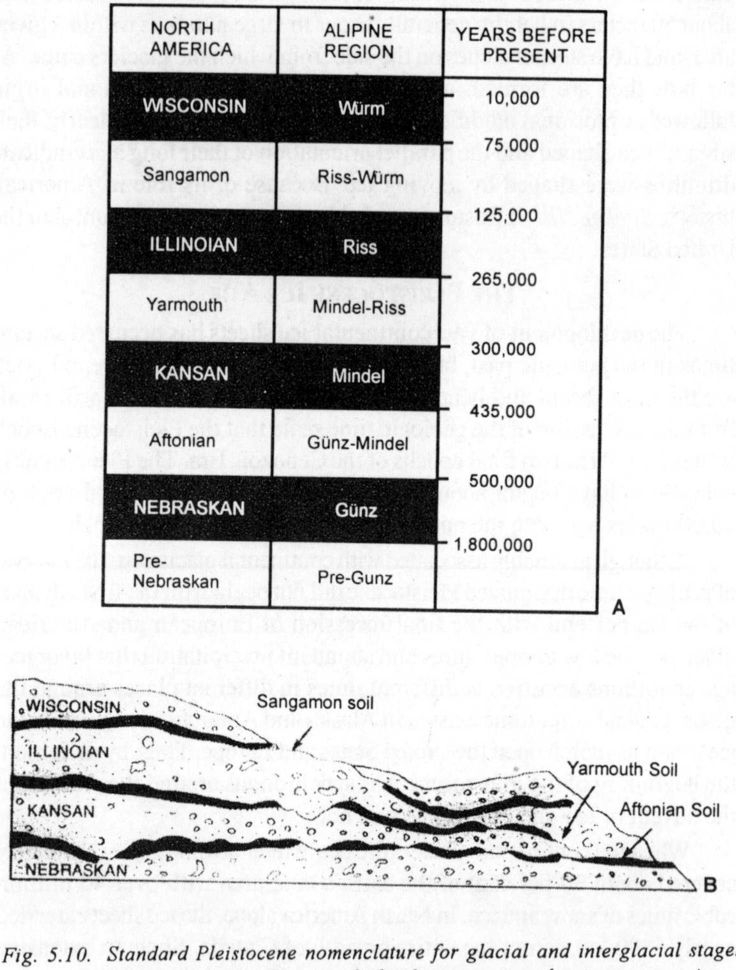

Fig. 5.10. Standard Pleistocene nomenclature for glacial and interglacial stages are shown in (A). (B) is an idealized cross-section showing a succession of deposits of glacial stages and interglacially developed soils.

Pleistocene sediments

Geologists studying the drift deposits of the United States and Europe have determined that during the Pleistocene Epoch there were at least four major advances of the ice separated by three warmer interglacial intervals. The deposits of each of these time intervals is called a stage, and each glacial and interglacial stage is named after a locality where deposits of that age are particularly well exposed for study.

Terrestrial deposits

Because they are characteristically unfossiliferous and generally similar-looking mixtures of coarse clastics, it is often difficult to say that a given blanket of drift is the equivalent of another at a distant location. Yet such correlations are essential if geologists are to determine the extent and nature of the various glacial advances. Usually, a single criterion for correlation will not suffice, and several lines of evidence, including superposition, must be employed. One method is to examine closely the extent to which a sheet of drift has been dissected by streams. Older layers of drift, if they have been exposed since the withdrawal of the glacier, are likely to have a greater number of streams per unit area than younger layers. Of course, climate and the amount of precipitation also influence stream density and must be taken into account in the evaluation of this method.

The depth of oxidation and amount of chemical weathering in blankets of drift may also provide criteria useful in evaluating the relative ages of deposits. Careful examination of fossil pollen grains in thick exposures of bog or lake deposits often clearly reflect fluctuations of climate and can be used to mark times of glacial advance and retreat. Varved clays deposited in lakes near the glaciers can sometimes be correlated to similar sediments of other lakes and in addition may provide an estimate of the time required for deposition of the entire thickness of lake deposits. However, the most accurate means of dating and correlating Pleistocene sediments is to extract pieces of wood, bone, or peat and determine their age by radio-carbon dating techniques. Unfortunately, even this method has its limitations, the most significant of which is the relatively short halflife (5570 years) of carbon 14. This limits the method to material less than about 100,000 years old and thus restricts the use of the carbon 14 technique to deposits of the Sangamon and Wisconsin.

Deep-sea sediments

Deep-sea sediments can be very useful in Pleistocene geochronology. The deep ocean basins are sites of a relatively continuous sedimentary record; the sediments contain abundant fossil remains; and the deposits can be dated by relating them to paleomagnetic data and also to radiometric isotopes having short half-lives.

Continuous sections of deep-sea sediments can be obtained by means of piston-coring devices. These tools can provide cores over 15 meters long. The cores can then be subjected to various kinds of analysis. One approach is to use the oxygen-isotope ratios of planktic calcareous foraminifers within the cored sediment to determine the water temperatures in which the foraminifers once lived. Such temperatures, plotted against depth, would indicate variation in temperature with time. Indications of cooler conditions are then correlated with glacial stages and decline in worldwide sea level.

Another way to use deep-sea sediments in Pleistocene chronology is to plot at each level in the core the relative abundance of species of foraminifera that are known to be especially sensitive to temperature. For example, the tropical species *Globoratalia menardii* is alternately present or absent within Pleistocene cores from the equatorial Atlantic. The absence of the species in part of a core is taken to indicate an episode of cooler climates and glaciation. Carbon14 dates in the upper part of such cores permit one to determine the rates of sedimentation. which is assumed to be uniform for the lower portions. Another foraminifera, *Globorotalia truncatulinoides,* also permits one to recognize alternate cooling and warming of the oceans. This species is trochospirally coiled, which means that it coils in a spiral with all the whorls visible on one side but only the last whorl visible on the other side. Individuals that coil to the right dominate in wormer water, whereas left-coiled individuals prefer colder water. During glacial advances, when ocean temperatures declined the right-coiled populations of G. *truncatulinoides* in middle and low latitudes were replaced by populations in which left coiling predominated. The record of such changes is clearly apparent in the deep-sea cores.

Remanent magnetism in some deep-sea sediments is sometimes sufficiently strong and stable that a particular section of the core can be correlated to a magnetic reversal documented on land in volcanic rocks of known age. However, the analysis is likely to be in error if the original orientation of detrital magnetic grains has been disturbed by burrowing organisms.

The effects of Pleistocene glaciations

Earlier it was noted that during maximal glacial coverage, over 40 million km^3 of ice and snow lay on the continents. This was equivalent to a tremendous amount of water. Removal of that water from the oceans had a multitude of effects on the environment. It has been estimated that sea level may have dropped at least 75 meters during maximal ice coverage. Extensive tracts of the present continental shelves became dry land and were covered with forests and grasslands. The British Isles were joined to Europe, and a land bridge stretched from Siberia to Alaska. During interglacial stages, marine waters returned to the low coastal areas, drowning the flora and forcing terrestrial animals inland.

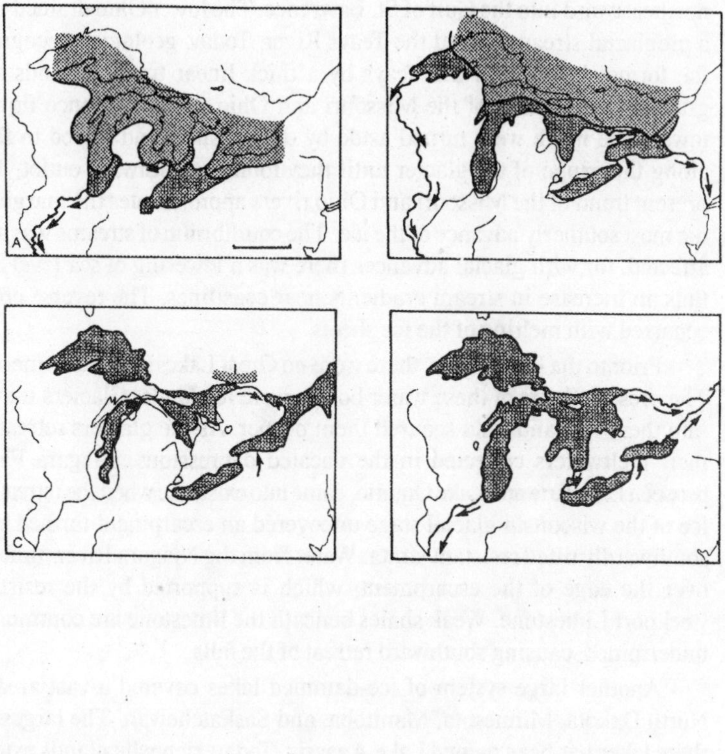

Fig. 5.11. Four stages in the development of the Great Lakes as the ice of the last glacial advance moved away.

The glaciers had a direct impact on the erosion of lands and the creation of glacial landforms. The great weight of the ice depressed the crust of the earth over large parts of the glaciated area, in some places to a level of 200 to 300 meters below the preglacial position. With the removal of the last ice sheet, the down-warped areas of the crust gradually began to return to their former positions. This rebound is dramatically apparent in parts of the Baltic, the Arctic, and the Great Lakes region of North

America, where former coastal features are now elevated high above former levels.

As the great continental glaciers advanced, they obliterated old drainage channels and caused streams to erode new channels. These dislocations are especially evident in the north-central United States. Prior to the Ice Age, the northern segment of the Missouri River drained northward into Hudson Bay, and the northern part of the Ohio River flowed northeastward into the Gulf of St. Lawrence. The lower Ohio drained into a preglacial stream named the Teays River. Today, geologists recognize the former location of the Teays by a thick linear trend of sands and gravels. Those parts of the Missouri and Ohio rivers that once flowed toward the north were turned aside by the ice sheet and forced to flow along the fringe of the glacier until they found a southward outlet. The present trend of the Missouri and Ohio rivers approximates the margin of the most southerly advance of the ice. The equilibrium of streams was also affected, for with glacial advances there was a lowering of sea level and thus an increase in stream gradients near coastlines. The reverse effect occurred with melting of the ice sheets.

Prior to the Pleistocene, there were no Great Lakes in North America. The present floors of these water bodies were lowlands. Glaciers moved into these lowlands and scoured them deeper. As the glaciers retreated, their meltwaters collected in the vacated depressions. Niagara Falls, between Lake Erie and Lake Ontario, came into existence when the retreating ice of the wisconsin glacial stage uncovered an escarpment formed by a southwardly tilted resistant strata. Water from the Niagara River tumbled over the edge of the escarpment, which is supported by the resistant Lockport Limestone. Weak shales beneath the limestone are continually undermined, causing southward retreat of the falls.

Another large system of ice-dammed lakes covered a vast area of North Dakota, Minnesota, Manitoba, and Saskatchewan. The largest of these lakes has been named Lake Agassiz. Today, rich wheatlands extend across what was once the floor of the lake. Other lakes developed during the Pleistocene, occupying basins that were not near ice sheets. These were formed as a consequence of the greatly increased precipitation and runoff that characterized regions south of the glaciers. Such water bodies are called pluvial lakes (Latin *pluvia*, rain). *Pluvial lakes* were particularly numerous in the northern part of the Basin and Range Province of North America, where faulting produced more than 140 closed basins. So-called pluvial intervals, when lakes were most extensive, were generally synchronous with glacial stages, while during interglacial stages many lakes shrank to small saline remnants or even dried out completely. Lake Bonneville in Utah was such a lake. It once covered over 50,000 km^2 and was as deep as 300 meters in some places. Parts of Lake Bonneville persist today as Great Salt Lake, Utah Lake, and Sevier Lake.

A rather spectacular event associated with Pleistocene lake formation occurred in the northwestern corner of the United States. Lobes of the southwardly advancing ice sheet repeatedly blocked the Clark Fork River, and the impounded water formed a long narrow lake extending diagonally across part of western Montana. The fresh water body, called Lake Missoula, contained an estimated 2000 km^3 of water. With the recession of the glacier, the ice dam broke, and tremendous floods of water rushed out catastrophically across more than 38,000 km^2 of what are now appropriately termed the channeled scablands.

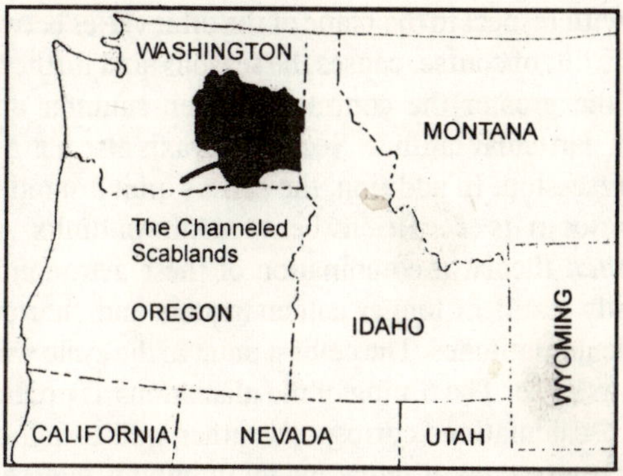

Fig. 5.12. Location of the channeled scablands.

The glacial conditions of the Pleistocene also had an effect on soils. In many northern areas, fertile topsoil was stripped off the bedrock and transported to more southerly regions, which are now among the world's most productive farmlands. Because of the flow of dense cold air coming off the glaciers, winds were strong and persistent. Fine-grained glacial sediments that had been spread across outwash plains and floodplains were picked up and transported by the wind and then deposited as thick layers of loess.

Cause of Pleistocene climatic conditionss

The result of oxygen isotope research indicate that world climates grew progressively cooler from Middle Cenozoic to the Pleistocene. The culmination of this trend was not a single sudden plunge into frigidity but rather an oscillation of glacial and interglacial stages. Any hypothesis that adequately explains glaciation must consider not only the long-term decline in worldwide temperatures but the oscillations as well. Further, the hypothesis must include reasons for the ideal combination of temperature and precipitation required for the build-up of continental glaciers. Although geologists, physicists, and meteorologists have been speculating about the cause of the Ice Age for over a hundred years, no single causative agent has been found. Indeed, it appears likely that Pleistocene climatic conditions came about as a result of several simultaneously occurring factors.

One particularly interesting hypothesis of Ice Age origin was developed by *M. Milankovitch*, a Yugoslavian astronomer who convincingly calculated that irregularities of the earth's movement could cause climatic cycles. Milankovitch drew attention to the fact that tilt of the earth's axis with respect to the plane of the orbit varies between about 22° and 24°. This tilt, of course, causes the seasons, and furthermore, the greater the tilt the greater the contrast between summer and winter temperatures at a particular latitude. Second, the axis also has a wobbling motion called precession. In addition, the earth's orbit around the sun is an ellipse that varies in its eccentricity between known limits. According to the *Milankovitch* theory, a combination of these astronomic factors would periodically result in longer colder winters and shorter warmer summers at particular latitudes. The coldest point in the cycle would occur every 40,000 years or so. The timing of the glaciations as predicted from the Milankovitch calculations correspond rather well to indications of cooling obtained from oxygen-isotope and foraminiferal analyses of deep-sea cores. However, there is one problem with the theory. If the Milankovitch effect has been in existence for billions of years, why haven't there been Pleistocene-like glaciations continuously down through geologic time? Apparently, other factor must also be involved.

One such factor might be variation in the amount of solar energy reflected from the earth back into space rather than being absorbed. The fraction of solar energy reflected back into space is termed the earth's *albedo*. At the present time, it is about 33 per cent. Theorists suggest that by the end of the Cenozoic, when continents were fully emergent, and hence highly reflective, temperatures may have been lowered enough for the Milankovitch effect to begin to operate. This is not an unreasonable suggestion, for only a 1 per cent lessening of retained solar energy could lead to as much as an 8°C drop in average surface temperatures. This would be sufficient to trigger a glacial advance if ample precipitation were available over continental areas. Still other geologists speculate that absorption of solar energy was hindered by could cover, volcanic ash and dust in the atmosphere, or fluctuations in carbon dioxide Adecrease in carbon dioxide content would cause a corresponding decrease in the warmth-gathering "greenhouse effect," for example. On the other hand, it is also possible that a build-up of carbon dioxide might trigger glaciation, for as warming occurred there might be more rapid evaporation and an increase in highly reflective cloud cover.

Chapter 6

The Global Ocean

Prelude. There is a majesty and omnipotence about the sea, Poet and scientist alike are moved by its breadth and power, its ever-changing aspect, and its apparent timelessness. It is difficult not to be fascinated by the multitude of strange creatures that inhabit its depths, or intrigued by the deep chasms and spectacular mountains that exist in the darkness of its abyss. The ocean was the cradle of life, and in many ways it continues to nurture the inhabitants of this planet.

Programs to study the world ocean comprehensively are generally considered to have begun in 1872 with the scientific expedition of the naval ship H.M.S. Challenger. The Challenger, a three-masted vessel with auxiliary steam power, was the research tool of a team of scientists charged by the British government to chart the ocean depths, measure movements of water masses, describe the sea's many creatures, and examine the ocean's chemistry and bottom deposits. In order to accomplish this formidable assignment, H.M.S. Challenger sailed over 110,000 km into all major ocean areas of the earth. During the 3.5 years of the expedition, enough data was collected to fill 50 heavy volumes. Over a century has elapsed since the Challenger expedition, yet scientists still refer frequently to the information provided in these reports.

The scientists aboard H.M.S. Challenger would have been astonished and envious of the sophisticated instrumentation now available for the study of the oceans. For example, they did not have the automated echo-sounding devices that are now regularly used in studying the topography of the ocean floors. Nor were they able to photograph the sea bottom, precisely measure subtle variations in magnetic and gravitational properties, or actually drill into the ocean floor and obtain core samples. The ability to accomplish these feats became possible with the tools aboard a modern research vessel named the Glomar Challenger as an obvious tribute to its predecessor, H.M.S. Challenger. The Glomar Challenger was outfitted solely for the collection of fundamental knowledge about the seas. It has permitted scientists to know the age, composition, and relations of rocks and sediments on the sea floors, and provided the means to verify concepts of sea floor spreading. Much of this information was derived from the vessel's capability for drilling into the ocean floor. In 1983, the Glomar Challenger was retired and was replaced two years later by the newly rechristened drillship, the *Joides Resolution*.

At first thought, drilling into the floor of the ocean does not seem a particularly difficult task. The difficulty becomes evident when one remembers that the drill ship floats at the surface with several thousand meters of drill pipe dangling below. The ship must be fixed in location and precisely positioned over the drill site so that the long "string" of pipe will not break during drilling. Periodically, worn bits must be replaced and the original bore hole reentered. To provide the necessary stability, drillships are provided with systems of motors that are electronically activated by sonar " distance sensors." One sonar beacon is dropped to the ocean floor. Three hydrophones attached to the ship's hull receive the sonar signal from the sonar beacon at slightly different times, thereby allowing the position of the ship to be determined relative to the beacon.

Since 1968, the Glomar Challenger and JOIDES Resolution have provided a rich store of samples of sediment and rock to depths of over 1300 meters below the ocean bottom. Very likely, geologists a hundred years from now will be studying these samples, just as today we continue to refer to the data collected a century ago by the scientists of the H.M.S. Challenger.

Ocean Water

The chemistry of sea water

The waters of the ocean are remarkably uniform in the kinds and proportions of dissolved elements. An average sample of sea water consists of about 35 parts per thousand dissolved matter. Of that dissolved matter, nearly 86 per cent consists of sodium and chlorine. The other major constituents in order of decreasing abundance are magnesium, sulfur, calcium, potassium, and bicarbonate. Minute quantities of almost all the other naturally occurring elements are also present.

Some of the elements in sea water are in the form of dissolved gases, the most important of which are carbon dioxide and oxygen. Carbon dioxide is essential to the growth of marine plants, a fact that is evident from the observation that the amount of this gas varies closely with the abundance of microscopic marine plants in any given area of the sea. By means of photosynthesis, plants replenish the supply of oxygen in sea water, and oxygen, of course, is essential to marine animal life.

Table 6.1. Dissolved solids in ocean water

Chemical constituent	*Content (Parts per Thousand)*
Calcium (Ca)	0.419
Magnesium (mg)	1.304
Sodium (Na)	10.710
Potassium (K)	0.390
Bicarbonate (HCO_3)	0.146
Sulfate (SO_4)	2.690
Chloride (Cl)	19.350
Bromide (Br)	0.070
Total dissolved solids (salinity)	35.079

The ocean has a great capacity for absorbing carbon dioxide from the air, and thus helps to regulate the amount of this gas in the earth's atmosphere. If the carbon dioxide content of the atmosphere rises, the rate at which it is dissolved in sea water also increases. Oxygen is also absorbed from the air above the oceans but in lesser amounts than carbon dioxide. Surface water tends to be richer in oxygen than deeper water because of its proximity to the air-water interface and also because marine plants flourish in the upper layers of water where there is abundant light for photosynthesis. Beneath the surface layer, however, the amount of oxygen dissolved in the water is lower because of the consumption of the element by animals and bacteria, as well as the reduction of organic waste as it sinks through the water column. Curiously, at depths greater than about 800 meters in many parts of the open ocean, oxygen concentrations increase somewhat, due to the transport of oxygen by deep currents from hight latitudes where dense oxygen-rich water sinks and flows generally toward the equatorial regions.

Physical properties of sea water

Because of the dissolved salt in sea water, it differs from pure water in several physical properties. The density of pure water, for example, is 1 gram per cubic centimeter at 4°C. In contrast, the density of sea water increases with increasing salinity and is 2 to 3 per cent greater than the density of fresh water.

The density of both sea and fresh water also changes slightly with variations in temperature. Once again the changes are somewhat different in sea water than in fresh water. As fresh water in cooled from a temperature of 20°C to a temperature of 4°C, its density gradually increases. The dense water will sink to the bottom of the pond or lake and be continuously replaced by water from above until the entire water mass has reached 4°C. If fresh water is cooled further, it will expand and its density will decrease. The lighter water will rise to the surface where it freezes after the temperature has reached 0°C. By comparison, sea water of average salinity has a freezing temperature of about –2°C. Water much colder than –2°C is rarely encountered in even the high latitudes of the ocean. Unlike fresh water, the density of sea water increases all the way down to its freezing point. It is evident from these relationships that the most dense water masses in the oceans are cold and have high salinity. Warm less saline waters have lower density.

Table 6.2. Comparison of per cent of dissolved solids in ocean and river water

Chemical constituent	*Per cent of total salt content* *Ocean water*	*River water*
Silica (SiO_2)	—	14.51
Iron (Fe)	—	0.74
Calcium (Ca)	1.19	16.62
Magnesium (Mg)	3.72	4.54
Sodium (Na)	30.53	6.98
Potassium (K)	1.11	2.25
Bicarbonate (HCO_3)	0.42	31.90
Sulfate (SO_4)	7.67	12.41
Chloride (Cl)	55.16	8.64
Nitrate (NO_3)	—	1.11
Bromide (Br)	0.20	—
Total	100.0	100.0

The temperature of the ocean varies both with latitude and depth and is strongly affected by oceanic circulation. Warmest water is found near the equator where temperatures average a balmy 28°C. Not unexpectedly, the coldest water are found in polar regions where temperatures may reach –2°C. In the open ocean, the temperature of surface water changes very little with the seasons. This is because of the great volume of the oceans and the constant mixing that occurs. The ocean reacts very slowly to changes in air temperature and therefore serves as a heat regulator for the atmosphere. Of course, in shallow regions of the seas, water temperature is more markedly influenced by air temperature changes of seasonal duration.

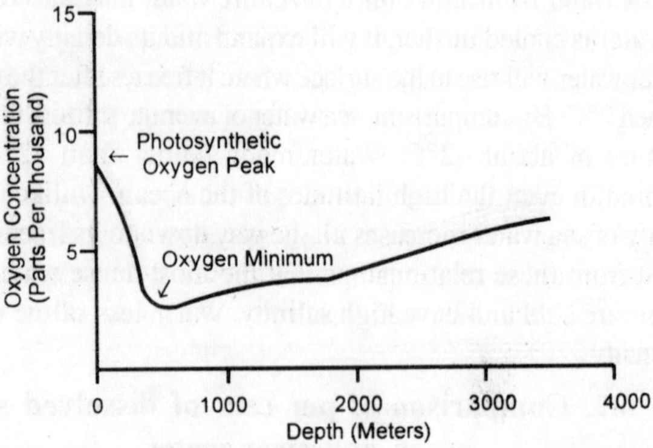

Fig. 6.1. Variation of oxygen (O_2) in the North Central Pacific.

In general, the temperature of ocean water decrease with depth. At moderate depths there is a layer of water in which the change of temperature with depth is at a maximum. This layer is called the *thermocline.* Temperatures decrease only very slowly below the thermocline, until at a depth of 5000 feet the temperature remains virtually constant at 1° to 3°C.

The Depth and Breadth of the Oceans

As land dwellers, we sometimes need to be reminded that over 71 per cent of the earth's surface is covered by ocean. The ocean is not only broad but also deep. Although the average depth of the ocean is about 4000 meters, the floor of some deep-sea trenches are over 11,000 meters below sea level. The ocean depths are measured with the aid of

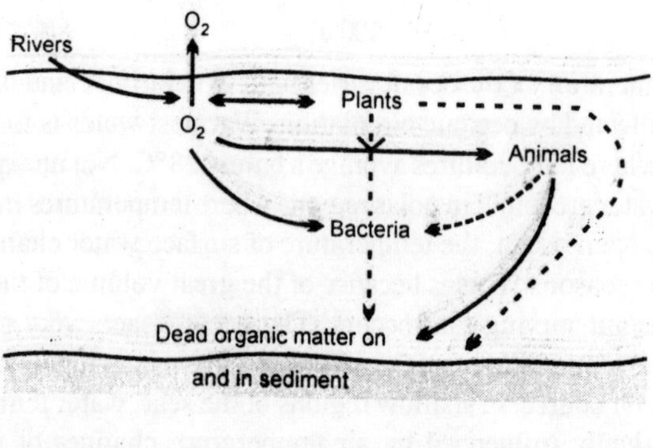

Fig. 6.2. Oxygen cycle in the sea. Solid arrows indicate flow of elemental oxygen; dashed arrows indicate flow of oxygen in organic matter.

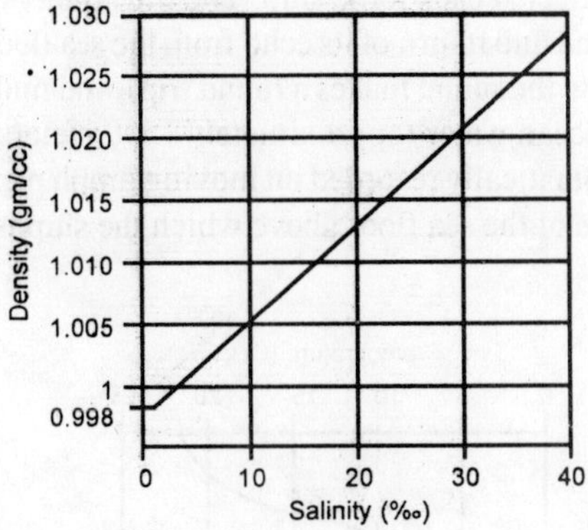

Fig. 6.3. Variation in the density of ocean water with salinity, assuming constant temperature and atmospheric pressure.

echosounding devices. The method is based on knowledge of the speed with which sound travels in water. A short sharp signal or "ping" is emitted about every $^1/_4$ second by the research vessel as it travels along. Sound waves from the signal move through the water column and, upon reaching

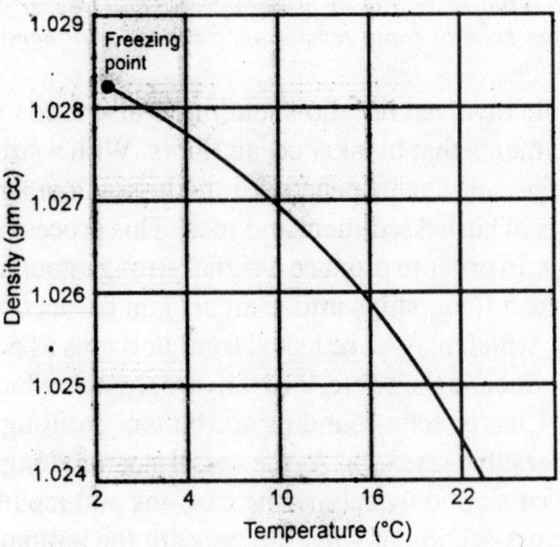

Fig. 6.4. Variation in the density of ocean water with temperature at constant salinity and atmospheric pressure.

the sea floor, are reflected back tothe ship. The time interval between the emission of the sound and return of its echo from the sea floor is recorded, divided by 2 (because the sound makes a round trip), and multiplied by the speed of sound in ocean water (approximately 1500 meters per second). The results are automatically recorded on moving graph paper to provide a continuous profile of the sea floor above which the ship is traveling.

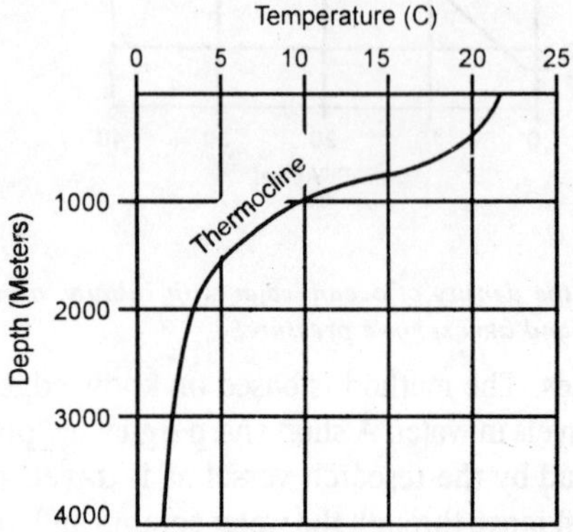

Fig. 6.5. Warm water in the ocean is less dense than cold water tends to stay at the surface, resulting in a layer of warm water over deeper cold water. The transition zone of rapid temperature change with depth is called the thermocline.

The principle involved in echo-sounding is also used to assist in the study of the sediments that blanket ocean floors. With a stronger signal, some of the energy can actually penetrate into the sea floor and is reflected off various layers of buried sediment and rock. This process is called *sub-bottom profiling.* In order to produce a signal strong enough to penetrate deep into the ocean floor, ships utilize an air gun or electric spark. The returned energy, which may be reflected from horizons as deep as 10 km below the ocean floor, is then detected by hydrophones, which are trailed behind the ship. Clearly, echo-sounding and bottom profiling are splendid tools for oceanographic research. As the vessel steams along, the moving graph paper reveals not only submarine canyons and mountains but an uninterrupted cross-section of what lies beneath the bottom of the sea.

The Sarth's Surface Beneath the Oceans

Eighteenth-century scientists had little knowledge of the topography of the ocean floors. They lived at a time when depth measurements were made by letting down a lead weight on the end of a rope. Not only was this method time consuming, but in the open ocean it was virtually impossible to prevent error from lateral drifting of the weight, the ship, or both. As a result of these problems, only a limited number of soundings were made, except in bays and offshore areas where such information was vital for safe navigation. Oceanographers interpreted the few measurements available as indicating that the ocean floors were monotonous flat plains. With the advent of continuous topographic profiles from echosounding devices, it was shown that the ocean floors are as irregular as the surface of the continents. Beneath the waves lay canyons deeper than the Grand Canyon and mountain systems more magnificent than the Rockies.

The sea floors near the continents

Continental shelves. As one departs on an ocean voyage from New York City, the first major oceanic topographic feature above which the ship travels is the continental shelf. The *continental shelves* are very gently sloping (an average of 0.1°) smooth surfaces that fringe the continents in widths that vary from only a few km to about 300 km and depths that range from low tide to about 200 meters. In a geologic sense, these shallow areas are not part of the oceanic crust but resemble the continents in their structure and composition. They are, in fact, the submerged edges of the continents and have a readily apparent continuity with the coastal plains. The outer boundaries of the shelves are defined by a marked increase in slope to greater depths. The smoothness of parts of the continental shelves seems to have been produced in part by the action of waves and currents during the last Ice Age. At that time, sea level was periodically lowered by as much as 140 meters as a result of water locked in glacial ice. Waves and currents sweeping across the shelves shifted sediment into low places and generally leveled the surface.

For geologists specializing in the study of sedimentary rocks, the continental shelves hold great interest. All of the sediment eroded from the continents and carried to the sea in streams must ultimately cross the shelves or be deposited on them. Study of depositional patterns on the shelves has provided valuable insights into the origin of features in ancient sedimentary rocks now found high and dry on the continents. The shelves also have enormous biologic importance. Over most of their area, sunlight can penetrate all the way to the sea floor. Algae and other forms of plant life proliferate. Here one finds the "pastures of the sea" on which, directly or indirectly, a multitude of swimming and bottom dwelling animals are dependent.

Within the last few decades, we have become increasingly aware of the value of the continental shelves. Over 90 per cent of the world's sea food is captured in the waters of the shelves. Photographs of enormous offshore drilling rigs remind us daily of the oil and gas resources that lie beneath this part of the sea floor.

Marginal seas and plateaus. The continental shelves are not the only marginal features of the oceans. For example, depressed areas of the continents near the continental borders are sometimes inundated to form *epicontinental marginal seas.* Example are the Gulf of St. Lawrence and the Gulf of Maine. Such areas are distinguished from the shelves by their greater topographic irregularity and depths. *Marginal plateaus* are also present here and there along the periphery of continents. The plateaus are shelf-like features that generally lie at greater depths than the shelves and are separated from shelves by a slight slope. The Blake Plateau east of Florida is a particularly fine example of a marginal plateau.

The continental slopes. Those areas of the ocean floor that extend from the seaward edge of the continental shelves down to the ocean deeps are named the *continental slopes.* Physiographic diagrams of the ocean floor are usually drawn with a large amount of vertical exaggeration, so that the continental slope appear as steep escarpments. Actually, the inclination of the surface is only 3° to 6°. From the sharply defined upper boundary of the continental slope, the surface of the ocean floor drops to depths of 1400 to 3200 meters. At these depths the inclination of the ocean floor becomes gentler. The less pronounced slopes comprise the *continental rises.* Most of these areas of lesser slope and low relief appear to be wedgelike accumulations of sediment that have been transported across the shelves and deposited in the deep ocean at the base of the continental slopes.

Submarine canyons and valleys

Marine geologists conducting submarine topographic surveys of the continental shelves have long been aware of the large canyons and deep valleys on the continental shelves and slopes. Some of these features, like the Congo Canyon at the mouth of the Congo River, and the submarine canyon seaward of the mouth of the Hudson River, are clearly delineated on profiles obtained by echo-sounding. Other canyonlike features are now filled with sediment and have been detected by drilling and sub-bottom seismic profiling. The majority of such features on the continental shelves appear to have been formed by rivers at times when sea level was lower and broad tracts of the shelves were exposed to subaerial erosion. The best evidence for their fluvial origin is their continuity with valleys on land. Indeed, about 80 per cent of submarine valleys appear to be extensions of land valleys. Those that are not associated with land valleys are most often found at the outer edge of the shelf and on the continental slope. These canyons are inferred to have been eroded by submarine processes such as sand slides, slumping, and currents of sediment-laden water called turbidity currents.

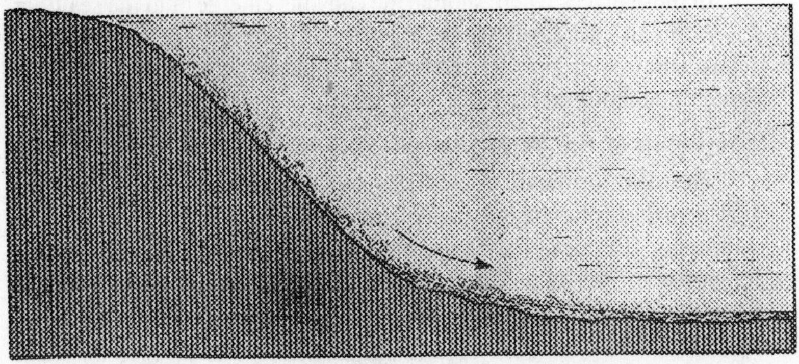

Fig. 6.6. A turbidity current is a mass of moving water that is denser than surrounding water because of its content of suspended sediment. Turbidity currents flow along the slopes of ocean (or lake) floors because of their density.

Water is said to be turbid when it contains an abundance of suspended particles, and a *turbidity current* is the movement of this dense mixture down a slope beneath clear or less turbid water. The sediment in suspension causes the moving mass to have greater density than less turbid water. The heavy water mass flows close to the sloping ocean floor, picking up additional loose material as it moves along and developing a characteristic turbulent motion. Turbidity currents can develop astonishing speed and are potent agents for the transport of sediment. A turbidity current initiated by an earthquake-triggered landslide off the Grand Banks of Newfoundland in 1929 crossed over and sequentially broke a series of trans-Atlantic telegraph cables. The time each cable was broken was automatically recorded, indicating the troublesome turbidity current was traveling 100 km per hour the steeper parts of the continental slope and continued out into the Atlantic for well over 600 km.

Submarine canyons formed by submarine processes are quite different from canyons and valleys formed subaerially on land. In most cases, their gradients are steeper, the canyon floors deepen consistently seaward, and the walls are more precipitous. Indeed, the height of the walls of submarine canyons may far exceed those of even the most magnificent of land canyons. The Grand Canyon of Colorado has a north wall that is about 1676 meters high, whereas the sides of the Great Bahama Submarine Canyon reach an astonishing height of 4400 meters above the canyon floor. Submarine canyons vary in length from only a few km to hundreds of km. The Bering Canyon north of the Bering Islands, for example, is 442 km long.

In those places where submarine canyons emerge onto the sea floor, the sediment carried down the canyons by turbidity currents may be deposited as *deep-sea fans* that resemble the alluvial fans found at the foot of mountains on land.

The floors of the ocean basins

The ocean basins are located between the continental rises. In general, they lie in the depth range from 4600 to 5500 meters. Unlike the crust of the continents, the ocean basins are underlain by igneous rocks of basaltic composition. The basalts are characteristically rather deficient in alkali elements like sodium and potassium and have been given the name *tholeiites.* There are a variety of topographic forms developed on the floors of the ocean basins, but the most distinctive are abyssal plains, abyssal hills, oceanic rises, and seamounts.

Abyssal plains

The *abyssal* plain are the vast flattish regions that extend seaward from the base of the continental rises. Their flatness can be attributed to sedimentation that has buried many of the irregularities that once existed on the ocean floor. Most of the sediment consists either of very fine mineral particles derived from land or of the microscopic remains of marine organisms. In addition, an appreciable amount of the sediment on the abyssal plains appears to be fine particles from nearly spent turbidity currents. Such currents do spread into thin sheetlike masses on reaching the deep-sea floor and would be effective agents in transporting and spreading sediment on the abyssal plains. Here and there, irregularities or extinct volcanoes interrupt the monotony of the abyssal plains. Such irregularities are called abyssal hills. They appear mostly in the areas where there has been insufficient sediment to cover them.

Oceanic rises, seamounts, and guyots

Oceanic rises are elevated tracts of the sea floor that are hundreds of square miles in area, that stand a few hundred meters above the surrounding abyssal plains, and that are distinctly separated from continental margins or oceanic ridges. The surface of a rise may be either relatively smooth or quite irregular. Rises are found around Bermuda (the Bermuda Rise), as well as in the Pacific, Indian, and South Atlantic oceans. They are thought to develop as gentle upwarpings of the ocean floor. Oceanic rises should not be confused with features like the East Pacific Rise, which is part of the ocean ridge system and not a true oceanic rise.

Among the most remarkable features of the sea floor are rather symmetric isolated volcanic peaks having a height of 900 meters or more. They are called *seamounts* if they are conical and *guyots* if, in addition, they have flat tops. Seamounts are known on the continental rises but are much more numerous on the ocean basin floors. Indeed, oceanographers estimate that more than 10,000 seamounts and guyots occur in the Pacific Ocean Basin alone. Many seamounts appear to have developed along fracture zones in the crust where lavas were able to issue forth and accumulate as undersea volcanoes. Others may have been formed in linear sequences as the ocean crust moved over "hot spots." Where the lava is built up above sea level, seamounts form islands such as those in the Hawaiian islands.

Guyots were named for the Swiss geographer *Arnold Guyot* (1807 to 1884). They are of special interest to geologists because of their remarkable flat tops. The most prevalent theories explain the flat tops as either drowned wave-beveled surfaces or coral reefs that had been built on the summits of barely submerged volcanoes. In support of these ideas, the top surfaces of many guyots are encrusted with the remains of ancient coral reefs, while a few others have yielded dredge samples of cobbles and pebbles that appear to have been shaped by wave action. Waves and coral reefs, however, are features that characterize the uppermost level of the sea. How then did the guyots reach the great depths at which they are now found? Either sea level rose to cover them, or the guyots were carried downward by subsidence of the oceanic crust. Because some guyots lie 2000 to 3000 meters below sea level, it seems quite unlikely that eustatic rise in sea level is the answer. A more likely explanation is that some guyots isostatically subsided simply because the oceanic crust has insufficient strength to support the weight of an entire volcano over long periods of geologic time. Clusters of guyots probably reached their present depths as a result of the gradual subsidence of oceanic crust when it cools and is conveyed off the elevated flanks of the mid-oceanic ridges.

Mid-oceanic ridges

Because of their impressive topography, distinctive structure, areal extent, and importance in global tectonics, the mid-oceanic ridges deserve a prominent place in any classification of this planet's major geologic features. Mid-oceanic ridges extend along 64,000 km of the sea floor and nearly equal the continents in total area. This world-encircling system can be traced down the middle of the Greenland Sea and the North and South Atlantic Oceans. It then swings eastward into the Indian Ocean basin and continues along between Australia and Antarctica to enter the Pacific Ocean. Once in the Pacific, the ridge is continued northward along the eastern side of the ocean basin, where it is called the East Pacific Rise.

The Mid-Atlantic Ridge is a widely studied segment of the ridge system and illustrates well many of the characteristics of mid-ocean ridges. In its southward trend down the Atlantic Ocean basin, it parallels the margins of Africa and South America. Altogether, the ridge occupies about a third of the Atlantic Ocean basin and rises over 3 km above the basin floors. Here and there some of its highest peaks project above sea level to form islands such as those of Iceland and the Azores.

In 1973 and 1974, the French-American Mid-Ocean Undersea Study (FAMOUS) undertook detailed mapping of the Mid-Atlantic Ridge southwest of the Azores. Included in the results of this study were cross-sectional profiles across the ridge that clearly showed the presence of a central rift valley resembling a huge graben. This central rift was bounded on either side by normal faults, along which basaltic melts rose from deep zones to form dikes, sills, and submarine lava flows. Similar rift zones have been inferred from echo-sounding profiles along many other segments of the world ridge system. They appear to mark the location of divergent plate boundaries. As lithospheric plates move apart, the crust is subjected to tension, normal faults develop, and basaltic lava is able to rise and become incorporated into the trailing edges of the diverging plates. From this lava, the mid-oceanic ridges are constructed.

Study of the world ridge system is not necessarily confined to the ocean floor. In places like the west coast of North America, eastern Africa, and the Red Sea, the ridges run into the continents. As is the case for the Mid-Atlantic Ridge, seismic refraction studies indicate that the rift occupied by the Red Sea is also characterized by normal faulting.

Deep-sea trenches

The deepest parts of the oceans are elongate, often arcuate troughs called *deep-sea trenches.* The floors of these great deeps lie as much as 11,000 meters below sea level. There is no light in the trenches, and pressures may exceed that at sea level by over 1000 times. Most deep-sea trenches are only 40 to 120 km in width, but a few are thousands of km in length. Trenches lie either along the oceanward side of volcanic island arcs, as exemplified by the Aleutian Trench, or adjacent to coastal ranges of continents, as is the case with the Peru-Chile Trench off the west coast of South America. The Mariana Trench in the North Pacific Ocean is particularly noteworthy for its record depth of 11,022 meters.

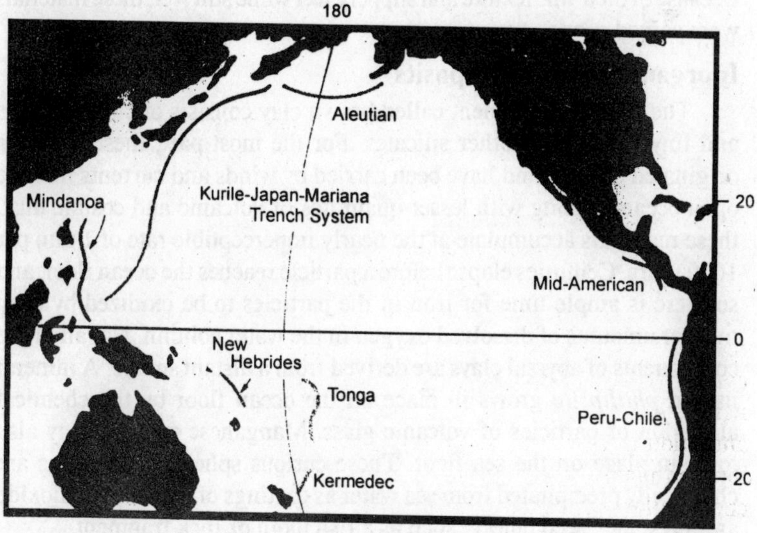

Fig. 6.7. Major trenches of the Pacific Ocean.

Deep-sea trenches and associated island arcs are vibrant with geologic activity. Volcanic eruptions and earthquakes are frequent events. When plotted on cross-sections of the trench and adjacent tracts, the foci of the earthquakes define a zone that slopes downward at an angle of 30° to 50° under the arcs and toward continental margins. Earlier we defined these trends as Benioff Seismic Zones. We also noted that strong negative gravity anomalies occur over deep-sea trenches. The Benioff Zones and negative anomalies indicate that, along the deep-sea trenches, the oceanic crust is bent and carried downward into the upper mantle. The result on the ocean floor is the elongate depression of the deep-sea trench. As discussed in previous chapters, deep-sea trenches are ocean floor manifestations of *subduction* zones They are one of several major global features that form along the *leading edges* of tectonic plates.

Deep-sea Sediments

Deposits of the deep ocean basins were first examined by scientists aboard the *H.M.S. Challenger*, who found that there were two abundant kinds of sediment on the basin floors. In the deepest regions, the *Challenger* crew brought up samples of clay, which they called "red clay." Actually, abyssal clays are more of a brownish color, and so the term *brown clay* is now preferred. In the shallower regions of the ocean basins, various kinds of very fine organic deposits were raised onto the deck of the *Challenger.* Because of their fine texture and slippery feel while still wet, these materials were named *oozes.*

Inorganic deep-sea deposits

The deep-sea sediment called brown clay consists of clay minerals and tiny particles of other silicates. For the most part, these particles originated on land and have been carried by winds and currents into the open oceans. Along with lesser quantities of volcanic and cosmic dust, these materials accumulate at the nearly imperceptible rate of 1 mm per 1000 years. Centuries elapse before a particle reaches the ocean floor, and so there is ample time for iron in the particles to be oxidized by even meager amounts of dissolved oxygen in the water column. Not all of the components of abyssal clays are derived from a distant source. A mineral named *phillipsite* grows in place on the ocean floor by the chemical alteration of particles of volcanic glass. Manganese nodules may also form in place on the sea floor. These curious spheric concretions are chemically precipitated from sea water as coatings of manganese dioxide around some "seed object" such as a fish tooth or rock fragment.

Occasionally, while examining the long cylindric cores of deep-sea sediments, geologists are startled to discover a layer of sand or silt-sized particles. In most cases, the coarser material was brought to the site of deposition by turbidity currents, as described earlier. Relatively large pebbles and cobbles are also sometimes found in deep-sea tracts near the poles. This kind of coarse debris has been dropped from drifting masses of melting glacial ice. It is especially prevalent on the floor of the ocean around Antarctica.

Organic deep-sea deposits

There are science students who have been so impressed by the beauty of the skeletal remains found in oozes that they have devoted their lives to the study of these minute organic structures. The principal contributors to deep-sea oozes are protozoans, tiny mollusks, and algae. Depending on the composition of their hard parts, these organisms contribute to the formation of either calcareous or siliceous oozes. By definition, an ooze must consist of at least 30 per cent of organically derived material. Therefore, oozes are not found in nearshore areas because the influx of terrigenous sediment is so great that the organic contribution does not reach the 30 per cent level.

Calcareous oozes

The principal constituents of calcareous oozes are the calcium carbonate coverings of foraminifers, coccoliths, and pteropods. Foraminifers are marine protozoans, whereas coccoliths are tiny calcite structures that encase the living cell of members of the algal family Coccolithophoridae. The term *Globigerina ooze* is frequently employed for a calcareous ooze composed of a mixture of coccoliths and tests of foraminifers. The "forams" in Globigerina ooze are species, which like *Globigerina* are adapted to a floating (planktonic) existence. The tests are

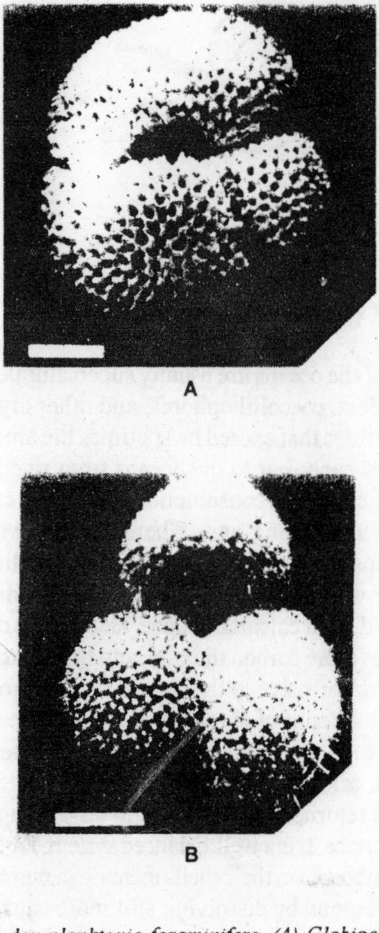

Fig. 6.8. Present-day planktonic foraminifers. (A) Globigerinoides conglobatus; (B) Globigerinoides rubra.

regularly vacated as part of the reproductive cycle of these organisms, and the abandoned shells settle to the sea floor. Only a very small percentage of the remains in oozes represent fatalities. The pteropods are a group of tiny marine gastropods (snails) that are adapted to a floating life. Their delicate shells are frequently found in Globigerina ooze, and locally the may be so abundant as to justify the name *pteropod ooze.*

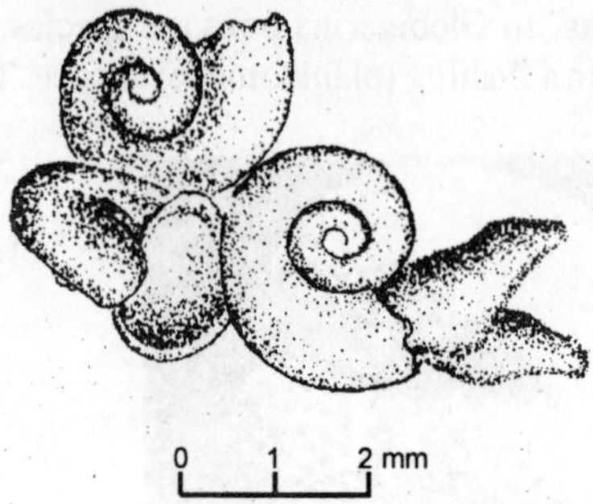

Fig. 6.9. Limacina, a tiny swimming marine snail with foot modified into a pair of winglike lobes or fins, shown in specimen at left. At the right are two empty conchs.

Surface waters of the oceans are usually supersaturated with calcium carbonate. Foraminifers, coccolithophores, and other organisms extract this material in quantities that exceed by six times the amount of calcium carbonate contributed each year to the oceans from rivers. Initially, one might surmise that the biologic consumption of calcium carbonate would have depleted the supply long ago. There is, however, a recycling mechanism that helps to maintain the supply. If the tiny shells settle through a column of water no deeper than about 3000 meters, they will accumulate intact and form calcareous ooze. Below that depth, however, the colder water holds more carbon dioxide, and this increases its acidity. These deep waters are corrosive to the fragile shells of foraminifers and coccolithophores. At a depth of about 4600 meters, the supply of shell materials from above is approximately balanced by the amount being dissolved. As a result, calcareous oozed cannot accumulate. The dissolved calcium carbonate is returned to the oceans to be used again by floating organisms near the surface. It is a well-balanced system, for if the organisms that utilize calcium carbonate in their shells increase in number, the depleted ocean water would respond by dissolving still more calcareous material on the ocean floor.

The ability of cold deep water to dissolve calcareous materials accounts for the fact that calcareous oozes are most extensive on the shallower regions of ocean basins. Tall submarine mountains may have their summits, which reach shallower levels, capped by calcareous ooze. They resemble snow-capped peaks, with "snow lines" at about 4600 meters below sea level.

Siliceous oozes

In order to be termed a siliceous ooze, a sediment must be composed of at least 30 per cent of organic silica. The two principal contributors to siliceous oozes are the unicellular diatoms, which are algae, and the microscopic protozoans known as radiolaria. Because the ocean is undersaturated at all depths with silica, microscopic siliceous shells are often dissolved before reaching the ocean floor. The rate of solution depends on the thickness of the skeletal structures and whether or not they have protective coatings of organic compounds. Siliceous oozes accumulate in colder or deeper oceanic regions where other sediments are lacking or in regions where an abundance of nutrients promotes high productivity of siliceous organisms.

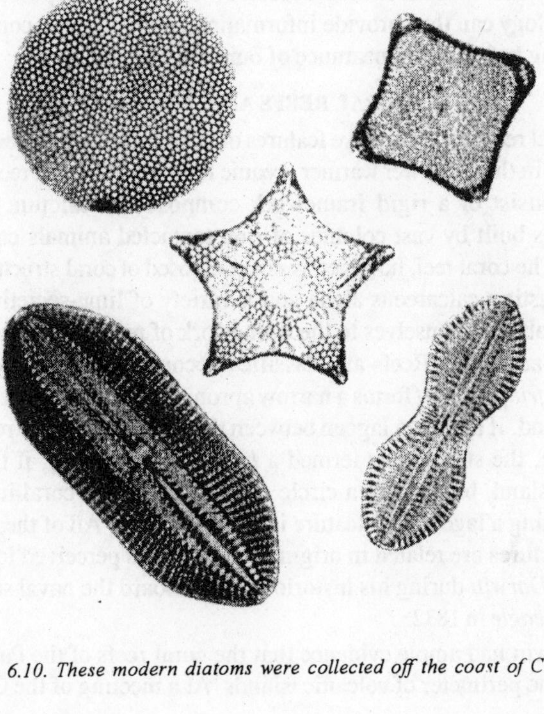

Fig. 6.10. These modern diatoms were collected off the coast of Crete.

Climatic history from deep-sea sediment

A core of deep-sea sediment can yield a bonanza of geologic information once it has been completely analyzed. Superposition tells us that the lower layers of sediment are older and the higher layers consecutively younger. Using radioactive dating methods, the actual period of time during which the sediments in the core accumulated can be determined. Next the foraminifers, radiolaria, diatoms, or coccolithophores are carefully identified at each successively higher level in the core. Because many species of these organisms were able to live only within certain limits of water temperature, their fossil remains are indicators of ancient temperature. The layers might, for example, suggest an ancient cooling trend if warm-water species in the lower parts of the core gave way to cold-water species in higher layers. Even where good temperature-indicator organisms are absent, the calcareous shells may provide chemical clues to ancient temperatures. Scientists have discovered that the ratio of the isotopes oxygen 16 and oxygen 18 dissolved in ocean water varies according to water temperature. Similarly, the ratio of these isotopes in the calcium carbonate shells will reflect the enclosing water's temperature at the time the carbonate was secreted. Oxygen isotope studies and paleontology can thus provide information about climatic conditions on earth long before the appearance of our own species.

Coral Reefs and Atolls

Coral reefs are distinctive features of the marine environment and are common in the shallower warmer oceanic regions. The coral reefs growing today consist of a rigid framework composed of calcium carbonate structures built by vast colonies of tiny tentacled animals called *coral polyps.* The coral reef, however, is not composed of coral structures alone, for encrusting calcareous algae and a variety of lime-secreting marine animals attach themselves to the framework of reef and contribute to its strength and mass. Reefs are classified according to their proximity to shore. A *fringing reef* forms a narrow apron directly around the perimeter of an island. If there is a lagoon between the inner edge of the reef and the shoreline, the structure is termed a *barrier reef.* Finally, if there is no central island, but merely a circle of coral reefs and coralline islands, surrounding a lagoon, the feature is called an *atoll.* All of these kinds of reef structures are related in origin. This fact was perceived long ago by *Charles Darwin* during his historic service aboard the naval survey ship *H.M.S. Beagle* in 1832.

Darwin had ample evidence that the coral reefs of the Pacific grew around the perimeter of volcanic islands. At a meeting of the Geological

Society of London during the summer of 1837, he proposed that volcanic islands tend to sink slowly because of the inability of the ocean floor to support their great weight. Before this begins to happen, however, free-swimming larvae of coral animals reach newly formed volcanic islands, attach themselves to the shallow submerged areas around the island, and begin their development into adult polyps. Gradually, the coralline framework is constructed and other organisms add their own skeletal structures to the reef. The corals, however, are essential to the vitality of the reef. *Darwin* was aware that corals are rather fussy creatures in that they thrive only in shallow, well lighted, relatively warm ocean waters. Depth of water is critical to the health of coral polyps. Thus, with the sinking of their volcanic island, the myriads of polyps might be doomed were it not for their astonishing efficiency in building their colonies upward so as to maintain an optimal habitat near the ocean surface As the process of subsidence and growth continues, a barrier reef would develop, as shown. Eventually, the island would sink beneath the waves, leaving only a circle of coralline islands-the *atoll*. In Darwin's own words, " . . . as the land with the attached reefs subsides very gradually from the action of subterranean causes, the coral building polypi soon raise again their solid masses to the level of the water: but not so the land; every inch of which is irreclaimably gone: as the whole gradually sinks, the water gains foot by foot upon the shore until the last and highest peak is finally submerged."

Several deep borings into atolls have validated Darwin's theory. A boring at Eniwetok in the Pacific encountered the basaltic summit of the volcano at depths of about 1200 meters. Eocene reef structures were directly above these igneous rocks.

It has been suggested that the subsidence associated with the development of some atolls is related to sea floor spreading. Spreading begins along the crest of a mid-oceanic ridge, and as the plate move away from the ridge, they subside very slowly due to thermal contraction and isostatic adjustment. The subsidence is estimated at about 9 cm per year for the first million years. Thus, a volcano formed at the crest of the mid-oceanic ridge is carried down the slight incline of the ocean plate until it is completely submerged. Coral growth that is able to keep pace with the subsidence will result in the formation of barrier reefs and atolls.

There is an alternate possibility for atoll formation. It is possible that corals might build fringing reefs around the perimeter of volcanic islands that had been erosionally truncated during an interglacial period of low sea level. If the sea level subsequently rose (as it did when the great Pleistocene ice sheets began to melt), then the corals would strive to build the reef upward in order to stay at their optimal living depth. It seems not unreasonable that particular atolls may be primarily the result of subsidence of the host island, while others may have formed in response to a rise in sea level.

Life in the Oceans

Biological realms of the sea

One need only view a Jacques Cousteau film on television or pause to examine the creatures in a tidal pool to appreciate the fact that the ocean teems with life. The multitude of marine creatures are not distributed uniformly through the oceans, but individual groups inhabit particular parts of the oceans according to their mobility and needs. Such variables as temperature, pressure, currents, light penetration, and nutrients limit the distribution of certain organisms. In addition, the different sediments that blanket the sea floor influence the distribution of organisms that live on, or burrow into, the ocean bottoms.

So that one may effectively communicate information about life in the oceans, scientists have developed a widely accepted classification of marine environments. In this classification, the entire ocean is divided into two broad environments: the *pelagic realm,* or water environment, and the *benthic,* or bottom, environment. The pelagic realm can in turn be divided into the neritic environment, which overlies the continental shelves, and the oceanic environment, which extends seaward beyond the shelves.

Bottom environments

The benthic environments are of particular importance to geologists because of the multitude of shell-building organisms that live there. In the past, these creatures have become the fossils that are now widely used in correlating strata and determining their relative ages. The benthic environment actually begins with a narrow zone above high tide which is called the *supratidal zone.* A few algae, other plants, and insects have adapted to this unique marine environment in which spray from waves or wetting during storms provides necessary moisture. Seaward from this supratidal belt is the intertidal or *littoral zone.* This zone is perhaps the most rigorous of marine environments, for its inhabitants must be able to tolerate the alternation of wet and dry conditions. Some creatures of the littoral zone are sufficiently mobile to move back and forth with the tides, whereas others will burrow into the moist sand in order to escape dessication during times of low tide. The littoral zone is the marine environment that we can all readily observe and on which we often play as well.

The greatest multitude of bottom-dwelling animals and plants in the ocean live on the relatively shallow continuously submerged *sublittoral zone.* This zone corresponds rather well to the continental shelf. The boundary of the sublittoral zone is drawn at the base of the zone of light penetration. Light does not penetrate as deeply in the littoral zone as in the open ocean, because of bottom turbulence and turbidity. In the benthic littoral zone one finds a host of blue-green, green, brown, and red algae, as well as abundant protozoans (foraminifers), sponges, corals and sea anemones, worms, mollusks, crustaceans, and various echinoderms (starfish, sand dollars, and sea urchins). All of these organisms that live on the ocean floor are *benthos.* Those that crawl about constitute the vagrant benthos, and those that are attached to the sea floor are called sessile benthos.

Beyond the continental shelves, the benthic environment is subjected to colder temperatures, little or no light penetration, and high pressures. Plants are unable to live at these depths. One encounters the *bathyal* environment from the edge of the shelf to a depth of about 4000 meters. Still deeper levels constitute the *abyssal* environment. The term *hadal* is reserved for the extreme depths found in oceanic trenches. Animals are less abundant in the abyssal and hadal realms. Mostly, they are carnivores and scavengers that depend on the slow fall of food from higher levels.

The drifters

The primarily microscopic drifting and floating organisms in the ocean are called plankton. Some do have feeble swimming abilities but not sufficient to permit them to migrate long distances against the pull of oceanic currents. As we have seen, both plants and animals are included in this category. The plants are called *phytoplankton* and include the Coccolithophoridae and diatoms. A group of phytoplankton not previously mentioned are the dinoflagellates. These creatures have whiplike flagella, which they use to move themselves feebly through the water. Most dinoflagellates lack mineralized skeletons and hence do not contribute to oceanic sediments. Some phytoplankton are quite large. The drifting *Sargassum,* a type of brown algae, has long branching stems with stalked bladders to help keep the massive growths afloat.

The foraminifers and radiolaria are true protozoan animals and thus are designated *zooplankton.* However, many other phyla of invertebrate animals are zooplankton either as adults or in there larval stages. Jellyfish of the Phylum Coelenterata, for example, are zooplankton, as are the larvae of certain segmented worms, the previously mentioned pteropods, the larvae of echinoderms (sea urchins and sea lilies), and many small crustaceans.

The swimmers

Almost all organisms in the oceanic realm are the prey of some other organism. Phytoplankton are consumed by zooplankton, which also consume one another and may ultimately become the food of *nekton.* Nekton are true swimming animals. They are able to move where they choose under their own power, and this is a very advantageous adaptation. A swimming creature can search for its food and does not have to depend on a drifting current to bring a chance morsel. It can escape predators at times and can move to more favorable areas when conditions become difficult. The nekton are a diverse group. For the most part, they are members of the Chordata, and include a vast array of fish and fewer numbers of reptiles and mammals. There are, however, nektonic nonchordates as well, the most numerous of which are squid, shrimp, and krill.

Ocean Currents

Because of the importance of ocean currents in navigation, they have been closely observed since the days of sailing ships. *Benjamin Franklin*, whose lively intelligence and interest in natural phenomena is well known, made one of the earliest studies of the Gulf Stream. Using ships' logs and notes provided by ships' captains, he mapped the Gulf Stream from the southeast coast of the United States northward to Cape Hatteras and thence eastward toward the northwest coast of Europe. Franklin's chart was useful in shortening the number of days required to sail from Boston to London. By avoiding the Gulf Stream on the return trip, these vessels also achieved a faster passage.

There are two major types of movements of ocean water. One kind is caused by differences in density. Where the density differences are the result of variations in salinity and temperature, these currents are termed *thermohaline.* People tend to be more aware of the second kind of ocean movements, which are the wind-driven or surface currents.

The role of wind

Surface currents are slow drifts of ocean water set in motion by winds that blow over the surface of the water. Energy is transferred from the moving air (wind) to the water. Because the energy transfer occurs at the surface, the topmost level of the ocean water moves the fastest, and successively lower levels have decreasing velocity. At depths of about 100 meters, the current can hardly be detected.

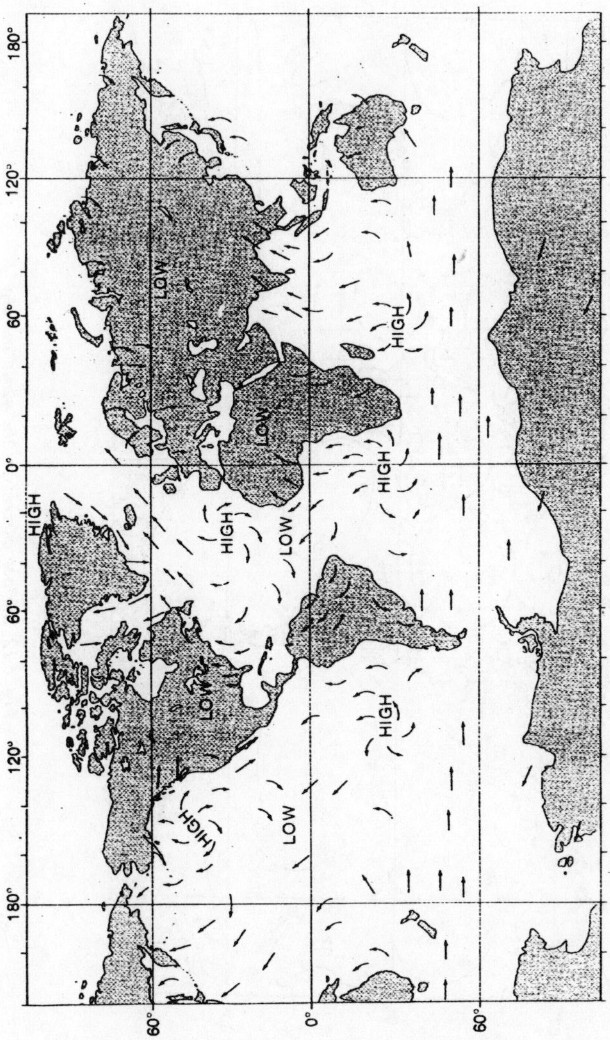

Fig. 6.11. Wind systems of the world in July.

If oceanic currents derive their energy largely from wind, then one should be able to see similarities between the global current pattern and the pattern of atmospheric circulation. In a very general way, such correlations do exist. In the low latitudes, trade winds blow from the east

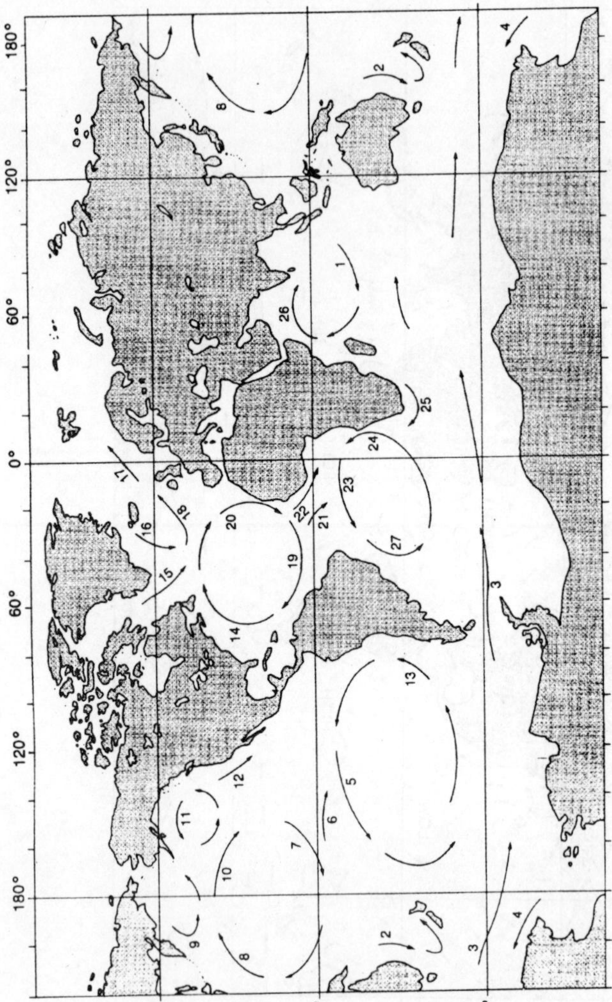

Fig. 6.12. Surface currents of the world in July.

diagonally toward the equator. To the north and south of the trades are the westerlies, which blow form the west diagonally away from the equator in the middle latitudes. The result is a system of large rather elliptic whirls of water circulation called *gyres*.

Influence of land masses

Wind is not the only factor that determines the global pattern of ocean currents. Land masses and the earth's rotation also play important roles. In considering the influence of land masses, one need only follow the path of currents indicated. The North Equatorial Current, for example, is deflected by the land areas of the Caribbean and North America and moves northeastward as the Gulf Stream. On approaching Europe, it is again deflected and divides into the northward-flowing North Atlantic Current and a southward-moving Canary Current. The Canary Current joins the North Equatorial current to complete the gyre.

In addition to such factors as wind direction and locations of continental barriers, oceanic currents are strongly influenced by the movement of the earth itself. The earth rotates from west to east, and as the solid earth moves eastward under the liquid oceans, water is more or less pushed toward the land mass on the west side of the oceans. Thus, the center of the gyres is usually offset to the west in ocean basins.

Influence of earth's rotation

An important effect resulting from the earth's rotation is the tendency of particles of matter in motion on the earth's surface to be deflected toward the right (clockwise) in the Northern Hemisphere and toward the left in the Southern Hemisphere regardless of the direction in which the body may be moving. This phenomenon has been named the *Coriolis effect* after the nineteenth century French mathematician *G.G Coriolis*, who first studied it. Because of the Coriolis effect, the subtropical gyres rotate in a clockwise sense in the northern half of our planet and counter-clockwise in the Southern Hemisphere.

Not only does the Coriolis force influence the horizontal pattern of ocean currents, but it also causes a vertical effect. We have already noted how the earth's rotation causes a concentration of major currents on the west side of ocean basins. As a result, the sea surface is not really level but is slightly higher in the center and on the west side of the ocean basins.

The Ekman spiral

As mentioned above, the major current systems of the oceans are generated by the frictional drag of the wind on the ocean surface. Because of the rotation of the earth, however, the water does not move in the direction of the wind, but rather the surface water moves 45° to the right of the wind direction in the Northern Hemisphere and 45° to the left in the Southern Hemisphere. In addition, as depth increase, each "layer" of water

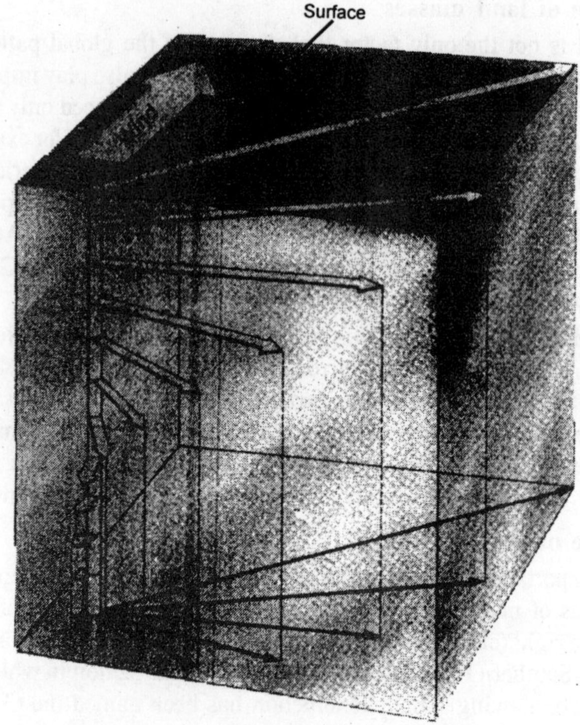

Fig. 6.13. The Ekman spiral as developed in the Northern Hemisphere.

undergoes a similar deviation, while simultaneously friction cause a decrease in velocity with depth. The successive shifts in direction and decrease in speed can be described as a spiral, which has been named the *Ekman spiral* after its discoverer. An important result of the Ekman phenomenon is that net transport of the water column moved by the wind is at right angles to the wind direction. This movement along the trends of the major current gyres causes a pileup of low-density water near the center of gyres. These "hills," as they are sometimes called, provide a slight slope along which water tends to move because of gravity. Once again, because of the Coriolis effect, the downward-moving water is deflected at right angles.

Thermohaline circulation

Thermohaline circulation of ocean water is caused by differences in the density of water masses. As described earlier, such density differences may result from variations in temperature or salinity. For example, sea water becomes more dense and sinks as result of evaporation (which increases salinity), cooling of the water, or freezing of sea water (which increases salinity by exclusion of salt from ice crystals). Warming of sea water or dilution with fresh water tends to decrease density. The density currents that result from these variations are exceptionally slow. They are unable to accomplish any significant geologic work but play an important role in the global exchange of water masses and transport of vital nutrients.

The Origin of the Ocean and Atmosphere

The histories of the ocean and atmosphere are closely related. The initial chapter of that history began about 4.6 billion years ago when the earth had accumulated most of its mass and was undergoing the internal changes involved in the formation of a core, mantle, and primordial crust. During this differentiation, large quantities of magma saturated with dissolved gases moved toward the surface of the earth and expelled their volatiles as they began to crystallize. The gases escaped in the course of volcanic eruptions or more slowly by rising through holes or vents above magmatic bodies. Such igneous activity would produce a mixture of gases that very likely changed somewhat as differentiation proceeded. For example, before iron in the planet had separated and descended to the core, this metal would have been more abundantly disseminated near the surface and would probably have combined with, and removed oxygen from, early volcanic exhalations. What was exhausted were gases rich in hydrogen (H_2), water, carbon dioxide, carbon monoxide, and hydrogen sulfide. Later, when the iron had melted and percolated toward the planet's center, the gases given off by volcanoes came to resemble those emitted during present-day eruptions. These include water vapor, carbon dioxide, sulfur dioxide, nitrogen, and small amounts of hydrogen chloride and carbon monoxide.

Such a water- and carbon-dioxide-rich atmosphere was suitable for the chain of chemical reactions required to produce life. However, it was an atmosphere quite different from that existing today in that it lacked abundant free (uncombined) oxygen.

Oxygen rich atmosphere

The change from an oxygen-poor to an oxygen-rich atmosphere began to take place about 1.8 billion years ago. The amount of oxygen in the atmosphere slowly increased and reached 3 to 10 per cent of present levels about 0.6 billion years ago. Oxygen was added to the atmosphere as a result of two processes. The first was dissociation of water molecules into hydrogen and oxygen. Termed *photochemical dissociation,* this process occurs in the upper atmosphere when water molecules are split by high-energy beams of ultraviolet light from the sun. Photochemical dissociation, however, does not produce free oxygen at a rate sufficient to balance loss of the gas by dissipation into space. Another far more important oxygen-generating mechanism came with the advent of life on earth and, more specifically, with life that had evolved the remarkable capability of dissociating carbon dioxide into carbon and free oxygen. We now know this process as *photosynthesis.* It has made the earth a truly unique planet in our solar system.

Geologic clues to the nature of ancient atmospheres

The oldest rocks that tell us something about the nature of earth's early atmosphere are 3.5 billion-year-old metamorphosed sediments from Africa. These rocks have retained evidence of having been deposited in water, and their component mineral grains have been formed or modified by weathering processes. They could not have developed in the absence of an atmosphere and hydrosphere. In these ancient formations, one can also find detrital particles of pyrite and uraninite. Such minerals would not survive in an oxygen-rich environment. They would be completely oxidized. Carbonate rocks such as dolostone or limestone are also absent. This also indicates that the atmosphere was rich in carbon dioxide and probably somewhat acidic. In such an environment, chert could form, but carbonate rocks could not. Indeed, the inferred abundance of carbon dioxide and water vapor in the atmosphere probably contributed to the formation of carbonic acids, which would have prevented the precipitation of carbonate minerals.

Iron in crustal rocks provides rather direct evidence of the advent of an oxygen-rich atmosphere. In the oldest rocks for which we have reliable radiometric dates, the iron is not deeply oxidized. Beginning in rocks that are about 3 billion years old, one observes evidence of periodic abundance of oxygen. Such formations exhibit an alternation of rusty red and gray colored bands. The former are colored by ferric iron oxide (Fe_2O_3) and indicate abundant free oxygen in the environment. The grayish layers contain oxygen-deficient iron compounds and suggest a lesser availability of oxygen. The alternation of color bands might have be caused by a fluctuating and perhaps season-related supply of oxygen. In the iron mining district north of Lake Superior, the ores above the banded iron deposits are uniformly oxidized. These rocks are about 1.8 billion years old and are evidence of the persistent presence of an oxygenic atmosphere by that time. In other parts of the world, one finds extensive outcrops of dolostone and limestone of about the same age. If carbon dioxide was still abundant in the atmosphere, these carbonate rocks would not have been deposited.

The Source of Ocean Water

If the water in the atmosphere was outgassed from the interior, then the bodies of water that accumulated on the surface of the earth were derived from the atmosphere after it had cooled sufficiently to condense and allow rain to fall. Gradually, the great depressions in the primordial crust began to fill, and oceans began to take form. One cannot help but wonder if the enormous volume of oceanic water could have all come from the interior. Calculations provide a very strong "yes" answer to this question. Vast amounts of water were locked within hydrous silicate minerals that were ubiquitous within the primordial earth. These waters, sweated from the earth's interior and precipitated onto the uplands, began immediately to dissolve soluble minerals and carry the solutes to the sea. In this way, the oceans quickly acquired the saltiness that is their most obvious compositional characteristic. They have maintained a relatively consistent composition by precipitating surplus solutes at about the same rate as they are supplied. Of course because of its high solubility, sodium chloride remains in sea water more readily than other common elements. However, the fossil record of marine organisms suggests that even this element has not varied appreciably in sea water for at least the past 600 million years.

The earth probably outgassed its present quantity of water rather early in its history and has been partially recycling it ever since. The heating that was required to melt the core, as well as possible stresses induced in the crust by the nearby moon, might have so disturbed the crust as to promote outgassing at a rapid rate. Soon thereafter, the oceans settled into a sort of "steady state" system and probably have not gained appreciably in volume. Water is continuously recirculated by evaporation and precipitation processes powered by the sun and gravity. Some of the water in the oceans is temporarily lost by being incorporated into hydrous clay minerals that settle to the ocean floors. However, even this water has not permanently vanished, for the sediments may be moved to orogenic belts and melted into magmas that return the water to the surface in the course of volcanic eruptions.

Chapter 7

THE HUMAN IMPACT ON THE WATERS

Deliberate modification of rivers

Although there are many ways in which humans influence water quantity and quality in rivers and streams-for example, by direct channel manipulation, modification of watershed characteristics, urbanization and pollution - the first of these is of particularly great importance (Mrowka, 1974). Indeed, there are a great variety of methods for direct channel manipulation and many of them have a long history. Perhaps that most widespread of these is the construction of dams and reservoirs. The first recorded dam was constructed in Egypt some 5000 years ago, but since that time the adoption of this technique has spead, whether to improve agriculture, to prevent floods, to generate power, or provide a reliable source of water. The construction of dams has increased markedly, especially between 1945 and 1971.

It is probable that around 700 dams are now being built worldwide each year, and dam-building has increased during the last half of the 1970s in several countries: Brazil, Republic of China (Petts, 1985). The estimate of the amount of stable runoff regulated by water reservirs in the continents of the world. The impact of human activities is especially marked in Africa and North America where about 20 per cent of the total runoff is now controlled by them. Stable runoff in this context is defined as river flow resulting largely from ground-water discharge.

One of the most striking features of dams and reservoirs is that they are becoming increasingly large. In the 1930s the Hoover or Boulder Dam in the USA (221m) was by far the tallest in the world. By the early 1980s it was exceeded in height by at least eighteen others. Of the eleven barrages over 5 km long only one, Forst Peck, USA, is more than 40 years old. A barrage at Kiev in the USSR is to be 41 km in length. Moreover, whereas Lake Mead, behind the Hoover Dam, was the largest in the world in 1936 with 38 billion m^3 of water, by the 1970s it was dwarfed. Kariba contained 160 billion m^3, Aswan's Lake Nasser contained 157 billion m^3, and Ghana's Akosombo 148 billion m^3 (Beckinsale, 1969).

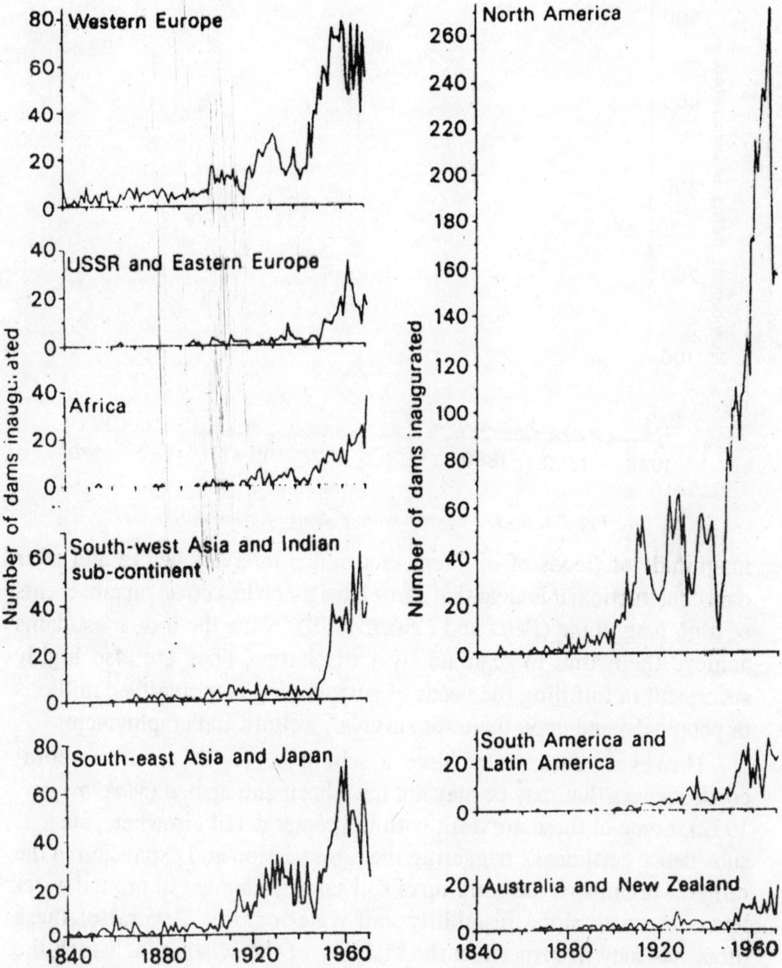

Fig. 7.1. (a) The construction of dams : for major regions.

Such large dams are capable of causing almost total regulation of the streams they impound, but in general the degree to which peak flows are reduced depends on the size of the dam and the impounded lake in relation to catchment characteristics. In Britain, peak flow reduction downstream from selected reservoirs varies considerably, with some tendency for the greatest degree of reduction to occur in those catchments where the reservoirs cover the largest percentage of the area. When considering the

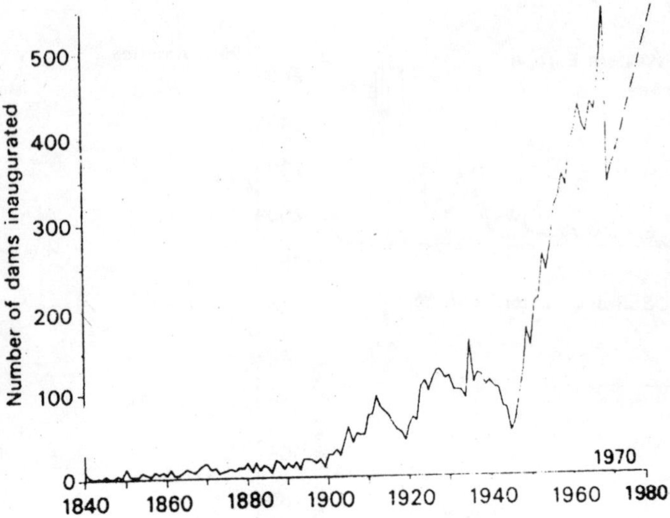

Fig. 7.1. (b) The construction of dams : for the world.

magnitude of floods of different recurrence intervals before and after dam construction, it is clear that dams have much less effect on rare events of high magnitude (*Petts* and *Lewin*, 1979). None the less, most dams achieve their aim: to regulate river discharge. They are also highly successful in fulfilling the needs of surrounding communities: millions of people depend upon them for survival, welfare and employment.

However, dams may have a whole series of environmental consequences that may or may not have been anticipated (*Makkaveyev*, 1972). Some of these are dealt with in greater detail elsewhere, such as subsidence earthquake triggering the transmission and expansion in the range of organisms the build-up of soil salinity changes in ground water levels creating slope instability and waterlogging. Several of these processes may in turn affect the viability of the scheme for which the dam was created.

A particularly important consequence of impounding a reservoir behind a dam is the reduction in the sediment load of the river downstream. A clear demonstration of this effect has been given for the South Saskatchewan River in Canada by *Rasid* (1979). During the pre-dam period, typified by 1962, the total annual suspended loads at Saskatoon and Lemsford Ferry were remarkably similar. As soon as the reservoir began to fill late in 1963, however, some of the suspended sediment began to be trapped, and the transitional period was marked by a progressive reduction in the proportion of sediment which reached Saskatoon. In the 4 years after the dam was fully operational the mean annual sediment load at Saskatoon was only 9 per cent that at Lemsford Ferry.

Table 7.1. Peak flow reduction downstream from selected British reservoirs

Reservoir	*% of catchment inundated*	*% of peak flow reduction*
Avon, Datmoor	1.38	16
Fernworthy, Dartmoor	2.80	28
Meldon, Dartmoor	1.30	9
Vynwy, mid-Wales	6.13	69
Sutton Bingham, Somerset	1.90	35
Blagdon, Mendip	6.84	51
Stocks, Forest of Bowland	3.70	70
Daer, Southern Uplands	4.33	56
Camps, Southern Uplands	3.13	41
Catcleugh, Cheviots	2.72	71
Ladybower, Peak District	1.60	42
Chew Magna, Mendips	8.33	73

Table 7.2. The ratio of post to pre-dam discharges for food magnitudes of selected frequency

	Recurrence interval (years)			
Reservoir	*1.5*	*2.3*	*5.0*	*10.0*
Avon, R, Avon	0.90	0.89	0.93	1.02
Stocks, R Hodder	0.83	0.86	0.84	0.95
Sutton Bingham, R. Yeo	0.52	0.61	0.69	0.79

Sediment retention is also well illustrated by the Nile both before and after the construction of the great Aswan High Dam. Until its construction the late summer and autumn period of high flow was characterized by high silt concentrations, but since it has been finished the silt load is rendered lower throughout the year and the seasonal peak is removed. *Petts* (1985, table XVIII) indicates that the Nile now only transports 8 per cent of its natural load below the Aswan High Dam, though this figure seems to be exceptionally low. Other rivers for which data are available carry between 8 and 50 per cent of their natural suspended loads below dams.

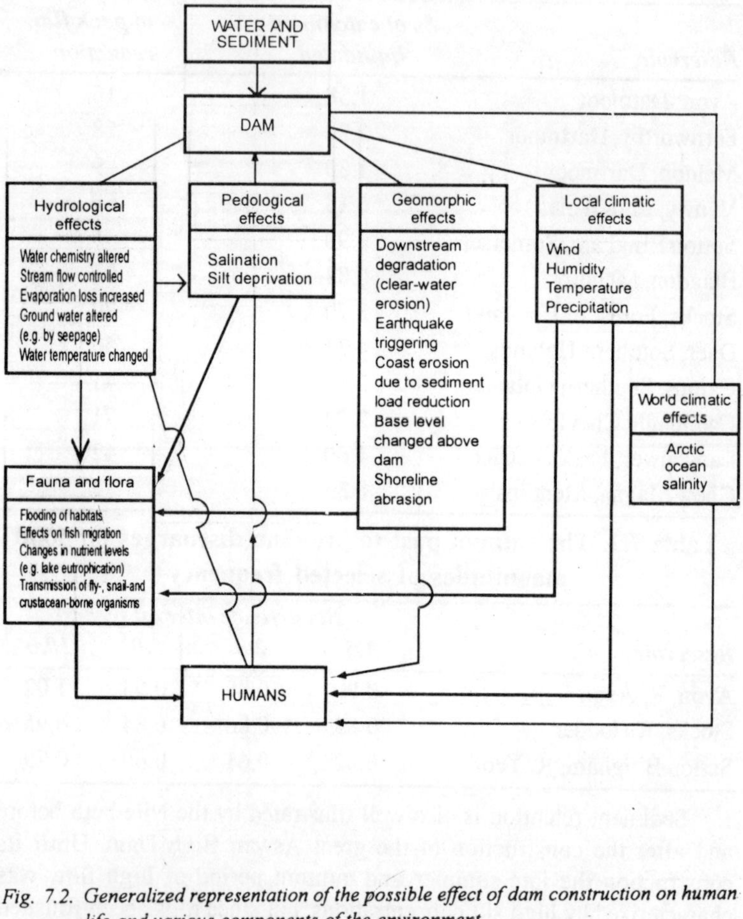

Fig. 7.2. Generalized representation of the possible effect of dam construction on human life and various components of the environment.

Sediment removal in turn has various possible consequences, including a reduction in flood-deposited nutrients on fields, less nutrients for fish in the south-cast Mediterranean Sea, accelerated erosion of the Nile Delta, and accelerated riverbed erosion since less sediment is available to cause bed aggradation. The last process is often called 'clear-water-erosion' (see *Beckinsale*, 1972), and in the case of the Hoover Dam it affected the river channel of the Colorado for 150 km downstream by causing incision. In turn such channel incision may initiate a rejuvenation of headward erosion in tributaries and may cause the lowering of ground-water tables and the undermining of bridge piers and other structures downstream of the dam. On the other hand, in regions such as northern China, where modern dams trap silt, the incision of the river channel downstream may alleviate the strain on levees and lessen the expense of levee strengthening or heightening.

Table 7.3. Total yearly suspended load (tons) of the South Saskatchewan River at Lemsford Ferry and Saskatoon, 1962–70

Period of record		*Lemsford Ferry*	*Saskatoon*	*Difference at Saskatoon (%)*
Pre-dam				
1962		1 813 305	1 873 278	+ 3
Transitional				
1963		4 892 159	446 788	– 8
1964		7 711 006	4 145 553	– 46
1965		9 731 837	2 721 021	– 72
1966		5 228 474	1 675 142	– 68
	Mean	6 890 869	3 254 626	– 53
Post-dam				
1967		12 618 814	445 967	– 96
1968		2 660 643	101 412	– 96
1969		10 562 413	2 146 496	– 80
1970		5 643 278	117 847	– 98
	Mean	7 871 287	702 930	– 91

However, clear-water-erosion does not always follow from silt retention in reservoirs. There are examples of rivers where, before impoundment, floods carried away the sediment brought in to the main stream by steep tributaries. Reduction of the peak discharge after the completion of the dam leaves some rivers unable to scour away the sediment that accumulates as large fans of sand or gravel below each tributary mouth (*Dunne* and *Leopold*, 1978). The bed of the main stream is raised and if water-intakes, towns or other structures lie alongisde the river they can be threatened again by flooding or channel shifting across the accumulating wedge of sediment. Rates of aggradation of a metre a year have been observed, and tens of kilometers of channel have been affected by sedimentation. One of the best documented cases of aggradation concerns the Colorado River below Glen Canyon Dam in the USA. Since dam closure the extremes of river flow have been largely eliminated so that the ten years' recurrence interval flood has been reduced to less than one-third. The main channel flow is no longer capable of removing sediment provided by flash-flooding tributaries, and deposits up to 2.6 m thick have accumulated within the upper Grand Canyon (*Petts*, 1985: 133).

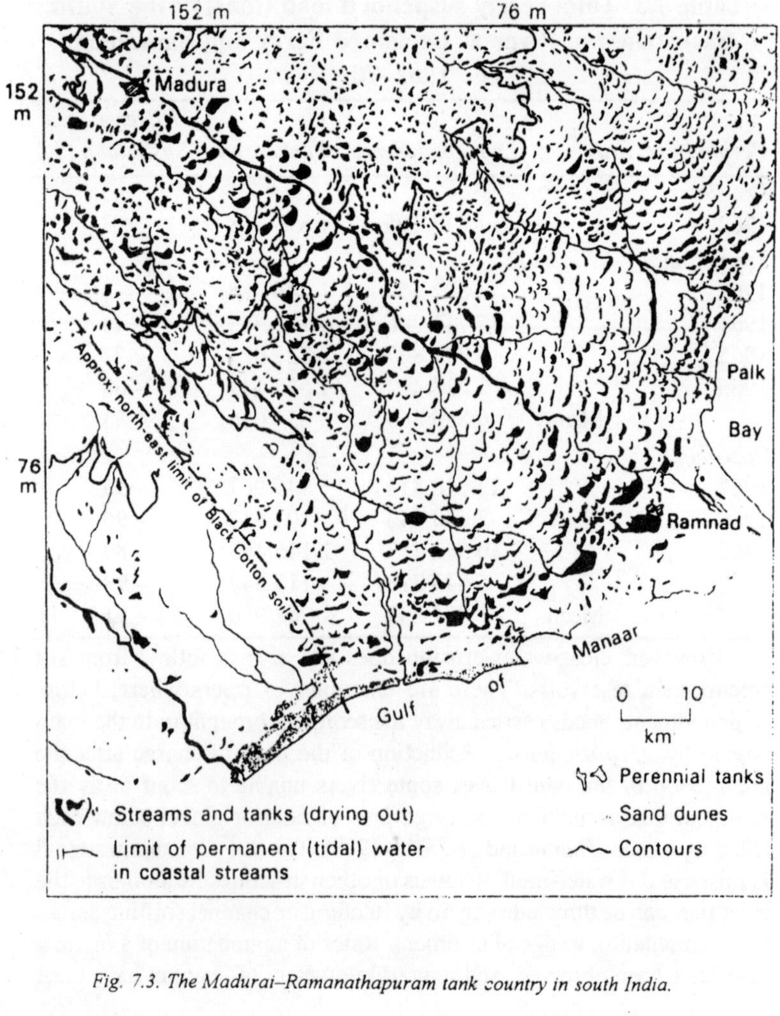

Fig. 7.3. The Madurai–Ramanathapuram tank country in south India.

Some landscapes in the world are dominated by dams, canals and reservoirs. Probably the most striking example of this is the 'tank' landscape of south-east India where myriads of little streams and areas of overland flow have been dammed by small earth structures to give what Spate (Spate and Learmonth, 1967: 778) has likened to 'a surface of vast overlapping fish-scales'.

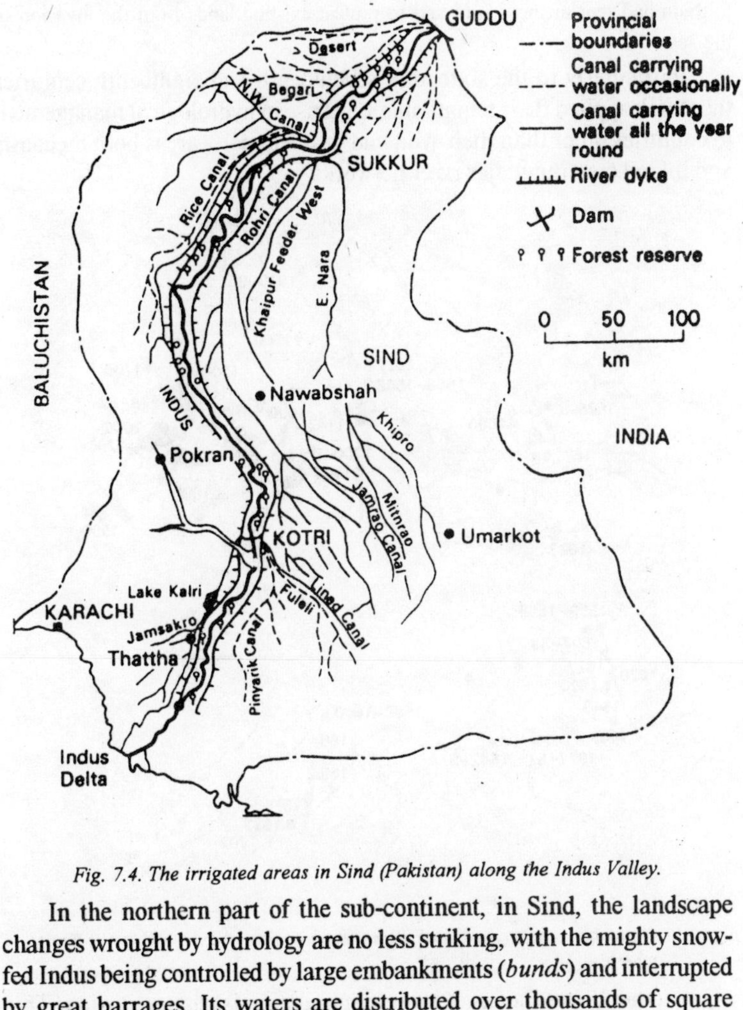

Fig. 7.4. The irrigated areas in Sind (Pakistan) along the Indus Valley.

In the northern part of the sub-continent, in Sind, the landscape changes wrought by hydrology are no less striking, with the mighty snow-fed Indus being controlled by large embankments (*bunds*) and interrupted by great barrages. Its waters are distributed over thousands of square kilometers by a canal network that has evolved over the past 4000 years.

Another landscape equally far-reaching changes have been wrought is the Netherlands. *Coates* (1976) has calculated that reclamation of that country from the sea, in the extension of drainage lines, involved, prior to 1860, the movement of 1000 million m³ of material. The area is dominated by human constructions: canals, rivers, drains and lakes. As *C.T. Smith* (1978: 506) has put it:

> It can be said of the Netherlands with more truth than of any other country that it is a creation of man, for it owes its existence to the long continued struggle to drain and reclaim new land and to protect existing lands from the invasion of the sea.

Particularly in the sixteenth, seventeenth and eighteenth centuries the Dutch applied their remarkable expertise in hydrological management to countries other than their won and drained many areas both on coasts and inland creating major river networks.

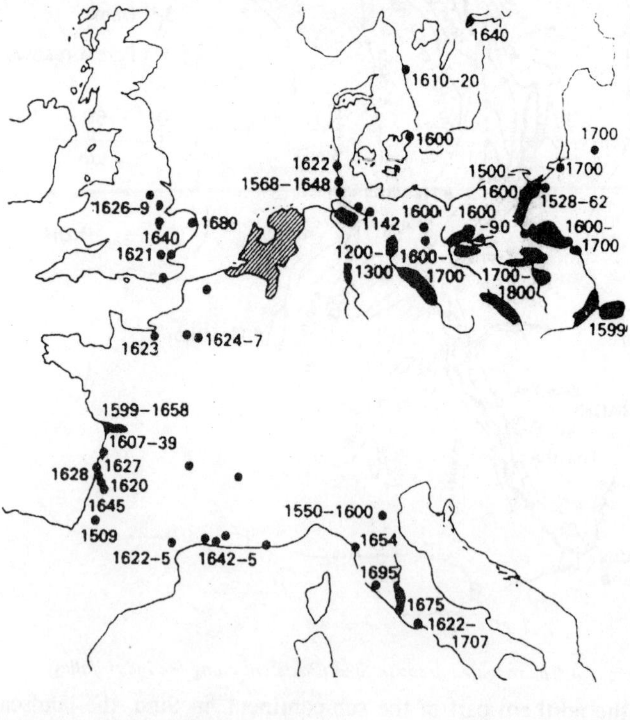

Fig. 7.5. Area where the great Dutch engineer were involved in wetland reclamation schemes.

Another direct means of river manipulation is channelization. This involves the construction of embankments, dikes, levees and floodwalls to confine floodwaters; and improving the ability of channels to transmit floods by enlarging their capacity through straightening, widening, deepening or smoothing.

Table 7.4. Selected terminologies for the methods of river channelization in the USA and UK.

American term	*British equivalent*	*Method involved*
Widening	Resectioning	Increase of channel capacity by manipulating width
Deepening	Resectioning	and/or depth variable
Straightening	Realigning	Increasing velocity of flow by Steepening the gradient
Diking	Embanking	Raising of channel banks to confine floodwaters
Bank stabilization	Bank protection	Methods to control bank erosion e.g. gabions and concrete structures
Clearing and snagging	Pioneer tree clearance Control of aquatic plants Dredging of sediments Urban clearing	Removal of obstructions from a watercourse, thereby decreasing the resistance and increasing the velocity of flow

Some of the great rivers of the world are now lined by extensive embankment systems such as those that run for more than 1000 km alongside the Nile, 7000 km along the Hwang Ho, 1400 km by the Red River in Vietnam, and over 4500 km in the Mississippi Valley (Ward, 1978). Like dams, embankments and related structures often fulfil their purpose but they may also create some environmental problems and have some disadvantages. For example, they reduce natural storage for floodwaters both by preventing water from spilling on to much of the floodplain, and by stopping bank storage in cases where impermeable floodwalls are used. Likewise the flow of water in tributaries may be constrained. In addition, embankments may occasionally exacerbate the flood problem they were designed to reduce by preventing floodwaters downstream of a breach from draining back into the channel once the peak has passed.

Channel improvement, designed to improve water flow, may also have unforseen or undesirable effects. For example, the more rapid movement of water along improved channel sections can aggravate flood peaks further downstream and cause excessive erosion. The lowering of water-tables in the 'improved' reach may cause over- drainage of adjacent agricultural land so that sluices must be constructed in the channel to maintain levels. On the other hand, lined channels may obstruct soil water movement (interflow) and shallow ground water and so cause surface saturation. *Brookes* (1985) and *Gregory* (1985) provide useful reviews on the impact of channelization.

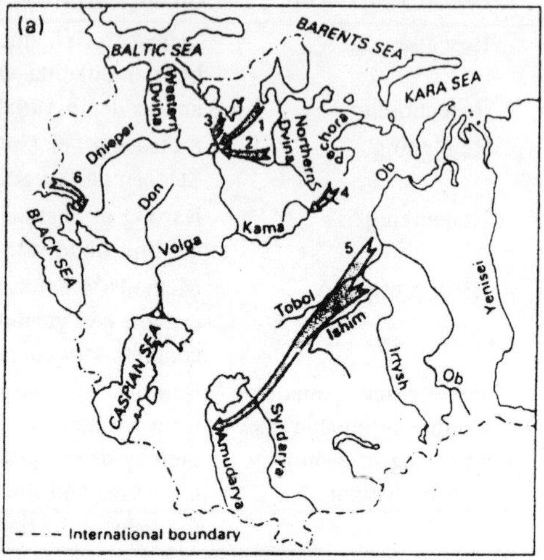

Fig. 7.6. (a) Some major schemes proposed for large-scale inter-basin water transfers : Projected water transfer system in the USSR. 1—from the Onega River, and in future from Onega Bay, 2—from the Sukhona and Northern Dvina Rivers, 3—from the Svir River and Lake Onega, 4—from the Pechora river, 5—from the Ob River, 6—from the Danube delta.

Channelization may also have miscellaneous effects on fauna through the increased velocities of water flow, reductions in the extent of shelter in the channel bed, and by reduced nutrient inputs due to the destruction of overhanging bank vegetation. In the case of large swamps, like those of the Sudd in Sudan or the Okavango in Botswana, the channelization of rivers could completely transform the whole character of the swamp environment. Illustrates some of the differences that exist between natural and artificial channels.

Another type of channel modification is produced by the construction of bypass and diversion channels to carry excess floodwater or to enable irrigation to take place. Such channels may be as old as irrigation itself. They may contribute to the salinity problems encountered in many irrigated areas.

Deliberate modification of a river regime can also be achieved by long-distance inter-basin water transfers (*Shiklomanov*, 1985), transfers necessitated by the unequal spatial distribution of water resources and by the increasing rates of water consumption. At present, the world water consumption for all human needs is 3500 km ^{3} y^{-1}: at the start of the century it was eight times less than this figure, and by the end of the century it is expected to be 6000 km^3 y^{-1}. The total volume of water in the various transfer systems in operation and under construction on a global scale is about 300 km^3 y^{-1}, with the largest countries in terms of volume of transfers being Canada, the USSR, the USA and India.

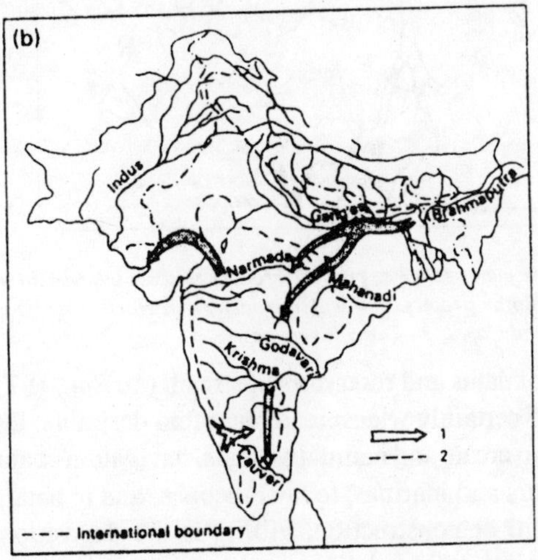

Fig. 7.6. (b) Some major schemes proposed for large-scale inter-basin water transfers : Projected systems for water transfers in India. 1—scheme of the national water network, 2—scheme of Grand Water Garland.

In future decades it is likely that many even greater schemes will be constructed route lengths of some hundreds of kilometres will be common, and the water balances of many rivers and lakes will be transformed. This is already happening in the USSR, where the operation of various anthropogenic activities of this type have caused runoff in the most intensely cultivated central and southern areas to decrease by 30-50 per cent compared to normal natural runoff. At the same time, inflows into the Caspian and Aral Seas have declined sharply, so that their levels have fallen and their areas decreased.

When one turns to the coastal portions of rivers, to estuaries, the possible effects of another human impact, dredging, can be as complex

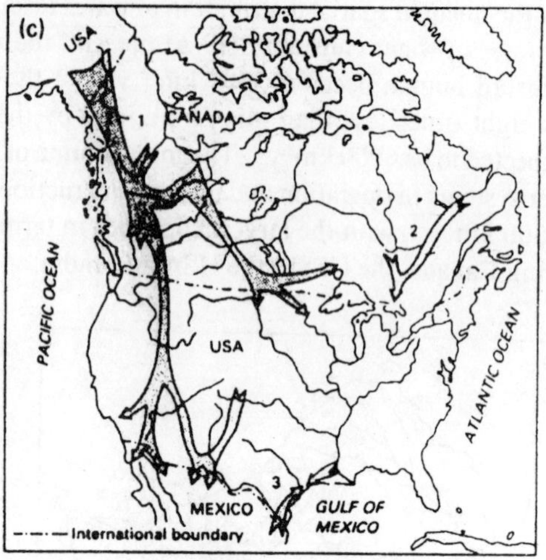

Fig. 7.6. (c) Some major schemes proposed for large-scale inter-basin water transfers : Some major projects for water transfers in North America. 1—NAWAPA, 2—Grand Canal, 3—Texas River, basins.

as the effects of dams and reservoirs upstream (*La Roe*, 1977). Dredging and filling are certainly widespread and often desirable. Dredging may be performed to create and maintain canals, navigation channels, turning basins, harbours and marinas; to lay pipelines; and to obtain a source of material for fill or construction. Filling is the deposition of dredged materials to create new land. There are miscellaneous ecological effects of such action. In the first place, filling directly disrupts habitats. Second, the generation of large quantities of suspended silt tends physically to smother bottom-dwelling plants and animals; tends to smother fish by clogging their gills; reduces photosynthesis through the effects of turbidity; and tends to lead to eutrophication by an increased nutrient release. Likewise, the destruction of marshes, mangroves and sea grasses by dredge and fill can result in the loss of these natural purifying systems. The removal of vegetation may also cause erosion. Moreover, as silt deposits stirred up by dredging accumulate elsewhere in the estuary they tend to create a 'false bottom'. Characterized by shifting, unstable sediments the dredged bottom, fill deposits or spoil areas are slowly - if at all - recolonized by fauna and flora. Furthermore, dredging tends to change the configuration of currents, the rate of fresh-water drainage and may provide avenues for salt-water intrusion.

Urbanization and its effects on river flow

The process of urbanization has a considerable hydrological impact, both in terms of controlling rates of erosion the delivery of pollutants to rivers and in terms of influencing the nature of runoff and other hydrological characteristics. An attempt to generalize some of these impacts using a historical model of urbanization is summarized usefully by *Savini* and *Kammerer* (1961) and reproduced.

Table 7.5. Stages of urban growth and their mescellaneous hydrological impacts

Stage	*Impact*
1. *Transition from pre-urban to early-urban stage :*	
(a) Removal of trees or vegetation	Decrease in transpiration and increase in strom flow
(b) Construction of scattered houses with limited sewerage and water facilities	
(c) Drilling of wells	Some lowering of water-table
(d) Construction of septic tansks, etc.	Some increase in soil moisture and perhaps some contamination
2. *Transition from early-urban to middle-urban stage :*	
(a) Bulldozing of land	Accelerated and erosion
(b) Mass construction of houses, etc.	Decreased infiltration
(c) Discontinued use and abandonment of some shallower wells	Rise in water-table
(d) Diversion of nearby streams for public supply	Decrease in runoff between points of diversion and disposal
(e) Untreated or inadequately treated sewerage into streams and wells	Pollution of streams and wells
3. *Transition from middle-urban to late-urban stage :*	
(a) Urbanization of area completed by addition of more buildings	Reduced infiltration and lowered water-table; higher flood peaks and lower low flows
(b) Larger quantities of untreated waste into local streams	Increased pollution
(c) Abandonment of remaining shallow wells because of pollution	Rise in water-table
(d) Increase in population requiring establishment of new water supply and distribution systems	Increase in local stream flow if supply is from outside basin

(e) Channels of streams restricted at least in part to artificial channels and tunnels	Higher stage for a given flow (therefore increased flood damage); changes in channel geometry and sediment load
(f) Construction of sanitary drainage system and treatment plant for sewage	Removal of additional water from area
(g) Improvement of strom drainage system	
(h) Drilling of deeper, large-capacity industrial wells	Lowered water pressure, some subsidence, salt-water encroachment
(i) Increased use of water for air-conditioning	Overloading of sewers and other drainage facilities
(j) Drilling of recharge wells	Raising of water-pressure surface
(k) Waste-water reclamation and utilization	Recharge to ground-water aquifers; more efficient use of water resources

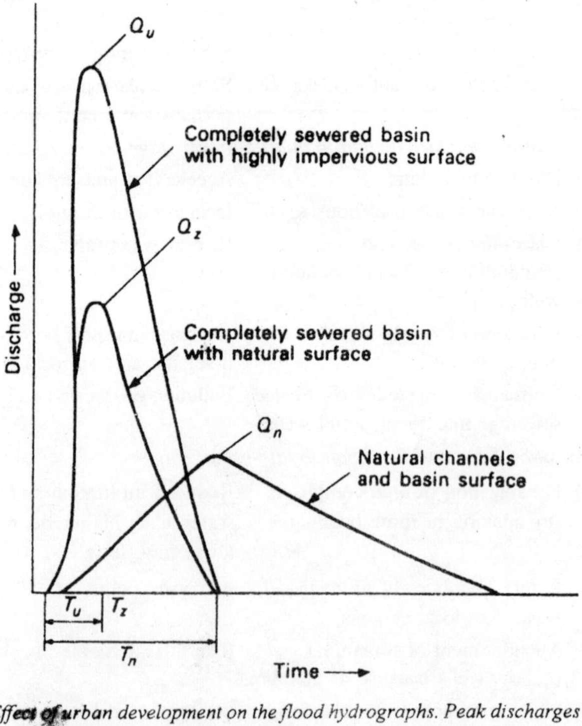

Fig. 7.7. Effect of urban development on the flood hydrographs. Peak discharges (Q) are higher and occur sooner after runoff starts (T) in basins that have been developed or sewered.

One of the most important effects is the way in which urbanization affects flood runoff. Research both in the United States and in Britain has shown that because urbanization produces extended impermeable surfaces of tarmac, tiles and concrete, so there is a tendency for flood runoff to increase in comparison with rural sites. City drainage densities may be greater than those in natural conditions (*Graf*, 1977) and the installation of sewers and storm drains accelerates runoff, as illustrated. The greater the area that is sewered the greater is the discharge for a particular recurrence level. Peak discharge are higher and occur sooner after runoff starts in basins that have been affected by urbanization and the installation of sewers. Some runoff may be generated in urban areas because low vegetation densities mean that evapotranspiration is limited.

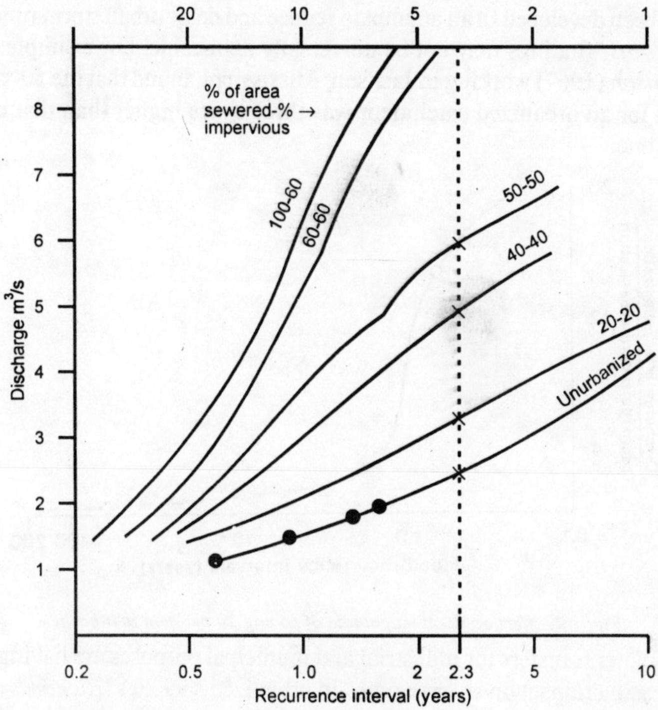

Fig. 7.8. Flood frequency curves for a 1 square mile basin in various states of urbanization.

However, in many cases the effect of urbanization is greater on small floods; as the size of the flood and its recurrence interval increase, so the effect of urbanization diminishes (*Martens*, 1968; *Hollis*, 1975). A probable explanation for this is that, during a severe and prolonged storm event, a non-urbanized catchment may become so saturated and its channel network so extended that it begins to behave hydrologically as if it were an impervious catchment with a dense surface-water drain network. Under these conditions, a rural catchment produces floods of a type and size similar to those of its urban counterpart. Moreover, a further mechanism probably operates in the same direction, for in an urban catchment it seems probable that some throttling of flow occurs in surface-water drains during intense storms, tending to attenuate the very highest discharges. Thus, *Hollis* believes, whilst the size of small frequent floods is increased many times by urbanization, large, rare floods (the ones likely to cause extreme damage) are not significantly affected by the construction of suburban areas within a catchment area. None the less, a whole series of techniques have been developed in an attempt to reduce and delay urban storm runoff, for *Hollis'* findings may not be universally applicable. For example, *K. V. Wilson* (1967) working in Jackson, Mississippi, found that the 50-year flood for an urbanized catchment was three times higher than that of a rural one.

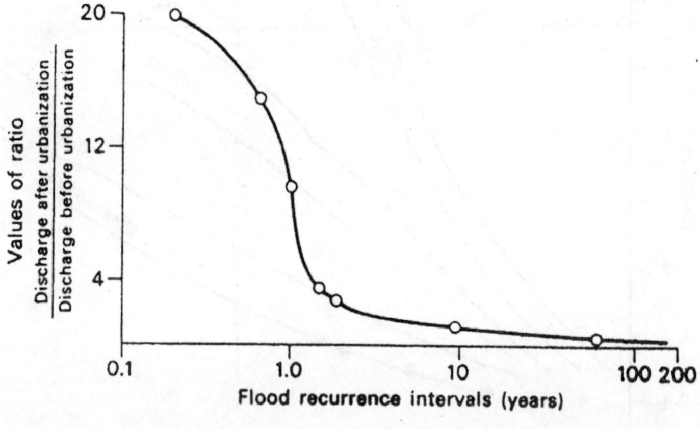

Fig. 7.9. Effect on flood magnitude of paving 20 per cent of a basin.

Water transfers for industrial and municipal purposes are having an increasing impact on river regimes in urbanized societies (*Richards* and *Wood*, 1977). Under dry weather flow conditions, stream flow in urban catchments in the Midlands and south-east England is mainly imported water. This is illustrated by the River Tame which contains about 90 per cent effluent in its 95 per cent duration flow. This proportion is increasing as more water is imported reduced in quality and added to low natural base-flows reduced by lack of recharge.

Table 7.6. Measures for reducing and delaying urban strom runoff

Area	*Reducing runoff*	*Delaying runoff*
Large flat roof	Cistern storage Rooftop gardens Pool storage or fountain storage Sod roof cover	Ponding on roof by constricted drainpipes Increasing roof roughness 1. rippled roof 2. gravelled roof
Car parks	Porous pavement 1. gravel car parks 2. porous or punctured asphalt Concrete vaults and cisterns beneath car parks in high value area Vegetated ponding areas around car parks Gravel trenches	Grassy strips on car parks Grassed waterways draining car parks Ponding and detention measures for impervious areas 1. rippled pavement 2. depressions 3. basins
Residential	Cisterns for individual homes or groups of homes Gravel drives (porous) Contoured landscape Ground-water recharge 1. perforated pipe 2. gravel (sand) 3. trench 4. poroush pipe 5. dry wells Vegetated depressions	Reservoir or detention basin Planting a high-delaying grass (high roughness) Grassy gutters or channels Increased length of travel of runoff by means of gutters, diversions and so on
General	Gravel alleys Porous pavements	Gravel alleys

Deforestation and its effect on river flow

As we have already noted one of the first major indications that humans could inadvertently adversely affect the environment was the observation that deforestation could create torrents and floods. The deforestation that gives rise to such flows can be produced both by felling and by fire.

The first experimental study, in which a planned land-use change was executed to enable observation of the effects of stream flow, began

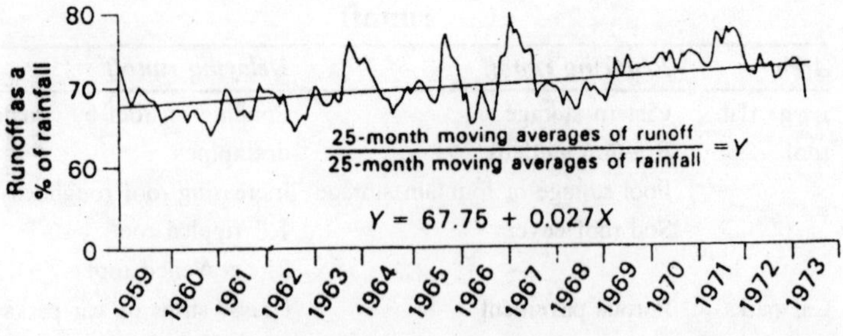

Fig. 7.10. Trends in 25-month moving averages of runoff as a percentage of 25-month moving averages of rainfall for the River Tame, Lee Marston, England, 1957–74. The trend reflects increasing amounts of imported 'runoff'.

at Wagon Wheel Gap, Colorado, in 1910 (*Pereira*, 1973). Here stream flow from two similar watersheds of about 80 hectares each were compared for 8 years. One valley was then clear-felled and the records were continued. After the clear-felling the annual water yield was 17 per cent above that predicted from the flows of the unchanged control valley. Peak flows are also increased. Studies on two small basins in the Australian

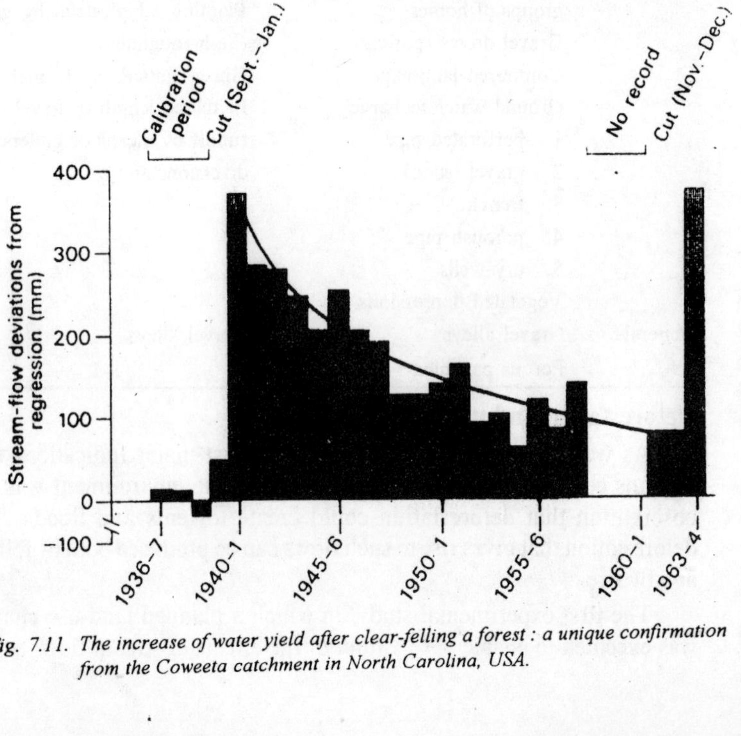

Fig. 7.11. The increase of water yield after clear-felling a forest : a unique confirmation from the Coweta catchment in North Carolina, USA.

Alps (Wallace's Creek - 41 km ^{2} and Yarrango Billy River - 224 km^2), which were burned over, showed that rain storms, which from previous records would have been expected to give rise to flows of 60-80 m^3 s^{-1} produced a peak of 370 m ^{3} s^{-1} (a five- or sixfold increase). Likewise catchment experiments in Arizona have shown that when chaparral scrub is burned there is a tenfold increase in water yield.

As vegetation regenerates after a forest has been cut or burned, so stream flow tends to revert to normal, though the process may take some decades. This is illustrated which shows the dramatic effects produced on the Coweeta catchments in North Carolina by two spasms of clear-felling, together with the gradual return to normality in between.

The substitution of one forest type for another may also affect stream flow. This can again be exemplified from the Coweeta catchments, where two experimental catchments were converted from a mature deciduous hardwood forest cover to a cover of white pine (*Pinus strobus*). Fifteen years after the conversion, annual stream flow was found to be reduced by about 20 per cent (*Swank* and *Douglass*, 1974). The reason for this notable change is that the interception and subsequent evaporation of rainfall is greater for pine than it is for hardwoods during the dormant season.

The reasons why the removal of a forest cover and its replacement with pasture, crops or bare ground have such important effects on stream flow are many. A mature forest probably has a higher rainfall interception rate, a tendency to reduce rates of overland flow, and probably generates soils with a higher infiltration capacity and better general structure. All these factors will tend to produce both a reduction in overall runoff levels and less extreme flood peaks. However, with careful management the replacement of forest by other land-use types need not be detrimental either in terms of sediment loss or flood generation. In Kenya, for example, the tea plantations with shade trees, protective grass covers, and carefully designed culverts were found to be 'a hydrologically effective substitute' for natural forest (*Pereira*, 1973: 127).

In many studies the runoff from clean-tilled land tends to be greater than that from areas under a dense crop cover, but tilling the soil surface does not always increase runoff (*Gregory* and *Walling*, 1973: 345). There are reports from the USSR suggesting that the reverse may be the case, and that autumn ploughing can decrease surface runoff, presumably because of its effect on surface detention and on soil structure.

Grazing practices also influence runoff, for heavy grazing can both compact the soil and cause vegetation removal. In general it tends to lead to an increase in runoff.

Changes in river-bank vegetation may have a particularly strong influence on river flow. In the south-west USA, for instance, many streams are lined by the salt cedar (*Tamarix pentandra*). With roots either in the water-table or freely supplied by the capillary fringe, these shrubs have full potential transpiration opportunity. The removal of such vegetation can cause large increases in stream flow. It is interesting to note that the salt cedar itself is an alien, native to Eurasia, which was introduced by humans. It has spread explosively in the south-west USA, increasing from about 4000 hectares in 1920 to almost 400 000 hectares in the early 1960s (*Harris*, 1966). In the Upper Rio Grande valley in New Mexico, the salt cedar was introduced to try and combat anthropogenic soil erosion, but it spread so explosively that it came to consume approximately 45 per cent of the area's total available water (*Hay*, 1973).

Reforestation of abandoned farmlands reverses the effects of deforestation: increased interception and evapotranspiration can cause a decline in water yield. In parts of the eastern USA, farm abandonment and recolonization of the land by pines, spruce and cedar has been occurring throughout the twentieth century, and this has reduced stream flow by important amounts at a time when water supplies for some eastern cities were becoming critically short (*Dunne* and *Leopold*, 1978).

A process which is often associated with afforestation is peat drainage. The hydrological effects of this are the subject of controversy, since there are cases of both increased and decreased flood peaks after drainage. It has been suggested that differences in peat type alone might account for the different effects. Thus it is conceivable that the drainage of a *Sphagnum* catchment would lead to increased flooding since *Sphagnum* compacts with drainage, reducing its storage volume and its permeability. On the other hand, in the case of non-*Sphagnum* peat there would be relatively less change in structure, but there would be a reduction in moisture content and an increase in storage capacity, thereby tending to reduce flood flows. The nature of the peat is, however, but one feature to consider (*Robinson*, 1979). The intensity of the drainage works (depth, spacing, etc.) may also be important. In any case, there may be two (sometimes conflicting) processes operating as a result of peat drainage: the increased drainage network will facilitate rapid runoff, and the drier soil conditions will provide greater storage for rainfall. Which of these two tendencies is dominant will depend on local catchment conditions.

It is not always easy to determine whether an increase in flood frequency or intensity is the result of land-use changes of the type we have been discussing, or whether some natural changes in rainfall have played a role. In central and south Wales there is some clear evidence of changes in flood magnitude and frequency over recent decades, and this has sometimes been attributed to the increasing amount of afforestation that has been carried out since the First World War, and to the drainage of upland areas that this has necessitated. While in the Severn catchment this appears to be a partial explanation (*Howe* et al., 1967), in other basins the main cause of more frequent and intense floods appears to have been a marked increase in the magnitude and frequency of heavy daily rainfalls. For example, in the case of the Tawe valley near Swansea, of 17 major floods since 1875, 14 occurred from 1929-81 and only 3 during the 1875-1928 period. Of 22 notable widespread heavy rainfalls in the Tawe catchment since 1875, only two occurred from 1875-1928, but 20 from 1929-1981 (*Walsh* et al., 1982).

The human impact on lake levels

One of the results of human modification of river regimes is that lake levels have suffered some change, though it is not always possible to distinguish between the part played by humans and that played by natural climatic changes.

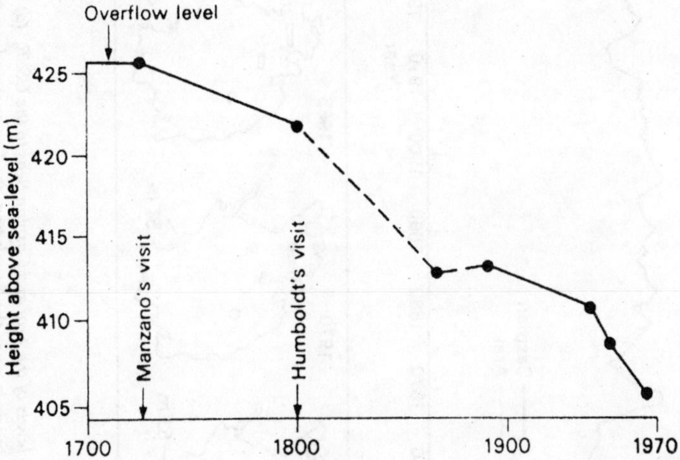

Fig. 7.12. Variations in the level of Lake Valencia, Venezuela, to 1968.

A lake basin for which there are particularly long records of change is the Valencia Basin in Venezuela (*Bockh*, 1973). It was the declining level of the waters in this lake which so struck the great German geographer, von Humboldt, in 1800. He recorded its level as being about

422 m above sea-level, and some previous observations on its level were made by Manzano in 1727, which established it as being at 426 m. The 1968 level was about 405 m, representing a fall of no less than 21 m in

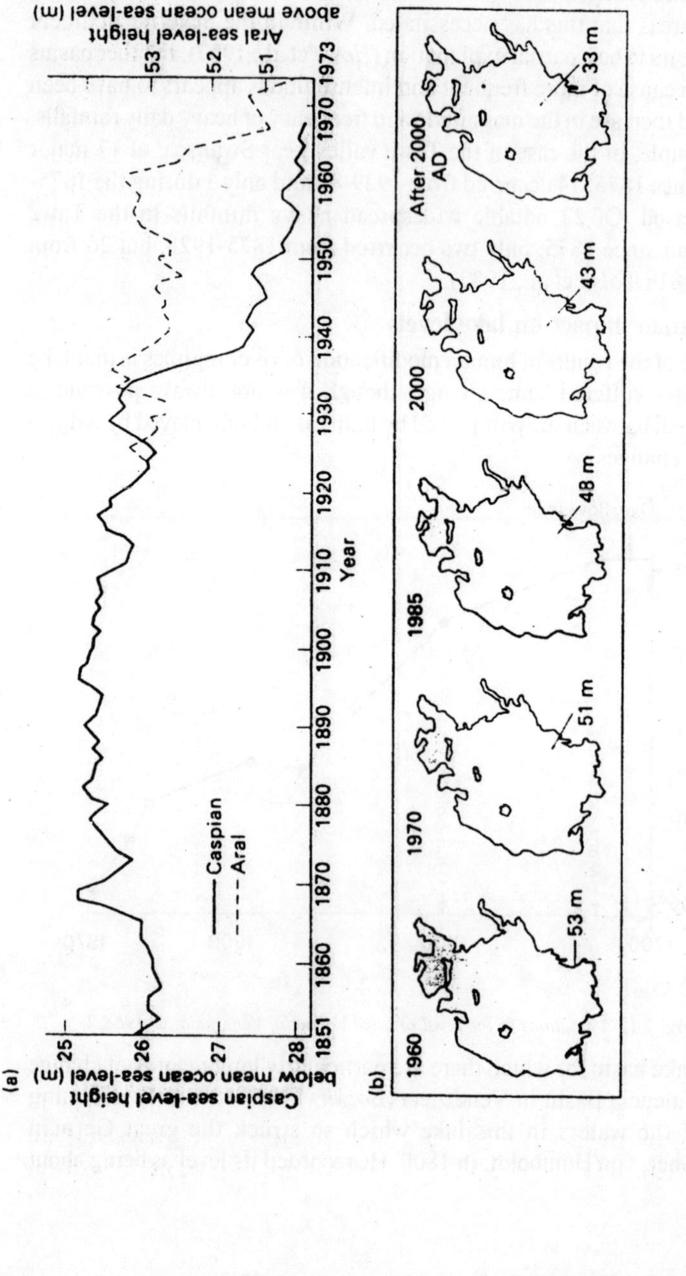

Fig. 7.13. The changing levels of the Aral and Caspian Seas in the USSR. (a) The nature of the changes until 1973, illustrating the very rapid decline in levels since the Revolution. (b) The past and predicted contraction of the Aral Sea as its level falls.

about 240 years. Humboldt believed that the cause of the declining level was the deforestation brought about by humans, and this has been supported by *Bockh* (1973), who points also to the abstraction of water for irrigation. This remarkable fall in level meant that the lake ceased to have an overflow into the River Orinoco. It has as a consequence become subject to a build-up in salinity, and is now eight times more saline than it was two and a half centuries ago.

Even the world's largest lake, the Caspian, has been modified by human activities. The most important change has been the fall of 3 m in its level since 1929. This decline is undoubtedly partly the product of climatic change (*Micklin*, 1972), for winter precipitation in the northern Volga Basin, the chief flow- generating area of the Caspian, has been generally below normal since 1930 because of a reduction in the number of moist cyclones penetrating into the Volga Basin from the Atlantic. None the less, human actions have contributed to this fall, particularly since the 1950s because of reservoir formation, irrigation, municipal and industrial withdrawals, and agricultural practices. In addition to the fall of level, salinity in the northern Caspian has increased by 30 per cent since the early 1930s. A secondary effect of the changes in level has been a decline in fish numbers due to the disappearance of the shallows. These are biologically the most productive zones of the lake, providing a food base for the more valuable types of fish and also serving as spawning grounds for some species. There are plans to divert some water from northward-flowing rivers in Siberia towards the Volga to corect the decline in Caspian levels, but the possible climatic impacts of such action have caused some concern.

Similar declines in inflow to those evident in the Caspian apply to the Sea of Azov (*Mote* and *Zumrunne*, 1977). The reduction of fresh-water inputs from inflowing rivers has permitted an increase in the ingress of saline water from the Black Sea. Salinity has increased at the rate of 30-40 per cent in 5 years in the early 1970s. As a consequence, the valuable sturgeon and carp fisheries have declined, while the numbers of unwelcome stinging Black Sea jellyfish have multiplied.

Water abstraction from the Jordan River for irrigation purposes has caused a decline in the level of the Dead Sea. Under natural conditions, fresh water from the Jordan constantly fed the less salty layer of the sea which occupied roughly the top 40 m of the 320 m deep body of water. Because the amount of water entering the lake via the Jordan was more or less equal to the quantity lost by evaporation, the lake maintained its stable, stratified state, with less salty water resting on the waters of higher salinity. However, with the recent human-induced diminution in Jordan discharge, the sea's upper layer has receded because of the intense levels of evaporation. Its salinity has approached that of the older and deeper waters. It has now been established that as a consequence the layered structure has collapsed, creating a situation where there is increased precipitation of salts. Moreover, now that circulating waters carry oxygen to the bottom, the characteristic hydrogen-sulphide smell has largely disappeared (*Maugh*, 1979).

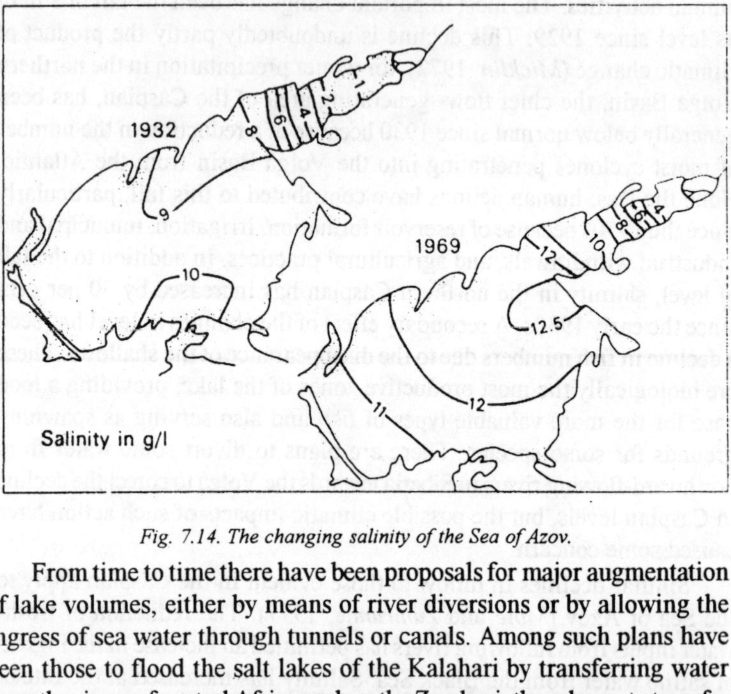

Fig. 7.14. The changing salinity of the Sea of Azov.

From time to time there have been proposals for major augmentation of lake volumes, either by means of river diversions or by allowing the ingress of sea water through tunnels or canals. Among such plans have been those to flood the salt lakes of the Kalahari by transferring water from the rivers of central Africa such as the Zambezi; the scheme to transfer Mediterranean water to the Dead Sea and to the Quattara Depression; and the Zaire-Chad scheme. Perhaps the most ambitious idea has been the so-called 'Atlantropa' project, whereby the Mediterranean would be empoldered, a dam built at the Straits of Gibraltar, and water fed into the new lake from the Zaire River (*Cathcart*, 1983).

Changes in ground-water conditions

In many parts of the world humans obtain water supplies by pumping from ground water (see, for example, *Drennan*, 1979). This has two main effects: the reduction in the levels of water-tables and the replacement, in coastal areas, of fresh water by salt water. Environmental consequences of these two phenomena include ground subsidence and soil salinization. Increasing population levels and the adoption of new exploitation techniques (for example, the replacement of irrigation methods involving animal or human power by electric and diesel pumps) has increased these problems.

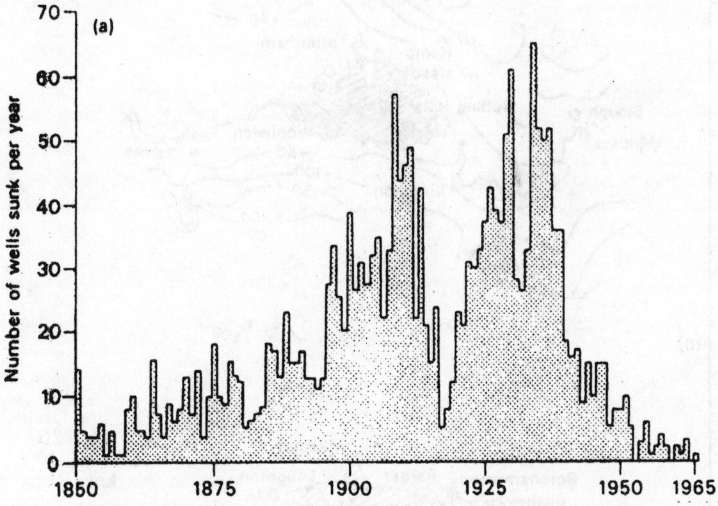

Fig. 7.15. (a) Changing ground-water conditions in the London area : construction of wells tapping the confined aquifer below London (1850–1965).

Some of the reductions in ground-water levels that have been caused by abstraction are considerable. A shows the rapid increase in the number of wells tapping ground water in the London area from 1850 until the Second World War, while figure illustrate the widespread and substantial changes in ground-water conditions that resulted. The piezometric surface in the confined chalk aquifer has fallen by more than 60 m over hundreds of square kilometres. Likewise, beneath Chicago, Illinois, pumping since the late nineteenth century has lowered the piezometric head by some 200 m.

The reduction in water levels that are taking place in the High Plains of Texas are some of the most serious, and threaten the long-term viability of irrigated agriculture in that area. Before irrigation development started in the 1930s, the High Plains ground-water system was in a state of dynamic equilibrium, with long-term recharge equal to long-term

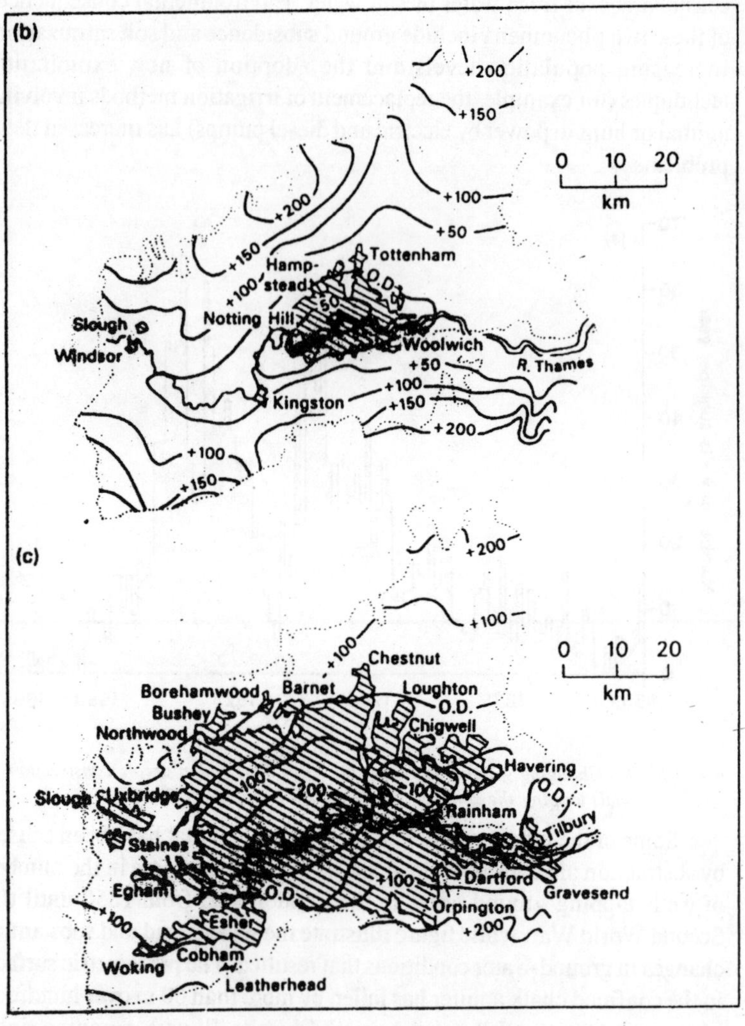

Fig. 7.15. (b) Changing ground-water conditions in the London area : ground-water contours in 1875, (c) ground-water contour in 1965.

discharge. However, the ground-water is now being mined at a rapid rate to supply centre-pivot and other schemes. In a matter of only fifty years or less, the water level has declined by 30 to 50 m in a large area to the north of Lubbock. The thickness of the aquifer has decreased more than 50 per cent in large parts of Castro, Crosby, Floyd, Hale, Lubbock, Parmer and Swisher counties, and already a decrease in the area irrigated by each well is taking place as a consequence of decreasing well yields (*The Gross Section*, Lubbock, 1982:1).

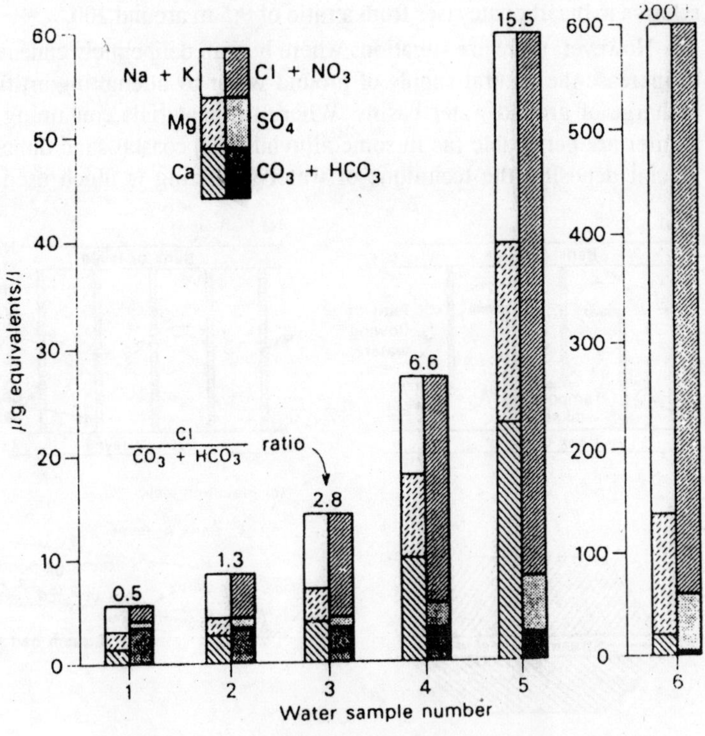

Sample number	Description
1	Normal good ground water in aquifer
2	Slightly contaminated ground water
3	Moderately contaminated ground water
4	Injuriously contaminated ground water
5	Highly contaminated ground water (near sea-shore)
6	Sea water

Fig. 7.16. Evidence of salt-water intrusion exemplified by chemical analyses of a line of well-waters from the Salinas valley, California, extending from the centre of the aquifer to the coast. Chloride— bicarbonate ratios are shown above each quality diagram.

The chemical changes in ground-water quality brought about by sea-water incursion may also be considerable. An example from the Salinas

Valley of California' is shown. The most notable feature, apart from the general overall increase in the total dissolved solids content by approximately tenfold, is the change in the ratio of chloride to bicarbonate. As the coast is approached, as one might expect, the quantity of chloride relative to bicarbonate rises from a ratio of 0.5 to around 200.

However, there are situations where human deliberately endeavour to increase the natural supply of ground water by attempting artificial recharge of ground-water basins. Where the materials containing the aquifer are permeable (as in some alluvial fans, coastal sand dunes or glacial deposits) the technique of water-spreading is much used. In

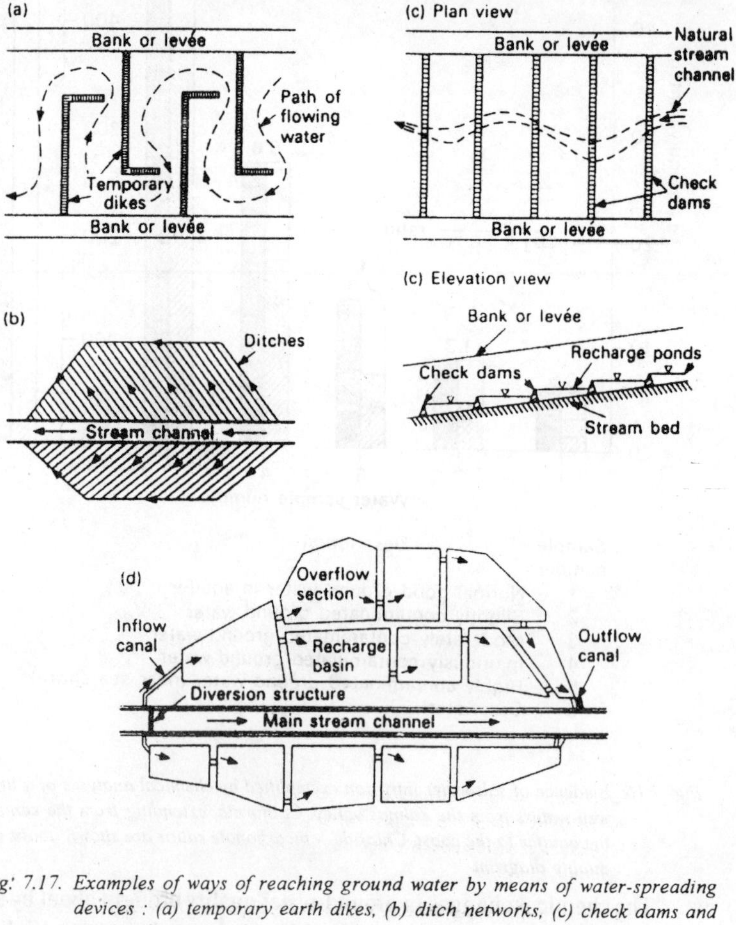

Fig.' 7.17. Examples of ways of reaching ground water by means of water-spreading devices : (a) temporary earth dikes, (b) ditch networks, (c) check dams and ponds, (d) connected recharge basins adjoining a stream channel.

relatively flat areas river water may be diverted to spread evenly over the ground so that infiltration takes place. Alternative water-spreading methods may involve releasing water into basins which are formed by excavation, or by the construction of dikes or small dams. On alluvial plains water can also be encouraged to percolate down to the water-table by distributing it to a series of ditches or furrows. In some situations natural channel infiltration can be promoted by building small check dams down a stream course. In irrigated areas surplus water can be spread by irrigating with excess water during the dormant season. When artificial ground-water recharge is required in sediments with impermeable layers such water-spreading techniques are not effective and the appropriate method may then be to pump water into deep pits or into wells. This last technique is used on the coastal plain of Israel, both to replenish the ground-water reservoirs when surplus irrigation water is available, and to attempt to diminish the problems associated with salt-water intrusion.

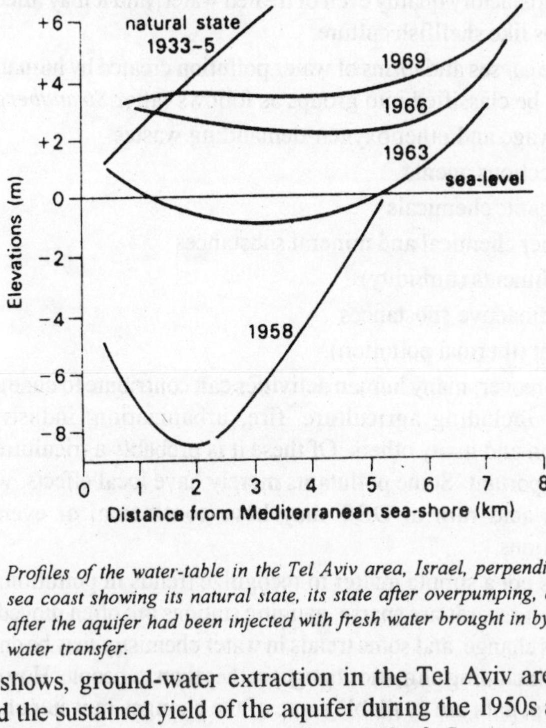

Fig. 7.18. Profiles of the water-table in the Tel Aviv area, Israel, perpendicular to the sea coast showing its natural state, its state after overpumping, and its state after the aquifer had been injected with fresh water brought in by inter-basin water transfer.

As shows, ground-water extraction in the Tel Aviv area greatly exceeded the sustained yield of the aquifer during the 1950s and water levels declined below sea-level over about 60 km². Sea-water intrusion became a problem. Completion of a new inter- basin water transfer scheme in the mid-1960s allowed the injection of fresh water into a line of wells 8 km long, in an attempt to provide a fresh-water 'barrier' along the coast. Other boreholes were injected to the landward of this 'barrier' to help fill the aquifer that had been depressed by over-pumping. This operation proved to be effective almost immediately (*Mandel*, 1977), and by 1969 the situation had definitely stabilized.

Water pollution

Water pollution is not new. During the reign of King George III a Member of Parliament reportedly wrote a letter to the Prime Minister complaining about the odour and appearance of the Thames. He wrote the letter, it is said, not with ink, but with water from the Thames itself (*Strandberg*, 1971).

Water pollution is frequently undesirable: it causes disease transmission through infection; it may poison humans and animals; it may create objectionable odours and unsightliness; it may be the cause of the unsatisfactory quality even of treated water; and it may affect economic activities like shellfish culture.

The causes and forms of water pollution created by humans are many and can be classified into groups as follows (after *Strandberg*, 1971):

1. Sewage and other oxygen-demanding wastes
2. Infectious agents
3. Organic chemicals
4. Other chemical and mineral substances
5. Sediments (turbidity)
6. Radioactive substances
7. Heat (thermal pollution).

Moreover, many human activities can contribute to changes in water quality, including agriculture, fire, urbanization, industry, mining, irrigation and many others. Of these it is probably agriculture that is the most important. Some pollutants merely have local effects, while others such as acid rain or DDT may have continental or even planetary implications.

It is not a simple matter to recognize trends in pollution. In general long-term records are sparse, gauging stations are often moved, analytical methods change, and some trends in water chemistry may be due to natural factors (including climatic change) rather than to people. However, where long-term data are available some of the changes in water chemistry are striking. In their study of the information collated on Lake Michigan, the Mississippi river, the Ohio River and the Illinois River, *Ackerman et al.*,

(1970) found that since the start of the twentieth century dissolved solids concentrations had risen markedly. For chlorides the increase has varied from 100 per cent in 52 years to 300 per cent in 70 years, while for sulphates it has increased from 80 per cent in 43 years to 155 per cent in 62 years.

It is also plainly not a simple matter to try and estimate the global figure for the extent of water pollution caused by humans. For one thing we know too little about the natural long-term levels of dissolved materials in the world's rivers. None the less, recent studies do give some general indication of the extent of the human impact. *Meybeck* (1979), for instance, has calculated that about 500 million tonnes of dissolved salts reach the oceans each year as a result of human activity. These inputs have increased by more than 30 per cent the natural values for sodium, chloride and sulphate, and have created an overall global augmentation of river mineralization by about 12 per cent.

Chemical pollution by agriculture and other activities

As has already been stated, agriculture may be one, if not the most, important cause of pollution, either by the production of sediments or by the generation of chemical wastes (Ministry of Agriculture, Fisheries and

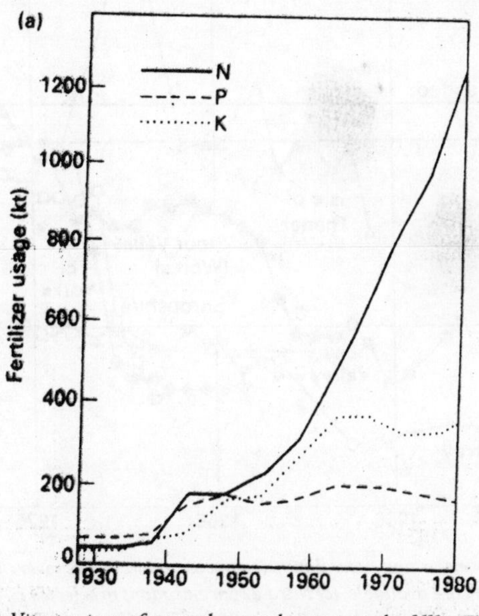

Fig. 7.19. (a) Nitrates in surface and ground waters in the UK : The trends in annual fertilizer usage in the UK during the period 1928–80.

Food, 1976). With regard to the latter, it has been suggested that denitrification processes in the environment are incapable of keeping pace with the rate at which atmospheric nitrogen is being mobilized through industrial fixation processes and being introduced into the biosphere in the form of commercial fertilizers (*Manners*, 1978). Nitrogen, with phosphorus, tends to regulate the growth of aquatic plants and therefore the eutrophication of inland waters. Excess nitrates can also cause health hazards to humans and animals, including methaemo-globinaemia in infants.

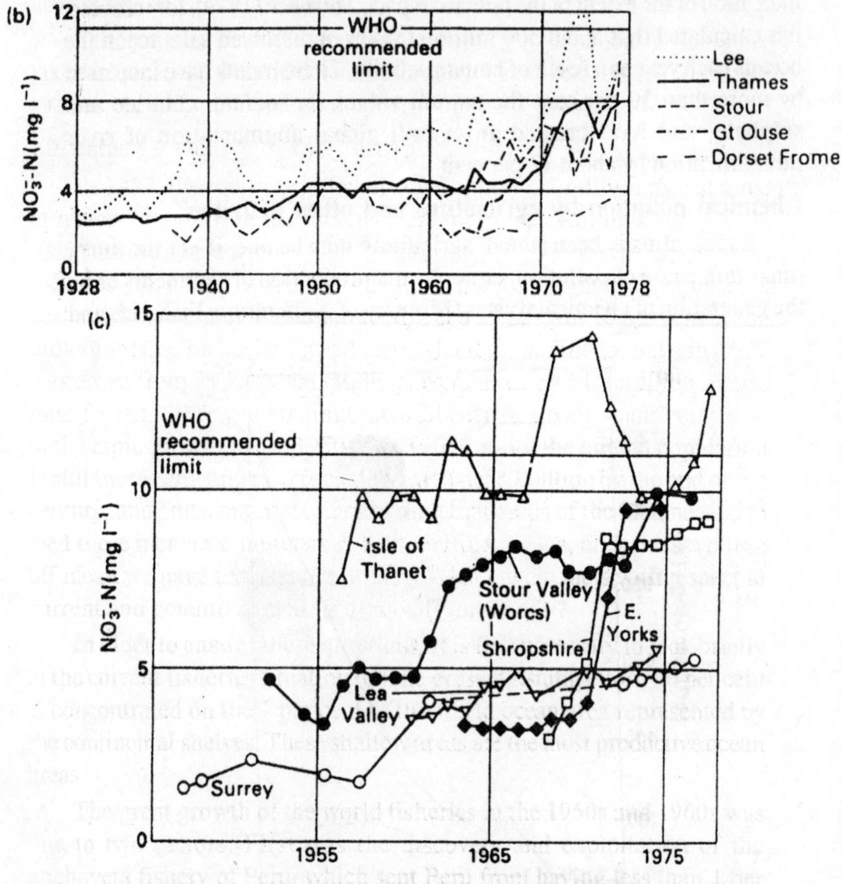

Fig. 7.19. (b) Trends in mean and annual nitrate concentration in five rivers for which long-term data are available. (c) Nitrate concentrations in selected public water supply abstraction boreholes in the Chalk and Triassic sandstone aquifers of the UK.

Eutrophication is the enrichment of waters by nutrients. The process occurs naturally during, for example, the slow aging of lakes, but it can be accelerated both by runoff from fertilized agricultural land and by the discharge of domestic sewage and industrial effluents (*Lund*, 1972). This process commonly leads to excessive growths of algae followed in some cases by a serious depiction of dissolved oxygen as the algae decay after death. Changes in diatom assemblages can also occur (see, particularly, *Battarbee*, 1977).

Increases in the application of nitrogenous fertilizers have almost amounted to a revolution (*Green*, 1976). The long-term trends in the UK are illustrated. The growth in fertilizer usage since the Second World War has been exponential, and in spite of the increasing costs of energy supplies and hydrocarbons in the 1970s world fertilizer production has continued to rise inexorably.

Table 7.7. Trends in nitrate concentrations in English rivers in relation to fertilizer use.

River	*Place*	*Period*	*Correlation coefficient with time*
Dee	Chester	1961–7	–0.77
Great Ouse	Bedford	1953–67	–0.22
Kennett	Reading	1953–67	+0.34
Rother	Horsham	1957–67	+0.90
Severn	Tewkesbury	1953–67	+0.78
Stour	Langham	1953–67	+0.73
Tees	Darlington	1958–67	–0.34
Thames	Hampton	1953–64	+0.22
Blithe	Newton	1953–67	+0.56
Derwent	Hathersage	1953–67	+0.26
Devon	Hawton	1953–67	+0.47
Dove	Monks Bridge	1953–67	+0.68
Dove	Stratton	1961–7	+0.47
Leen	Newstead Abbey	1957–63	–0.16
Manifold	Iham	1956–67	+0.25
Poulter	Elkesley	1953–67	+0.41
Tyne	Wylam	1956–67	+0.08
Wensum	Norwich	1953–67	+0.05

When one examines the evidence to see whether increasing nitrate fertilizer applications are indeed leading to widespread upward trends in nitrate concentrations in river and ground waters, it is often conflicting (*Manners*, 1978; *Rodda et al.*, 1976). This may be because soil and vegetation have a large storage capacity for nitrogen, while a great deal probably depends on local soil, climate and land-management conditions. Further problems are presented by the inadequacy of long-term data. This complexity in the evidence is brought out strongly in Tomlinson's analysis of trends of nitrate concentrations in English rivers (1970). In six of his rivers nitrate concentrations increased significantly with time, in eight the correlation coefficients were positive but not significant, in three cases the correlations were negative and not significant, while in one case the correlation was negative and significant. However, the situation since Tomlinson has now become rather clearer (Royal Society Study Group, 1983), and although there are considerable fluctuations from year to year, the trend in nitrate levels in English rivers is clearly apparent. They are 50 to 400 per cent higher than they were 20 years ago. Also causing concern is the trend in nitrate concentrations in British ground waters. Investigations have revealed a large quantity of nitrate in the unsaturated zone of the principal aquifers (mainly Chalk and Triassic sandstone), and this is slowly moving down towards the main ground-water body. The slow transit time means that in many water supply wells increased nitrate concentrations will not occur for 20 to 30 years, but they will then be above acceptable levels for human health.

However, even if an increase in nitrate levels is evident this may not necessarily be because of the application of fertilizers. Some nitrate pollution may be derived from organic wastes. There has also been some anxiety in Britain over a possible decline in the amount of organic matter present in the soil, which could limit its ability to assimilate nitrogen. Moreover, the pattern of tillage may have affected the liberation of nitrogen. The increased area and depth of modern ploughing accelerates the decay of residues and may change the pattern of water movement in the soil. Finally, tile drainage has also expanded in area very greatly in recent decades in England. This has affected the movement of water through the soil and hence the degree of leaching of nitrates and other materials (*Edwards*, 1975).

Given the uncertainties surrounding the question of nitrate pollution, and bearing in mind the major advances in agricultural productivity that they have permitted, attempts at controlling their use have not been received with complete favour. Indeed, as *Viets* (1971) has pointed out, if fertilizer use were curtailed there would be less vegetation cover and increased erosion and sediment delivery to rivers. This, he suggests, would necessitate an increase in land hectarage to maintain production levels which would also cause greater erosion; at the same time the increased ploughing would lead to greater nitrate loss from grasslands. Nevertheless some farmers are inefficient and wasteful in their use of fertilizers and there is scope for economy (*Cooke*, 1977).

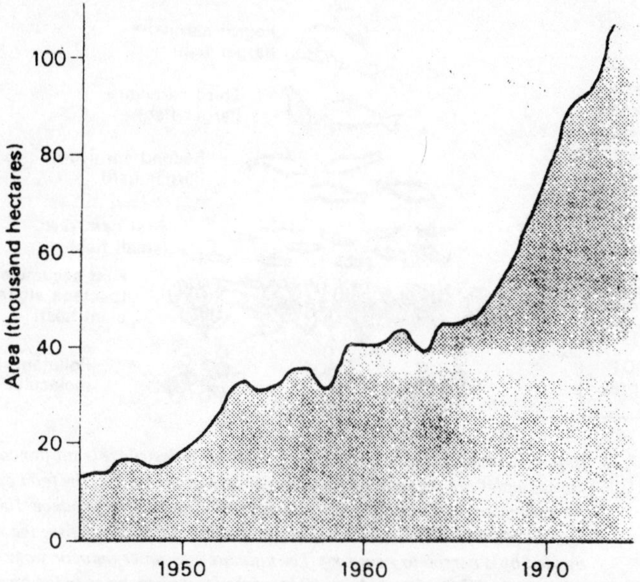

Fig. 7.20. Annual total area of field drainage by tile drains in England and Wales.

Pesticides are another source of chemical pollution brought about by agriculture. There is now a tremendous range of pesticides and they differ greatly in their mode of action, in the length of time they remain in the biosphere, and in their toxicity.

Much of the most adverse criticism of pesticides has been directed against the chlorinated hydrocarbon group of insecticides, which includes DDT, Dieldrin and various others. These insecticides are toxic not only to the target organism but to other insects too (that is, they are non-specific). They are also highly persistent. Appreciable quantities of the original application may survive in the environment in unaltered form for years. This can have two rather severe effects: global dispersal, and the 'biological magnification' of these substances in food chains (*Manners*, 1978). This last problem is well illustrated for DDT.

In addition to the influence of nitrate fertilizers, the confining of animals on feedlots results in tremendously concentrated sources of

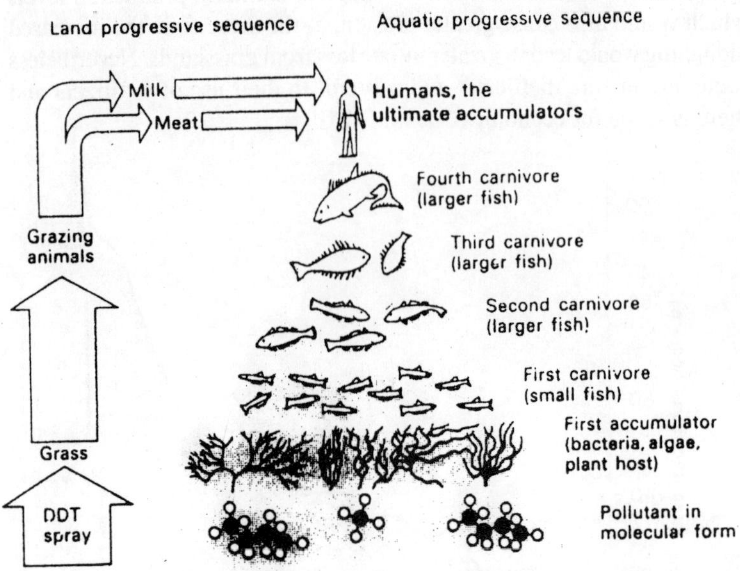

Fig. 7.21. Biological concentration occurs when relatively indestructible substances (DDT for example) are ingested by lesser organisms at the base of the food pyramid. An estimated 1000 kg. of plant plankton are needed to produce 100 kg of animal plankton. These, in turn, are consumed by 10 kg of fish, the amount needed by a person to gain 1 kg. The ultimate consumer (man or woman) then takes in the DDT taken in by 1000 kg of the lesser creatures in the base of the food pyramid, when he or she ingests enough fish to gain 1 kg.

nutrients and pollutants. Animal wastes in the USA are estimated to be as much as 1.6 billion tonnes per year, with 50 per cent of this amount originating from feedlots. It needs to be remembered that 1000 head of beef produce the equivalent organic load of 6000 people (*Sanders*, 1972). The number of cattle fed on feedlots in the USA is rapidly increasing partly because *per capita* consumption of meat has moved sharply upward, and partly because the confinement of cattle on small lots, on which they are fed a controlled selection of feeds, leads to the greatest possible weight gains with the least possible cost and time (*Bussing*, 1972). Cattle feedlot runoff is a high-strength organic waste, high in oxygen-demanding material, and has caused many fish kills in rivers in states such as Kansas. There has been a marked increase in Britain in the phosphorus content of some rivers since the early 1950s, an increase related to the use of detergents.

Other changes in surface-water chemistry may be produced by the washing out of acids that pollute the air in precipitation. This is particularly clear in the heavily industrialized area of north-western Europe, where there is a marked zonation of acid rain with pH values that often fall below 4 or 5. A broadly comparable situation exists in North America (*Johnson*, 1979).

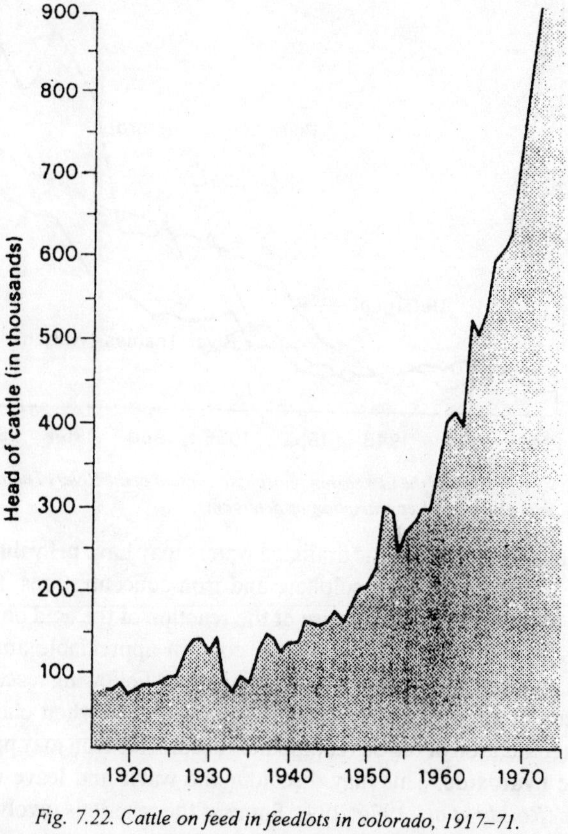

Fig. 7.22. Cattle on feed in feedlots in colorado, 1917–71.

Mining can also create serious chemical pollution. In the stripmining area of Kentucky, for example, *Collier* (1964) found that oxidation of the iron sulphide in the spoil banks and other parts of the mining area produced an excess of hydrogen ions. The ions then reacted with the mineral matter of the spoil bank, releasing soluble products at a rate 10 to 15 times greater than in the non-mined area. Such pollution was not entirely undesirable in its effects. *Collier* found that this release of minerals was good for tree growth, increasing their rate of development.

In Britain, coal seams and mudstones in the coal measures contain pyrite and marcasite (ferrous sulphide). In the course of mining the water-table is lowered, air gains access to these minerals and they are oxidized. Sulphuric acid may be produced.

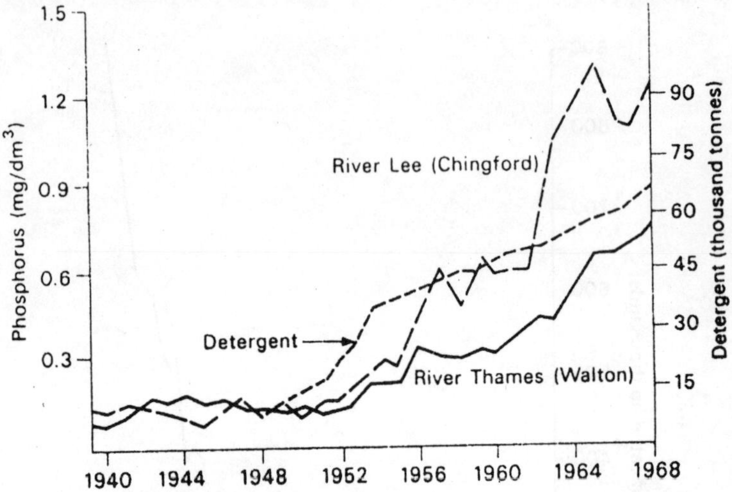

Fig. 7.23. Comparison of the increasing phosphate content of the Rivers Thames and Lee with the annual consumption of detergents.

As a consequence, mine drainage waters may have pH values as low as 2 or 3. They have high sulphate and iron concentrations, they may contain toxic metals, and because of the reaction of the acid on clay and silicates in the rocks, they may also contain appreciable amounts of calcium, magnesium, aluminium and manganese. Following reactions with sediments or mixing with alkaline river waters, or when chemical or bacterial oxidation of ferrous compounds occurs, the iron may precipitate as ferric hydroxide. This may discolour the water and leave unsightly deposits (*Rodda et al.*, 1976: 299). Some of the reactions involved in the development of acid mine drainage have been set down by Down and Stocks as follows (1977: 110-11):

1. Oxidation of the sulphide (usually FeS_2) in a wet environment producing ferrous sulphate and sulphuric acid.

$$2FeS_2 + 2H_2O + 7O_2 = 2FeSO_4 + 2H_2SO_4$$

2. Ferrous sulphate, in the presence of sulphuric acid and oxygen, can oxidize to produce ferric sulphate, especially in the presence of the bacterium, *Thiobacillus ferrooxidus*.

$$4FeSO_4 + 2H_2SO_4 + O_2 = 2Fe_2(SO_4)_3 + 2H_2O$$

3. The ferric iron so produced combines with the hydroxyl $(OH)^-$ ions of water to form ferric hydroxide, which is insoluble in acid and precipitates.

$$Fe_2(SO_4)_3 + 6H_2O = 2Fe(OH)_3 + 3H_2SO_4$$

The use of salt for de-icing roads has increased the chloride content of runoff in some areas. For example, the chloride content of Lough Neagh, Northern Ireland, almost doubled between 1958 and 1969 because of salt application to roads in its catchment. In the USA some 6 million tonnes of salt are applied to the roads each year, and in those states where it is applied the quantities amount to some 32 tonnes km^{-1}. Sugar maples seem susceptible to such high levels of salt and ancient specimens are dying along rural roads all over New England (*Wagner*, 1974: 99).

Similarly, storm-water runoff from urban areas may contain large amounts of contaminants, derived from litter, garbage, carwashings, horticultural treatments, vehicle drippings, industry, construction, animal droppings and the chemicals used for snow and ice clearance. Comparison of contaminant profiles for urban runoff and raw domestic sewage, based on surveys throughout the USA, indicates the importance of pollution from urban runoff sources. Further data for a variety of world cities are listed.

Table 7.8. Comparison of contaminant profiles for urban surface runoff and raw domestic sewage, based on survey throughout the USA

Constituent	*Urban surface runoff*	*Raw domestic sewage*
Suspended solids	250–300	150–250
BOD	10–250	300–350
Nutrients		
(a) Total nitrogen	0.5–5.0	25–85
(b) Total phosphorus	0.5–5.0	2–15
Coliform bacteria (MPN/100 ml)	104–106	106 or greater
Chlorides	20–200	15–75
Miscellaneous substances		
(a) Oil and grease	yes	yes
(b) Heavy metals	(10–100) times sewage conc.	traces
(c) Pesticides	yes	seldom
(d) Other toxins	potential exists	seldom

In New York City some half million dogs leave up to 20000 tonnes of pollutant faeces and up to 3.8 million litres of urine in the city streets each year, all of which is flushed by gutters to storm water sewers.

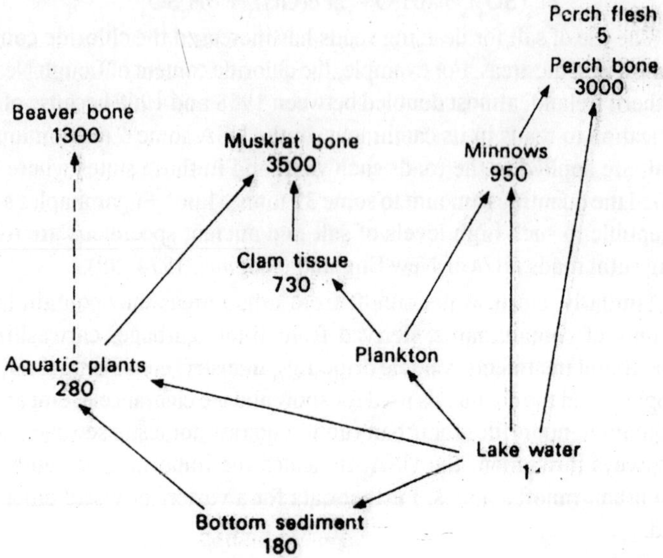

Fig. 7.24. The biological concentration of strontium 90 in the Perch Lake food web.

The nuclear industry has also caused some water pollution and its effects may be compounded by the process of biological concentration and magnification effects to which we have already referred in the context of DDT. This is illustrated by the case of Perch Lake, Ontario, which is fed by a stream that contains radioactive material seeping from a nearby liquid disposal area. Strontium 90 is one of these polluting radionuclides and it becomes concentrated in its movement up the food chain into the muskrat and perch.

Sewage is still a major pollutant. The New York Metropolitan area alone produces 6.8 billion litres of sewage per day of which about 16 per cent is raw. Much of this enters the Hudson and East Rivers around New York. In addition the city produces many tons of sewage sludge, fly ash and dredge waste per day, and 8.6 million tonnes of waste are dumped each year into the New York bight, off the mouth of the Hudson River. In an area of about 100 km² there is a black toxic sludge which smothers all forms of marine life (*Southwick*, 1976: 16).

The world's oceans are becoming increasingly prone to contamination by oil as world production, transport and utilization of this material expands. The effects of this pollution on animals have been widely studied. The sources of pollution include tanker collisions with other ships, the explosion of individual tankers because of the build-up of gas levels, the wrecking of tankers on coasts through navigational or mechanical failure, seepage from offshore oil installations, and the flushing of tanker holds. There is no doubt that the great bulk of the oil and related materials polluting the oceans results from human action (*Blumer*, 1972), though humans should not be attributed with all the blame, for natural seepages are reasonably common (*Landes*, 1973). Paradoxically, human actions mean that many natural seepages now cause less pollution than formerly; natural seepages have diminished as wells have drawn down the levels of hydrocarbons in the oil-bearing rocks. Likewise, the flow of asphalt that once poured from the Trinidad Pitch Lake into the Gulf of Paria has also ceased because mining of the asphalt has lowered the lake below its outlet.

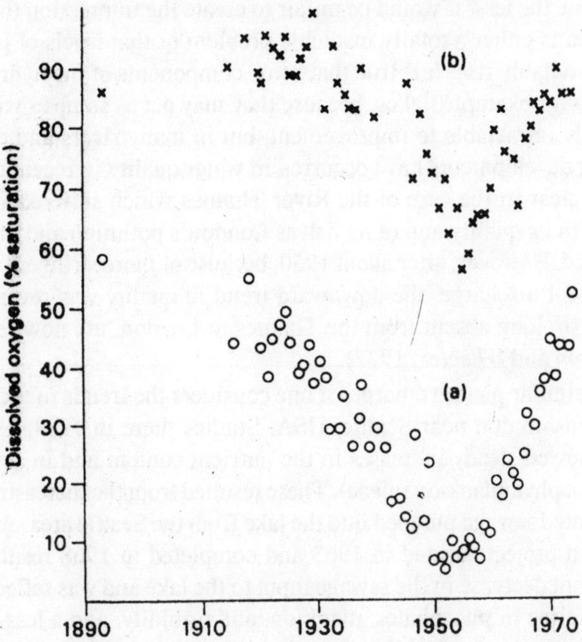

Fig. 7.25. The average dissolved oxygen content of the River Thames at half-tide in the July–September quarter since 1890. (a) 79 km below Teddington weir, (b) 95 km below Teddington weir.

Of the various serious causes of oil pollution, a more important mechanism than the much-publicized role of tanker accidents is the discharge of the ballast water taken into empty tankers to provide stability on the return voyage to the loading terminal (*Pitt*, 1979). It is in this field, however, that technical developments have led to most amelioration. For example, the quantity of oil in tanker ballast water has been drastically reduced by the LOT (load on top) system, in which the ballast water is allowed to settle so that the oil rises to the surface. The tank is then drained until only the surface oil in the tank remains, and this forms part of the new cargo. In the future large tankers will be fitted with separate ballast tanks not used for oil cargoes, called segregated or clean ballast systems. Given such advances it appears likely that an increasing proportion of oil pollution will be derived from accidents involving tankers of ever-increasing size, such as the spillage of 300 million litres, which came from the wreck of the *Amoco Cadiz* in 1978. It is to this problem that more attention needs to be directed.

None the less, it would be unfair to create the impression that water pollution is either a totally insoluble problem or that levels of pollution must inevitably rise. It is true that some components of the hydrological system - for example, lakes, because they may act as sumps - will prove relatively intractable to improvement, but in many rivers and estuaries striking developments have occurred in water quality in recent decades. This is clear in the case of the River Thames which suffered a serious decline in its quality and in its fish as London's pollution and industries expanded. However, after about 1950, because of more stringent controls on effluent discharge, the downward trend in quality was reversed and many fish, long absent from the Thames in London, are now returning (*Gameson* and *Wheeler*, 1977).

A similar picture emerges if one considers the trends in the state of Lake Washington near Seattle, USA. Studies there in 1933, 1950 and 1952 showed steady increases in the nutrient content and in associated growth of phytoplankton (algae). These resulted from the increasing levels of untreated sewage pumped into the lake from the Seattle area. A sewage diversion project, started in 1963 and completed in 1968 resulted in a significant decrease in the sewage input to the lake and was reflected in a rapid decline in phosphates, plankton, and turbidity, and a less marked decline in nitrate levels. Likewise, a long-term study of the levels of many heavy metals in sea water off the British Isles suggests that levels are generally low and that concentrations do not seem to he increasing (*Preston*, 1973).

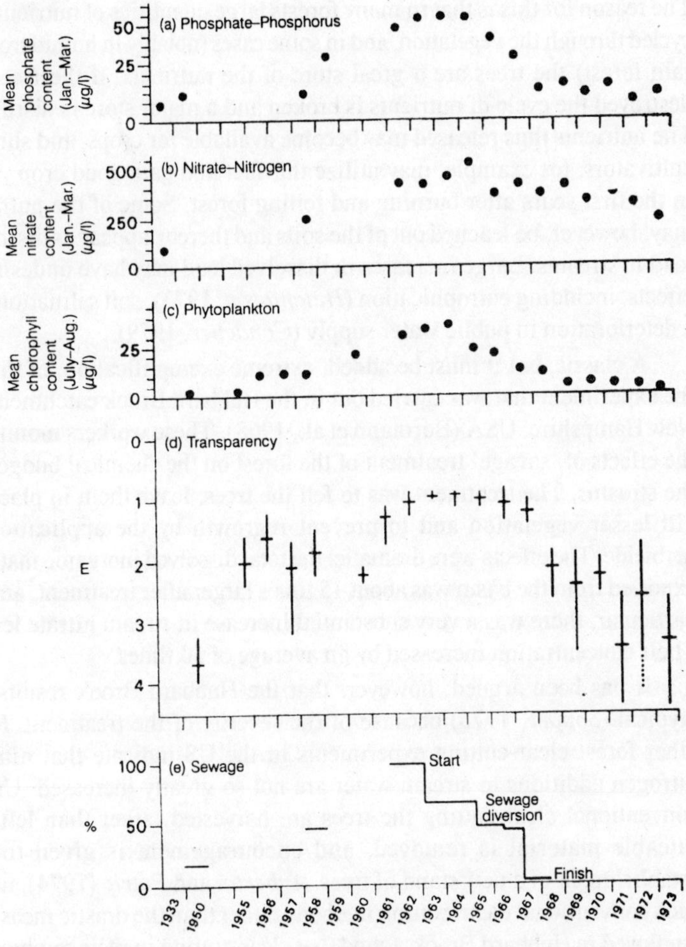

Fig. 7.26. Changes in the state of Lake Washington, USA, associated with levels of untreated sewage from 1933 to 1973. The relative amount of treated sewage entering the take is shown as a percentage of the maximum rated capacity of the treatment plants, 76 million litres per day.

Deforestation and its effects on water quality

The removal of a tree cover not only may affect river flow and stream-water temperature, it may also cause changes in stream-water chemistry. The reason for this is that in many forests large quantities of nutrients are cycled through the vegetation, and in some cases (notably in humid tropical rain forest) the trees are a great store of the nutrients. If the trees are destroyed the cycle of nutrients is broken and a major store is disrupted. The nutrients thus released may become available for crops, and shifting cultivators, for example, may utilize this fact and gain good crop yields in the first years after burning and felling forest. Some of the nutrients may, however, be leached out of the soils and thereby appear as dissolved load in streams. Large increases in dissolved load may have undesirable effects, including eutrophication (*Hutchinson*, 1973), soil salination and a deterioration in public water supply (*Conacher*, 1979).

A classic, but it must be added, extreme exemplification, of this, is the experiment that was carried out in the Hubbard Brook catchments in New Hampshire, USA (Bormann et al., 1968). These workers monitored the effects of 'savage' treatment of the forest on the chemical budgets of the streams. The treatment was to fell the trees, leave them in place, to kill lesser vegetation and to prevent regrowth by the application of herbicide. The effects were dramatic: the total dissolved inorganic material exported from the basin was about 15 times larger after treatment, and, in particular, there was a very substantial increase in stream nitrate levels. Their concentration increased by an average of 50 times.

It has been argued, however, that the Hubbard Brook results are atypical (*Sopper*, 1975) because of the severity of the treatment. Most other forest clear-cutting experiments in the US indicate that nitrate-nitrogen additions to stream water are not so greatly increased. Under conventional clear-cutting the trees are harvested rather than left, all saleable material is removed, and encouragement is given to the establishment of a new stand of trees. *Aubertin* and *Patric* (1974), using such conventional clear-cutting methods rather than the drastic measures employed in Hubbard Brook, found that clear-cutting in their catchments in West Virginia had a negligible effect on stream), pH and the concentrations of most dissolved solids.

Even if clear-cutting is practised, there is some evidence of a rapid return to steady-state nutrient cycling because of quick regeneration. As *Marks* and *Bormann* (1972) have put it:

Because terrestrial plant communities have always been subjected to various forms of natural disturbances, such as wind storms, fires, and insect outbreaks, it is only reasonable to consider recovery from disturbances as a normal part of community maintenance and repair.

Likewise *Hewlett et al.*, (1984) found no evidence in the Piedmont region of the USA that clear-cutting would create such extreme nitrate loss that soil fertility would be impaired or water eutrophication caused. They point out that rapid growth of vegetation minimizes nutrient losses from the ecosystem by three main mechanisms. It channels water from runoff to evapotranspiration, thereby reducing erosion and nutrient loss; it reduces the rates of decomposition of organic matter through moderation of the microclimate so that the supply of soluble ions for loss in drainage water is reduced; and it causes the simultaneous incorporation of nutrients into the rapidly developing biomass so that they are not lost from the system.

Thermal pollution

The pollution of water by increasing its temperature is called thermal pollution. Many fauna are affected by temperature so that this environmental impact has some significance (*Langford*, 1972).

In industrial countries probably the main source of thermal pollution is from condenser cooling water released from electricity generating stations. Water discharged from power stations has been heated some 6-9°C, but usually has a temperature of less than 30°C. The extent to which such water affects river temperatures depends very much on the state of flow. For example, below the Ironbridge power station in England, the Severn River undergoes a temperature increase of only 0.5°C during floods, compared with an 8°C increase at times of low flow (*Rodda et al.*, 1976).

Over the past two decades or more (see Royal Commission on Environmental Pollution, 1972), both the increase in the capacity of individual electricity power-generating units, and the improvements in their thermal efficiency, have led to a diminution in the heat rejected in relation to the amount of cooling water per unit of production. Economic optimization of the generating plant has cut down the flow of cooling water per unit of electricity, though it has raised its temperature. This increased temperature rise of the cooling water is more than offset by the reduction achieved in the volume of water utilized. None the less, the expansion of generating capacity has meant that the total quantity of heat discharged has increased, even though it is much less than would be expected on a simple proportional basis.

Table 7.9. Colling water used per unit of power generation in the UK.

Yes	Temperature rise (°C)	Specific water circulation Per unit of power generation (m^3)
(a) Coal and oil-fired		
1950	7	0.21
1960	9	0.15
1970	10	0.12
1980 (estimated)	12 –14	0.08–0.09
(b) Nuclear		
1962	8	0.33
1967	9	0.24
1980 (estimated)	12 –14	0.09–0.14

Thermal pollution of streams may also follow from urbanization (*Pluhowski*, 1970). This results from various sources: changes in the temperature regime of streams brought about by reservoirs according to their size, their depth and the season; changes produced by the urban heat island effect; changes in the configuration of urban channels (for example, their width-depth ratio); changes in the degree of shading of the channel, either by covering it over or by removing a natural vegetation cover; changes in the volume of storm runoff; and changes in the ground-water contribution. Pluhowski found that the basic effect of cities on river-water temperatures on Long Island, New York, was to raise temperatures in summer (by as much as 5-8°C) and to lower them in winter (by as much as 1.5-3°C).

Table 7.10. Effect of forest-cutting on mean monthly maximum rever-water temperature in the USA.

Location	Temperature increase (°C)
Coweeta (North Caronlina)	4
Fernow (West Virginia)	5.5
Penn State (Pennsylvania)	6
Hubbard Brook (New Hampshire)	6
H.J. Andrews (Oregon)	6.7
Coastal Range (Oregon)	8
Mean	6.03

Reservoir construction can also affect stream-water temperatures. *Crisp* (1977) found, for example, that as a result of the construction of a reservoir at Cow Green (Upper Teesdale, northern England) the temperature of the river downstream was modified. He noted a reduction in the amplitude of annual water- temperature fluctuations, and a delay in the spring rise of water temperature by 20-50 days, and of the autumn fall by up to 20 days. In rural areas human activities can also cause significant modifications in river-water temperature. Deforestation is especially important (*Lynch* et al., 1984). *Swift* and *Messer* (1971), for example, examined stream temperature measurements during six forest-cutting experiments on small basins in the southern Appalachians, USA. They found that with complete cutting, because of shade removal, the maximum stream temperatures in summer went up from 19 to 23°C. They believed that such temperature increases were detrimental to temperature-sensitive fish like trout. On the other hand, the temporary shutdown of power plants may create severe cold-shock kills of fish in discharge-receiving waters in winter (J. R. *Clark*, 1977). Moreover, an increase in water temperature causes a decrease in the solubility of oxygen which is needed for the oxidation of biodegradable wastes. At the same time, the rate of oxidation is accelerated, imposing a faster oxygen demand on the smaller supply and thereby depleting the oxygen content of the water still further.

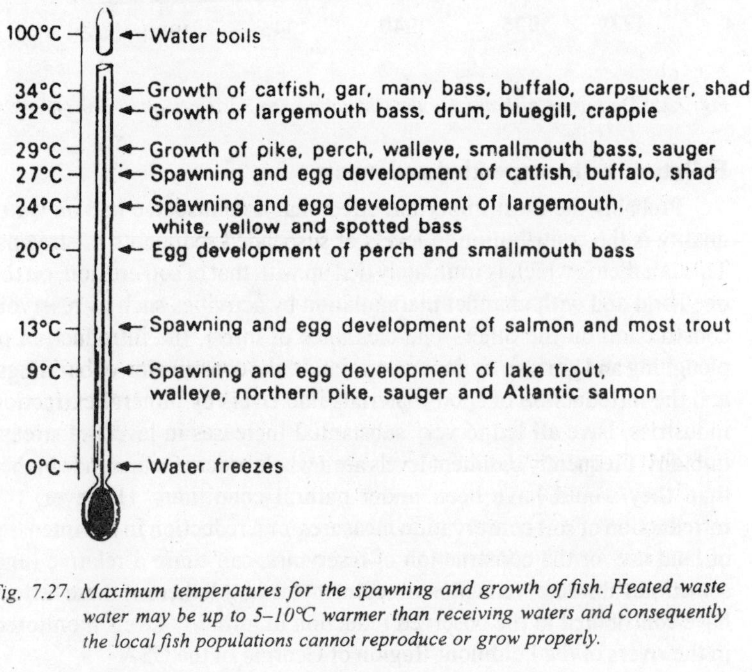

Fig. 7.27. Maximum temperatures for the spawning and growth of fish. Heated waste water may be up to 5–10°C warmer than receiving waters and consequently the local fish populations cannot reproduce or grow properly.

Temperature also affects the lower organisms, such as plankton and crustaceans. In general the more elevated the temperature is, the less desirable the types of algae in water. In cooler waters diatoms are the predominant phytoplankton in water that it not heavily eutrophic; with the same nutrient levels, green algae begin to become dominant at higher temperatures and diatoms decline; at the highest water temperatures, blue-green algae thrive and often develop into heavy blooms. One further ecological consequence of thermal pollution is that the spawning and migration of many fish are triggered by temperature and this behaviour can be distrupted by thermal change.

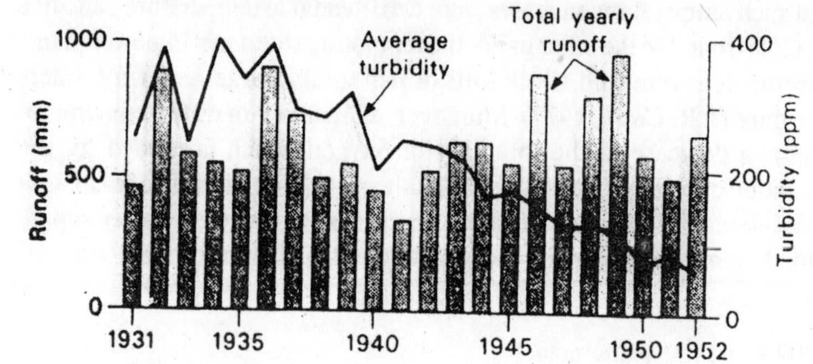

Fig. 7.28. Decline of turbiditry in the Chattaboochee Basin, Atlanta, Georgia, USA, 1931–52.

Pollution with suspended sediments

Probably the most important effect that humans have had on water quality is the contribution to levels of suspended sediments in streams. This is a theme which is intimately tied up with that of soil erosion, on the one hand and with channel manipulation by activities such as reservoir construction on the other. The clearance of forest, the introduction of ploughing and grazing by domestic animals, the construction of buildings, and the introduction of spoil materials into rivers by mineral extraction industries, have all led to very substantial increases in levels of stream turbidity. Frequently sediment levels are a whole order of magnitude higher than they would have been under natural conditions. However, the introduction of soil conservation measures, or a reduction in the intensity of land use, or the construction of reservoirs, can cause a relative (and sometimes absolute) reduction in sediment loads. All there of these factors have contributed to the observed reduction in turbidity levels monitored in the rivers of the Peidmont Region of Georgia in the USA.